EMPOWERED

EMPOWERED

POPULAR FEMINISM

AND POPULAR MISOGYNY

Sarah Banet-Weiser

Duke University Press Durham and London 2018

Designed by Courtney Leigh Baker
and typeset in Warnock Pro and Avenir
by Westchester Publishing Services

Library of Congress Cataloging-in-Publication Data
Names: Banet-Weiser, Sarah, [date] author.
Title: Empowered : popular feminism and popular misogyny /
Sarah Banet-Weiser.
Description: Durham : Duke University Press, 2018. |
Includes bibliographical references and index.
Identifiers: LCCN 2018014915 (print)
LCCN 2018016343 (ebook)
ISBN 9781478002772 (ebook)
ISBN 9781478001683 (hardcover : alk. paper)
ISBN 9781478002918 (pbk. : alk. paper)
Subjects: LCSH: Feminism—United States. | Misogyny—
United States. | Popular culture—United States. |
Feminism. | Misogyny. | Popular culture.
Classification: LCC HQ1421 (ebook) | LCC HQ1421 .B355 2018
(print) | DDC 305.420973—dc23
LC record available at https://lccn.loc.gov/2018014915

Cover art: "Empowered" necklace by Fierce Deer (etsy.com
/shop/FierceDeer).

This book is dedicated to my mother,

ANNE LAVERNE BANET.

She is the strongest person I know,
and taught me the two crucial things about life:

believe in yourself,
and don't take shit from anyone.

CONTENTS

On November 9, the day after Donald Trump was elected president of the United States, I wrote the following:

> On election night, on my way home from work, my 15 year old daughter texted me. Her text read: "OMG. I yelled at my entire team about Donald. It was so cool!" I responded with encouragement. A bit later, she texted me again and said "it will be bad if he wins." I replied immediately: "he won't." Another while later, she texted "I'm scared." I replied that I was on my way. She texted back: "momma hurry he's winning." In a short text trajectory, my remarkably mature, self-possessed daughter moved from a position of empowerment to one of a frightened child, wanting her mom to rescue her from what was starting to look like a national catastrophe. But I couldn't rescue her—I could only cry with her.
>
> It's hard for me not to read the election of Donald Trump as President through the lens of my 15 year old daughter, or my young female undergraduate students. It is difficult to explain to young women, who see and experience a volume of messages and initiatives telling them to be confident, to lean in, to just *be* empowered, why a known misogynist and racist has just been elected president. Popular feminism exists most spectacularly in an economy of visibility, where it often remains just that: visibility. Popular misogyny, on the other hand, seems to fold into state and national

structures with terrible efficiency—like the election of Donald Trump as president.[1]

I wrote this short piece because the election of Trump as US president initially derailed me (as it did many others) from finishing this book, from thinking in intellectual ways about what just happened. But I have been a feminist theorist for longer than I have been anything else. The first two university classes I taught were Introduction to Women's Studies and Women of Color in the United States. While I've written on topics other than gender, I have approached all of those topics with a feminist methodology. My personal relationships are shaped within a feminist worldview. The politics of feminism informs the way I think, the way I write, the way I organize my life. And the contemporary moment is in many ways a remarkable one in which to be a feminist. After so many years of defending feminism to others, and struggling to make it visible as an expansive politics, rather than a niche politics, this is an exciting time, one in which I think, "Finally, finally."

All that is to say: it was often difficult for me to write this book, in which I critique some of the processes and practices of feminism today. Even though I believe that critique is warranted, I cannot deny that I also feel ambivalent about it. For instance, when Verizon launched an ad campaign pointing out the gender disparity within the technology industry— of which the company is a part—the more cynical side of me found it ironic and unsettling, but another side of me also thought, "Well, at least that's something." I recognize the importance in the goals of "girl empowerment" organizations, because it is essential to see the asymmetries of power in culture, politics, and everyday life. Yet I also think it is actually *disempowering* to focus on the empowerment of girls who are privileged because of race and class. And while I worry that the ever-expanding reach of neoliberalism is *restructuring* today's feminist politics as an individual politics rather than a collective one, I remain hopeful that I am not alone in my unease, and I am bolstered by the presence of collectivities that protest this very shift all around the globe. It is ambivalence—both in my own intellectual critique of popular feminism and in the ambivalent spaces these politics create—that is the feminist project for me. Because of this ambivalence, it is unproductive to simply dismiss popular feminism as just another branding exercise that serves the ever-expanding reach of neoliberal markets, or to try to determine the authenticity of certain feminisms over others. Rather, the overlaps and intersections of affect, desire, critique, and ambivalence that characterize popular feminism are potentially opening spaces for, and connections to, mobilizing feminist practice.

I began this project with a focus on popular feminism; I quickly learned that this focus would necessarily require me to engage with a contemporary response to popular feminism: popular misogyny. If I thought being a feminist made it difficult to intellectually critique popular feminism, it turned out to be much, much more difficult to analyze popular misogyny. I had to read, see, hear, and experience misogyny in a multitude of forms, and because I identify as a woman, it often felt viscerally personal. The expressions of popular misogyny, from men's rights activism to comments on social media to #GamerGate to the growing state-by-state retraction of abortion rights, are often terrifying, and give me a what-the-fuck-kind-of-world-are-we-living-in kind of feeling. I found myself a bit unprepared as a scholar to know what to do with and how to think about this version of misogyny and the way in which it is created and expressed within a context of the popular. And aside from feeling overwhelmed by the wide and varied continuum of popular misogyny, I felt unequipped as well to think through the best coping mechanisms when researching popular misogyny so as not to incur lasting psychic damage. I had to change my typical method of doing research, which is taking a deep dive into a topic, because the water I dove into was so toxic. I often found myself in tears, or sick to my stomach, or generally in despair. Still, as I moved closer to finishing this book, it was clear that recognizing, and then theorizing, popular misogyny as a deep structuring force in culture and politics is politically important. While I may feel ambivalent about critiquing popular feminism, my experience researching popular misogyny was not at all ambivalent; I feel quite certain in my critique of misogyny.

I also feel strongly that it is important to challenge the typical journalistic move that treats misogynistic acts as individual anomalies. In this book, I approach popular misogyny as a *structural* force. Of course, not all practices of heteronormative masculinity are misogynistic. Part of what makes this moment feel different is the vast amount of information, the sheer volume of expressions, that comprises practices of masculinity. I attempt in this book to parse through some of these expressions as a way to demonstrate how popular misogyny functions to shore up hegemonic masculinity while also creating new ways to objectify and devalue women. And understanding popular misogyny as a structural force, one often invisible *as* misogyny, is crucial in a moment when popular feminism has gained such spectacular visibility. This book is about the relationship between popular feminism and popular misogyny; it is necessary to take a structural approach to popular misogyny at a time when popular feminism is visible across multiple media platforms. Misogyny has existed for centuries, to be sure. In the current moment, however, popular misogyny responds to, reacts against, and challenges popular feminism—precisely because it is so visible.

Understanding the structural power of popular misogyny became all the more urgent for me on November 8, 2016. Again, I initially felt that a book on popular feminism and popular misogyny was beyond the point. For me, critical writing has captured my optimism, my hope for social change. But I then realized that the relationship of popular feminism and popular misogyny that I write about in this book is about the ascendency of someone like Trump to president of the United States, and it was worth writing about.

This book is my attempt to make sense of this relationship, as well as an attempt to remain optimistic in a time when politics often feel hopeless. It is my attempt to think through, and to somehow challenge, the dynamics of power that provide the context for a fifteen-year-old girl to go from feeling empowered to feeling vulnerable and powerless. And it is my hope that the visibility of popular feminism will continually remind us that the struggle is worth it.

ACKNOWLEDGMENTS

This is an intensely personal book for me. It was, without a doubt, the most exhilarating—and the most difficult—intellectual project I've done. During the five years I was writing and researching this book, many of my worlds collapsed, others changed radically, and still others were rebuilt. Relationships I never thought would end did just that, my children became adults, and I found joy and inspiration in new partners, friends, and places. As with everything I have ever written, this book is the result of a collaboration—with friends, lovers, children, scholars, students, and people I've never met but have read or listened to. But this collaboration is also different, and even more rewarding: I have found, and been nurtured by, an amazing feminist community during the book's journey, so while it is the angriest book I have ever written, it is also the most hopeful. My friends enabled me to survive writing about misogyny, and their feminism sustains me and convinces me that things will get better. I know I will forget some people here, and for that I apologize. But I am grateful to have an opportunity to thank those who continue to make a profound impact on my life and my thinking.

There are a few people who were, quite simply, essential to this book; I literally couldn't have written it without them. Jack Bratich, with his brilliant, capacious mind, was loving, supportive, and deeply engaged in this project. So many chapters began as conversations with him; so many points I was able to clarify because of his gentle provocations. Collaborating with him has made me smarter, more nuanced, and open to so many new thoughts and experiences. I am forever grateful to him. Inna Arzumanova, my wonderful, smart, generous friend, has been patient and kind through-out all of my freak-outs about life and love, not to mention the book. It is so rare to have someone in your life who, when you feel lost, pushes you to find your own voice in not only your work but your life as well. Also rare is my friendship with Daniela Baroffio, which is unbelievably sustaining to me—our many conversations about love, parenting, politics, and friendship make my life so much richer. I can't imagine doing any of this without her. My dear friend Josh Kun has been an essential support and friend during this process; more than that, he provides all of us with an incredible model of what it means to be a public intellectual and do necessary political work. I'm not sure what I'd do if I didn't have him to make fun of me. During the course of writing and researching this book, I became friends with the lovely, brilliant Rosalind Gill. It was her important, crucial femi-nist work that inspired me to write this book in the first place; it was her expansive, compassionate heart that made me love her. She opened her house, and her incredible friendship network, to me in London, and I will never forget it. It is always lovely to experience the transformation in one's relationship with an advisee to one of a cherished friend, and I am so lucky to have this experience with Laura Portwood-Stacer. She was an essential editor of this book—it is in much, much better shape due to her efforts. She was also a great partner in life issues, from outfits to parent-ing to text coaching. Finally, my editor at Duke University Press, Courtney Berger, is simply fantastic. She has been an incisive reader, a source of support, and endlessly patient throughout this project. The day after the US presidential election, I texted her, "My work is hope for me but now it feels hopeless. Tell me to keep writing." She immediately texted back, "You MUST keep writing. It is even more important now." It was moments like these that kept me writing in these distressing times, and I hope she knows how much it means to me.

There are some friends who generously read entire drafts of this book, at different stages, and their feedback has made this a much better book. David Lobenstine, a truly gifted editor, read this book at a too-early stage and managed to be incredibly helpful and thoughtful anyway. The book has definitely benefited from his thoughts and provocations. Dana Polan has read every manuscript I've written—I cannot express how grateful I am to him. He is the most generous person I know. Melina Sherman, my pas-sionate feminist student, not only read the manuscript but also engaged in spirited conversations about feminism, life, and politics. Kate Miltner provided incisive feedback on the entire manuscript and also coauthored a piece with me—I am so grateful to her for thinking through networked misogyny with me and for our many conversations about, well, everything. Perry Johnson also read the entire manuscript and offered many useful suggestions; her own work on popular feminism has been an inspiration. I am also grateful to the two anonymous readers of the manuscript, who pushed me to clarify my thinking and my key concepts.

This is a book about feminism, and it wouldn't have been possible without my incredible feminist community. My friends helped me not only with navigating the theories that frame this work but also with navigating my personal life in times of upheaval. I am forever grateful to my rock, my comfort, my personal finance planner, and my best friend, Joyce Campion. I don't know what I would do without my unstoppable, intrepid girlfriends Laurie Ouellette and Roopali Mukherjee. Our many collaborations and friendship rituals have helped give this book a truly personal form. I am grateful for my cherished friend Alison Trope, who is my model for feminism and social justice, and is also the bravest person I know. I am so privileged to know and love Val Hartouni (who, years ago, gave me a vocabulary for my feminism), Marita Sturken, Carrie Rentschler, Alison Hearn, Herman Gray, Barbie Zelizer, Karen Tongson, Anne Balsamo, Nitin Govil, and Sarah Sharma. The book—and my life—also benefited from my friendships with Cynthia Chris (who generously read my introduction), Shana Redmond, Kara Keeling, Wendy Hui Kyong Chun, Nayan Shah, Safiya Noble, Tara McPherson, Tania Modleski (who read the introduction at a late stage and gave crucial feedback), Aniko Imre, Sara de Benedictis, Rachel O'Neill, Angela McRobbie, Jonathan Sterne, Michael Delli Carpini, Jessa Lingel, Nancy Baym, Diane Negra, Jo Littler, Jayson Harsin, Karine Lacherchere, Nic Sammond, Stephanie Schulte, Steve Duncombe, Brenda Weber, Lisha Nadkarni, Sue Dvonch, Keri Ravelo, Stephanie Lees, Julie Main, Catherine Rottenberg, David Craig, and Mauricio Mota.

I am so grateful to all of my colleagues, staff, and friends at the Annenberg School for Communication and Journalism. First and foremost, they recognized that in order for me to be a good director of the school I needed to maintain my identity as a scholar, and I am so fortunate that I was given the time and resources to do this work. The staff in the director's office—Imre Meszaros, Billie Shotlow, Ally Arguello, Sarah Holterman, Christine Lloreda, Jordan Gary, and Anne Marie Campian—literally made my job possible; I cannot thank them enough. From my (very complicated!) travel plans to their vast institutional knowledge to their patience and compassion in listening to me complain, they have been my rock. Many others at the Annenberg School have made my life and my job so much easier, and I am grateful to them: Tracy Mendoza, Deb Lawler, James Vasquez, Dave Racewicz, Bruce Massagia, Anna Kanauka, Diana O'Leary, Cindy Martinez, Marisa Evans, Charles Peyton, Ray Barkley, and Bryan Sylvester. I am so thankful for my colleagues, especially François Bar, Hernán Galperin, Colin Maclay, Mike Ananny, Ben Carrington, Hye Jin Lee, Tom Hollihan, Patti Riley, Rebecca Weintraub, Geoff Cowan, and Ernie Wilson, for their support and guidance along the way. Larry Gross and Sandra Ball-Rokeach are cherished friends and incredible mentors. Henry Jenkins has been, as usual, a warm and supportive friend and interlocutor; he read parts of this book and gave me frank and important suggestions. It has been so lovely to become friends and colleagues with Christina Dunbar-Hester; I'm sad that my time with her at USC is short, but I'm confident that we have become lifelong friends. Stacy Smith's work on difference in Hollywood is an inspiration; I'm grateful for all of our many conversations. My treasured friend Taj Frazier has shown me what true dedication to racial justice means at an institution of higher education. Gordon Stables has become a cherished friend; I absolutely rely on him and his expert, considerate guidance on all the academic labyrinths we have to navigate each day. Becoming friends with Willow Bay over the past four years has been wonderful; she has been a source of inspiration and guidance. Collaborating with her on this adventure has been a true gift. My dear friend Manuel Castells has also been a remarkable source of support and guidance, and I look forward to all our future collaborations.

My students, undergraduate and graduate, former and present, have sustained me throughout my entire career. Their passion, intelligence, and investment in a more just world motivated me to begin—and finish—this book. I want to thank Melissa Brough, John Cheney-Lippold, Cara Wallis, Travers Scott, Lori Lopez, Dayna Chatman, Brittany Farr, Evan Brody, Kate Miltner, Melina Sherman, Perry Johnson, Courtney Cox, Garrett Broad, Nick Busalacchi, Tisha Dejmanee, Sam Close, Simi Dosekun, Lauren Sowa, Lauren Leavitt, Tyler Nygaard, Anjali Nath, Anna Loup, Bianca Nasser, Kate Oh, Clare O'Connor, Sarah Myers West, Lin Zhang, Renyi Hong, Stefania Marghitu, Lara Bradshaw, and Paromita Sengupta.

This book took shape over the course of many years, but especially the last five. I was fortunate to have the opportunity to workshop these ideas in talks and lectures during this time, and I am grateful to the individuals and institutions who supported my visits: the first presentation of these ideas was at the invitation of Carrie Rentschler from the Institution of Gender, Sexuality and Feminist Studies at McGill University; Jayson Harsin supported me at the American University of Paris and has since engaged in fruitful conversations with me about the work; Nick Couldry and our collaborative Communication Futures research group between USC and the London School of Economics gave me an opportunity to present a version of this work; Clementine Tholas invited me to present at the Sorbonne University in Paris; Michel Wieviorka at the Fondation Maison des sciences de l'homme generously hosted me for two summers in Paris so that I could write; Tarleton Gillespie and Hector Postigo gave me the opportunity to get my ideas out early in my first blog ever on Culture Digitally; and the faculty and students in the first three years of the Annenberg Summer Institute on Difference and the Media offered crucial feedback in framing this project. I would also like to thank Melissa Click and Julie Elman at the Console-ing Passions conference; Sarah Sharma, the amazing director of the McLuhan Center at the University of Toronto; Gustavo Cordosa at the University of Lisbon; Stewart Hoover, Deborah Whitehead, and Nabil Echchaibi at CU Boulder and the Center for Religion and Media; Mónica Moreno Figueroa from Cambridge University and the Politics of Beauty conference; Cheryl Cooky from the North American Society for the Sociology of Sport; Lawrence Wenner from Loyola Marymount University Forum on Media Ethics and Social Responsibility; George Mason University and the Critiquing Culture conference; Jonathan Gray and the media studies department at the University of Wisconsin–Madison; and Nancy Baym, Mary Gray, danah boyd, and Kate Crawford at Microsoft Research/New England. I am also grateful to the New England Science Club for Girls and the Lower East Side Girls Club for opening their doors to me and allowing me to experience the hope and inspiration that goes on there.

One of the things I learned through writing this book was that I needed both personal and professional renewal in my life. I am so immensely grateful that my colleagues and friends in the Department of Media and Communications at the London School of Economics are giving me the opportunity to do both. They have been incredibly supportive and inviting, and I am looking forward to the next stage of my career with them.

I am especially grateful to Nick Couldry, Terhi Rantanen, Sonia Livingstone, Shani Orgad, Charlie Beckett, Myria Georgiou, Ellen Helsper, Lilie Chouliaraki, Robin Mansell, Seeta Gangadharan, Bart Cammaerts, and all of the faculty there.

Duke University Press has been a gift to me; I've already mentioned the extraordinary talent of Courtney Berger. I also want to thank Ken Wissoker, Sandra Korn (who has been very patient with me and all my requests), my excellent production editor Liz Smith, and the copyeditors for the press. Courtney Baker designed a truly beautiful cover for this book. Anne Metcalf was a fantastic indexer; I was so pleased to work with her.

Not everyone is lucky enough to have a supportive and loving family. I am. My family, my love for them and their love for me, has literally made this possible. My sisters, Angela, Suzannah, Genevieve, Yurima, and Candice, are the embodiment of what sisterhood truly means. My brothers, Matt, Joey, Sean, Cary, and Ron, have loved me and supported me throughout. All of my nieces and nephews (thirteen of them!) are a constant source of joy and inspiration. Bill Weiser has been very supportive during a very difficult time. My own children have shown me what strength, love, and brilliance look like every day: Sam and his incredible light; Luke and his steadfast generosity; and Lily and her exuberant joy of life and love have not only sustained me but have given me real hope, and I have found true friends in each of them. My other daughters, Whitney Kistner and Payton Smith, in their beauty, kindness, and love for my sons, also give me hope. My father, who passed away ten years ago, continues to pop up in my life and in my mind, encouraging me to keep going. And finally, my mother, Anne Laverne Banet, the strongest woman I know. She raised seven children by herself with no money, she encouraged us—especially her daughters—to be strong and resilient, and she never, ever lost faith in us. She taught me what it means to be a feminist. This book is dedicated to her.

A SMALL PORTION of this work appeared in earlier versions in previous publications. I am fortunate to have a bi-monthly column with the *Los Angeles Review of Books*, where I discuss popular feminism and misogyny. Sections of the introduction and the conclusion earlier appeared in that column ("Popular Feminism: #MeToo," January 27, 2018; "Popular Feminism: Structural Rage," March 30, 2018), but have been significantly revised for this book. Part of the introduction appears as my keynote address published as "Keynote Address: Media, Markets, Gender: Economies of Visibility in a Neoliberal Moment" in *Communication Review* 18, no. 1 (2015). Part of "Am I Pretty or Ugly? Girls and the Market for Self-Esteem," published in *Girlhood Studies* 7, no. 1 (Summer 2014), appears in chapter 2. Chapter 2 also includes some parts of my article "'Confidence You Can Carry!': Girls in Crisis and the Market for Girls' Empowerment Organizations" published in *Continuum: Journal of Media and Cultural Studies* 29, no. 2 (2015). Finally, my ideas about networked misogyny were originally fleshed out with my coauthor Kate Miltner in "#MasculinitySoFragile: Culture, Structure, and Networked Misogyny" in a "Comments and Criticisms" section of *Feminist Media Studies* 16, no. 1 (2016). I am grateful for all these publishers.

INTRODUCTION

In 2018, we are living in a moment in North America and Europe in which feminism has become, somewhat incredibly, *popular*. It feels as if everywhere you turn, there is an expression of feminism—on a T-shirt, in a movie, in the lyrics of a pop song, in an inspirational Instagram post, in an awards ceremony speech. Feminism is "popular" in at least three senses: One, feminism manifests in discourses and practices that are circulated in popular and commercial media, such as digital spaces like blogs, Instagram, and Twitter, as well as broadcast media. As such, these discourses have an accessibility that is not confined to academic enclaves or niche groups. Two, the "popular" of popular feminism signifies the condition of being liked or admired by like-minded people and groups, as *popularity*. And three, for me the "popular" is, as cultural theorist Stuart Hall (1998) argued, a terrain of struggle, a space where competing demands for power battle it out. This means that there are many different feminisms that circulate in popular culture in the current moment, and some of these feminisms become more visible than others. Popular feminism is networked across all media platforms, some connecting with synergy, others struggling for priority and visibility. Popular feminism has, in many ways, allowed us to imagine a culture in which feminism, in every form, doesn't have to be defended; it is accessible, even admired.

But feminism isn't the only popular phenomenon we need to contend with in the early twenty-first century. Each time I began to investigate a popular feminist practice or expression, there was always an accompanying hostile rejoinder or challenge, regardless of the mediated space in which it occurred—whether that was social media, the legal realm, or corporate culture. For every Tumblr page dedicated to female body positivity, there were fat-shaming and body-shaming online comments. For every confidence organization for girls, there was yet another men's rights organization claiming that men are the "real" victims. For many women—and more than a few men—a broader acceptance of feminism as an identity, concept, and practice is exhilarating; yet, for those who find feminism to be a threat, this acceptance also stimulates fear, trepidation, aggression, and violence. When feminism is "in the water," so to speak, as it is in popular culture today, it is not surprising to witness a backlash from patriarchal culture. It is not surprising because opposition to feminism is not new. There is clearly a relationship between the creation and expression of popular feminism and what I began to call "popular misogyny."

Misogyny is popular in the contemporary moment for the same reasons feminism has become popular: it is expressed and practiced on multiple media platforms, it attracts other like-minded groups and individuals, and it manifests in a terrain of struggle, with competing demands for power. For me, popular misogyny in some ways follows a conventional definition of misogyny: a hatred of women. But I also want to make a more nuanced case for popular misogyny: it is the instrumentalization of women as objects, where women are a means to an end: a systematic devaluing and dehumanizing of women. Popular misogyny is also, like popular feminism, networked, an interconnection of nodes in all forms of media and everyday practice. Of course, misogyny is not only expressed and practiced by men; women are also part of this formation. Misogyny is also challenged and critiqued by many, even as it is often expressed as an invisible norm.

The relationship between popular feminism and popular misogyny is deeply entwined: popular feminism and popular misogyny battle it out on the contemporary cultural landscape, living side by side as warring, constantly moving contexts in an economy of visibility. This economy of visibility, as I elaborate later, is a media landscape that is many things at once: a technological and economic context devoted to the accumulation of views, clicks, "likes," etcetera; a backdrop for popular feminism and popular misogyny; the battlefield for the struggles between them; a set of tactics used by some feminisms and some misogynies to move into the spotlight with more ease than others. Both feminism and misogyny deploy the popular, albeit in different ways. The sheer popularity of popular feminism provides spaces for a specific kind of political action along themes that resonate within an economy of visibility, such as empowerment, confidence, capacity, and competence. As such, popular feminism is *active* in shaping culture. However, the "popular" of popular misogyny is *reactive*.

The contemporary networked media context in which popular feminism and popular misogyny are expressed makes for a particular manifestation of the struggle between feminism and misogyny that has existed for centuries. While networked culture has provided a context for a transfigured feminist politics, it has also provided a context for misogyny to twist and distort the popular in ways that seem new to the contemporary era. Because popular misogyny is reactive, it doesn't have the same consistency, history, and political motion as popular feminism. Clearly, the intensification of misogyny in the contemporary moment is in part a reaction to the culture-wide circulation and embrace of feminism. Every time feminism gains broad traction—that is, every time it spills beyond what are routinely dismissed as niched feminist enclaves—the forces of the status quo position it as a peril, and skirmishes ensue between those determined to challenge the normative and those determined to maintain it. This happened with suffrage and abolition, with the US civil rights movement and the liberal feminist movement of the 1960s and '70s. It happened in the 1980s, as Susan Faludi (1991) and others have documented, and these challenges continue into the current moment, where among other things, US states such as Texas and Arkansas, in their fight to eliminate abortion rights for women, have decimated women's health care in general. Feminism is framed, by media and society alike, as a set of risks—risks that emerge anywhere and everywhere: feminism threatens conventional definitions and performances of masculinity; it threatens work culture, especially perilous in a global recession because when women have jobs this is somehow seen as taking away a man's natural right to have a job; and it threatens conventional performances of heteronormative femininity, particularly in the ways that femininity functions to reassure men of their dominant position.[1] Such efforts to dismantle and delegitimize feminism have been occurring at regular intervals for centuries. Misogyny has certainly long existed as a norm, built into our structures, laws, policies, and normative behavior. As such, it has been relatively invisible as a politics, existing rather as common sense, the "way things are." But the contemporary version of misogyny is also a new outgrowth of its reactive nature. The contemporary networked visibility of popular feminism, available across multiple media platforms, has stimulated a reaction, mobilizing misogyny to compete for visibility within these same mediated networks.

In the following pages I contend with how, and in what ways, the rise of popular feminism has encouraged both a response and an intensification of popular misogyny. I attempt to show some of the social, cultural, and economic conditions that define and describe particularly visible forms of popular feminism and popular misogyny. *Empowered* is organized around some of the key themes I have recognized within popular feminism: *shame*, *confidence*, and *competence*. These are also themes that are then taken up by popular misogyny, though the meaning of them is distorted, and deflects attention away from women and toward men, and is then targeted actively *against* women. In turn, each of these themes is dependent on a logic that revolves around the twinned discourses of *capacity* and *injury*. By this I mean that both popular feminism and popular misogyny tap into a neoliberal notion of individual capacity (for work, for confidence, for economic success), but both also position injury—for women, the injury of sexism; for men, the injury of feminism and "multiculturalism"—as a key obstacle to realizing this capacity. I also situate popular feminism and popular misogyny as practices that are simultaneously residual and emergent: there are clear ways that both feminism and misogyny have been engaged in a particular dynamic for centuries—just as it is clear that the current networked moment shifts this dynamic in important ways.

Popular feminism exists along a continuum, where spectacular, media-friendly expressions such as celebrity feminism and corporate feminism achieve more visibility, and expressions that critique patriarchal structures and systems of racism and violence are more obscured (see McRobbie 2009; Gill 2011; Rottenberg 2014). Seeing and hearing a safely affirmative feminism in spectacularly visible ways often eclipses a feminist critique of structure, as well as obscures the labor involved in producing oneself according to the parameters of popular feminism. The visibility of popular feminism, where examples appear on television, in film, on social media, and on bodies, is important, but it often stops there, as if *seeing* or purchasing feminism is the same thing as changing patriarchal structures. To be clear: the popular feminism I discuss in this book focuses on media expressions and their circulation, the social, cultural, and economic conditions that provide a context for a specific version of popular feminism to emerge as highly visible. That is, this book is not about the political intentions that energize a variety of feminist practices; it is about how some of these political intentions are marshaled by institutions and structures, and what they make available and what they foreclose in terms of politics. Yet, while popular feminisms are often framed by this kind of ambivalence, popular misogyny, in contrast, frames itself in deterministic and resolute terms. The spaces that are opened up by contemporary iterations of popular misogyny are framed not in ambivalent terms but as a zero-sum game: according to popular misogyny, men are suffering because of women in general, and feminism in particular. Women are taking over space, jobs, desire, families, childrearing, and power. For popular misogynies, every space or place, every exercise of power that women deploy is understood as taking that power *away* from men. In this historical moment, popular feminism is in defense against, among other things, structural gendered inequalities. Popular misogyny is in defense against feminism and its putative gains.

The risks posed by popular feminism share some similarities with historical moments, but it is also clear to me that we are in a new era of the gender wars, an era that is marked by a dramatic increase in the visible expression and acceptance of feminism, and by a similarly vast amount of public vitriol and violence directed toward women. Both feminism and its repudiation abound online and offline, which means that our avenues for expression—indeed, our very means of expression, from emoji to the media platforms on which we type them—are radically different from the wars of generations past. Misogyny, once a social formation that was expressed primarily in enclosures (home, locker room, board room, etc.) now increases via the connection, circulation, publicness, networks, and communication across and through those enclosures.[2] But while it circulates with relative ease in digital networks, misogyny is also reified in institutional structures: the workplace (unequal pay, sexual harassment, glass ceilings); organized religions (many of which continue to denigrate women); state politics (where women remain in the vast minority, and, as we have seen in the Trump administration, are often interrupted, diminished, and outright silenced).

Because I conducted research for this book while living in the United States, many of the examples are US-based, though popular feminism is not confined to the United States. Popular feminism and popular misogyny are expressed and practiced around the world in different ways, in a variety of contexts. Indeed, not a single day has gone by in the last several years that there hasn't been new material in both popular feminism and popular misogyny across the globe; it has been difficult to determine which examples to include, and which to leave out. Ultimately, I selected some of the examples that became particulary visible within the popular, be that a social media–shared campaign, a cable reality television show, or a confidence organization that made headlines. Some of these enjoyed an especially heightened visibility, such as the Always #LikeAGirl campaign, which aired during the Super Bowl in 2015, the annual US football championship, which is one of the most watched events on American television, and one of very few broadcast events that is widely watched by diverse (rather than niche) audiences; for this reason, the event has become particularly known for the very expensive advertisements aired during the broadcast. Others, such as the #DontMancriminate campaign I discuss in chapter 1, were the creation of a small online magazine based in India. However, the images from #DontMancriminate circulated widely and swiftly on social media, and they were then picked up by popular blogs and websites—so it became quite visible as an example of popular misogyny. I do not attempt to be exhaustive with my examples, nor do I present examples that are necessarily equal in their popularity and visibility. Indeed, this variety is part of the point I am making: the examples gesture to a set of networked cultures rather than to a specific political mechanism. I use them as a lens through which we can see the active response and reactive call of popular feminism and popular misogyny operating. In other words, the examples I analyze in this book are not characterized by their specificity or uniqueness but rather by how they form a broad contemporary context, one that shares similarities with histories of feminisms and misogynies, but also one that represents a shift happening now.

Popular Feminism

I began this introduction with three senses of the "popular" in popular feminism: as media visibility and accessibility, as popularity, and as a struggle for meaning. Surely there are other meanings of "popular," but in surveying the cultural landscape over the past decade, it is these three that signify most powerfully with popular feminism; thus I will use them as a map to clarify what I mean by "popular feminism." What does popular feminism look like? How does it circulate? Who are its ideal constituents? What are its goals? These questions have been asked more and more over the past decade, as versions of popular feminism have circulated more broadly through American and European culture. A key signifying moment in popular feminism, for many girls and women, was when Beyoncé performed at the MTV Video Music Awards in 2014 with the word "feminist" lit up behind her. Despite the fact that I've spent many years investigating commodity feminism, there seemed to be something special about that moment (a specialness that was then replicated in thousands of memes and images on social media). After the performance, columnist Jessica Valenti (who is herself part of popular feminism) proclaimed in the *Guardian*, "The zeitgeist is irrefutably feminist: its name literally in bright lights" (Valenti 2014, n.p.). Earlier, in February 2014, the popular blog *Jezebel* asked, "What does it mean for feminism if feminism becomes trendy?" (Beusman 2014, n.p.). Valenti similarly wondered, "If everyone is a feminist, is anyone?" (Valenti 2014, n.p.). So while Beyoncé's performance was spectacular, it was only one of many popular feminist images and expressions within the contemporary media landscape; in asking these questions, the authors refer to popular feminist practices, from organizing marches to hashtag activism to T-shirts. Indeed, these questions have only grown more urgent, as feminist manifestos have crowded most media platforms, making a specific version of feminist subjectivity and its parent political commitments both hypervisible and normative within popular media.

Of course, the architecture of many of these popular media platforms is capitalist and corporate. As we have seen historically, specific messages of feminism are often incorporated into advertising and marketing, and contemporary popular feminism is no different. One after another, major global companies—from the technology company Verizon to the beauty corporations CoverGirl and Dove to the automobile companies Chevrolet and Audi—have churned out emotional advertising campaigns, urging us to pay closer attention to girls and the opportunities available to them (or the lack thereof). American girls, this new marketing narrative typically goes, have been excluded from a plethora of professional and personal fields, from science, technology, engineering, and math (STEM) careers to music to athletics, because they feel unqualified and have low self-esteem. However, these ads declare, an answer is at hand, and with only the right products, anything is possible.

Successful female entrepreneurs have become eager spokeswomen for the cause: Facebook's Sheryl Sandberg (2013) wrote a best-selling memoir and feminist ode, offering her own brand of motivational and aspirational

FIGURE INTRO.1. Beyoncé, MTV Video Music Awards, 2014.

corporate feminism, pleading with girls and women to overcome "imposter syndrome" and to "lean in." Girl empowerment organizations, in both US and global development, insist that focusing on gender equality is "smarter economics," and again, that girls and women need to "lean in" to be economically successful. Teaching girls and women to code in computing, as a way to address the marginalization of women in technology industries, became a hot new industry itself. Social media has exploded with feminist campaigns, from #bringbackourgirls to #solidarityisforwhitewomen to #yesallwomen to the campaign in 2016, inspired by US president Donald Trump's casual dismissal of sexual assault, #NotOkay, to the 2017 (and continuing) explosive movement about sexual harassment in the workplace, #MeToo. Blogs and websites, such as *Black Girl Dangerous*, *Feministing*, *Feminist Current*, *Crunk Feminist Collective*, and *Jezebel*, are filled with passionate defenses and celebrations of feminism and exhortations toward feminist and antiracist activism. Meanwhile, the question du jour for female (and some male) celebrities has become: "Are you a feminist?" *Cosmopolitan* magazine and the Ms. Foundation, in an unlikely partnership, announced a "top ten" list of celebrity feminists at the end of 2014, with actress Emma Watson awarded as the "celebrity feminist of the year" (Filipovic 2014). Last but certainly not least for our particular era, feminist ideology is now sartorial—and just a click away. Etsy and others offer feminist tank tops, buttons, and entire wardrobes. High fashion has also taken note: as part of collections in 2017, designer Christian Dior created a $710 T-shirt that proclaimed "We Should All Be Feminists," and Prabal Gurung's more modestly priced version (at only $195) stated "This Is What a Feminist Looks Like." The manifestations of popular feminism are numerous, from hashtag activism to corporate campaigns to intersectional political and social action. Surely an ad campaign from Dove about body positivity is seen by far more viewers than critical commentary on sexual violence toward women of color. Yet it is important to see these two manifestations of feminism as related; to consider them as completely discrete is to simplify the context that enables and propels both of them into a simultaneous existence, even if this existence is asymmetrical in terms of visibility.

In other words, there are many different feminisms that are popular in the current moment. Indeed, media platforms such as Twitter and Facebook have enabled a visibility of feminisms that have long struggled for a broader space and place in culture, which makes it often difficult to distinguish between and among them. This mediated circulation around and within different spaces is crucial to popular feminism. J. K. Gibson-Graham envisioned feminist politics as one that is about a kind of network; a "vast set of disarticulated economic 'places'—households, communities, ecosystems, workplaces, civic organizations, enterprises, public arenas, urban spaces, diasporas, regions, government agencies—related analogically rather than organizationally and connected through webs of signification" (2006, 38). Popular feminism is analogical, in that feminist practices share similar experiences and particularities, but it is also more broadly networked, connected through webs of signification. *Empowered* explores and theorizes this networked characteristic of popular feminism and locates it within a dynamic relationship with a similarly networked popular misogyny.

The Popular as Media Accessibility

It is important to analyze the "popular" in popular feminism to see how it is distinct from other feminist practices and expressions. What are its boundaries, its borders? Is it defined by its politics, its visibility, where it emanates from? The popular feminism I analyze in this book generally materializes as a kind of *media* that is widely visible and accessible. It appears on broadcast media, in television and advertising. It appears in popular music. In the contemporary context, it appears perhaps most urgently in social media, with media companies such as Instagram, Tumblr,

FIGURE INTRO.2.
Emma Watson,
"The Fresh Face
of Feminism," *Elle*
magazine, 2014.

Facebook, and Twitter providing platforms for its circulation. As I expand on below, popular feminism circulates in an economy of visibility. Yet visibility is never simple. Media scholars, feminists, critical race scholars, LGBTQ scholars, and others have worked over many decades in the name of visibility; in a media context in which if you are visible, you *matter*, visibility matters indeed (e.g., Grewal 2005; Hegde 2011; Gross 2012; H. Gray 2013; Smith, Pieper, and Choueiti 2017). Part of this visibility means being accessible to a large, popular audience. As a set of practices and expressions that circulate in an economy of visibility, popular feminism is part of the larger "attention" economy, where its sheer accessibility—through shared images, "likes," clicks, followers, retweets, and so on—is a key component of its popularity. And this popularity and accessibility are measured in and through their ability to increase that visibility; popular feminism engages in a feedback loop, where it is more popular when it is more visible, which then authorizes it to create

FIGURE INTRO.3.
"Empower Women"
T-shirt, H&M
retailers, 2017.

ever-increasing visibility. Visibility is not a static thing; it has to be in a constant state of growth.

But, as we also know, in a media context in which most circuits of visibility are driven by profit, competition, and consumers, simply *becoming* visible does not guarantee that identity categories such as gender, race, and sexuality will be unfettered from sexism, misogyny, and homophobia. The popular feminisms I explore in this book are typically those that become visible precisely because they do not challenge deep structures of inequities. That is, in order for some images and practices to become visible, others must be rendered invisible.

In this sense, the popular feminism I discuss throughout this book is not disruptive to capitalism or mainstream politics, but rather follows what Catherine Rottenberg (2014) has called neoliberal feminism. Rottenberg argues that neoliberal feminism is one in which the values and assumptions of neoliberalism—ever-expanding markets, entrepreneurialism, a focus on the individual—are embraced, not challenged, by feminism. In her words, "Unlike classic liberal feminism whose *raison d'être* was to pose an immanent critique of liberalism, revealing the gendered exclusions within liberal democracy's proclamation of universal equality, particularly with respect to the law, institutional access, and the full incorporation of women into the public sphere, this new feminism seems perfectly in sync with the evolving neoliberal order. Neoliberal feminism, in other words, offers no critique—immanent or otherwise—of neoliberalism" (Rotten-berg 2014, 419).

While the popular feminism I analyze in this book clearly connects to neoliberal principles of individualism and entrepreneurialism, it also does, in fact, owe a debt to liberal feminism's critique of gendered exclusions in the public and corporate spheres. That is, this corporate-friendly popular feminism emanates from an increasing visibility of a gendered disparity in dominant economic spheres—a lack of female CEOs, a lack of female Hollywood directors, a lack of women in technology and media fields, and an increased awareness of sexual harassment within corporate industries such as media and technology. The popular feminisms I ana-lyze in this book are, like liberal feminism, in many ways a call to bring more women to the table, simply because they are women. It thus has a history in what feminist historian Joan Scott has called an "add women and stir" kind of liberal feminism, in which the presence of women is suf-ficient to call feminism into being (Scott 1991). The inclusion of women becomes the solution for all gender problems, not just those of exclusion or absence. It is, of course, important to have bodies at the table, but their mere presence doesn't necessarily challenge the structure that supports, and builds, the table in the first place; as Scott points out, merely includ-ing women does not address "the framework of (historically contingent) dominant patterns of sexuality and the ideology that supports them" (But-ler and Scott 1992, 25). In this way, popular feminism and its exhortations to simply have *more* women in various cultural, political, and economic realms is similar to liberal efforts to include people of color within a wid-ened field of whiteness, one that continues to shape representation, work, and politics without interrogating the racism that forms the boundaries of whiteness from the ground up.

The focus on inclusion by popular feminism makes it specifically cor-porate friendly; it has benefited from decades of neoliberal commodity activism, in which companies have taken up women's issues, especially those that have to do with individual consumption habits, as a key selling point for products (Mukherjee and Banet-Weiser 2012). I explore many of these recent campaigns in this book and argue that there is a market for feminism; the popular feminisms I discuss mainly contribute to, rather than challenge, this market. This historical context of commodity feminism provides a backdrop for the expansion of popular feminism into other capitalist, consumerist realms. Within neoliberal brand culture, specific feminist expressions and politics are brandable, commensurate with market logics: those that focus on the individual body, those that connect social change with corporate capitalism, and those that emphasize individual attributes such as confidence, self-esteem, and competence as particularly useful to neoliberal self-reliance and capitalist success. In a capitalist, corporate economy of visibility, those feminisms that are most easily commodified and branded are those that become most visible. This means, most of the time, that the popular feminism that is most visible is that which is white, middle-class, cis-gendered, and heterosexual.

The Popular as Popularity

Popular feminism is also about specific *exclusions*, which leads to the second definition of "popular" in popular feminism: that of *popularity*. A basic definition of popularity is being admired by like-minded individuals. But a more practiced definition of popularity recalls for many of us the cliques and exclusionary practices of high school. Memorialized in films from *Grease* to *Pretty in Pink* (and the rest of the John Hughes oeuvre) to *Mean Girls*, popularity means the privilege of some to say to others, as the character Gretchen Wieners did in *Mean Girls*, "You can't sit with us." One can't sit with the popular clique unless one conforms to the norms of that group; again, the dominant culture of the popular feminism I examine in this book is primarily white, middle-class, cis-gendered, and heteronormative. This is the popular feminism that seizes the spotlight in an economy of visibility and renders other feminisms less visible. We witness this kind of exclusion in the popular feminist insistence on a universal definition of "equality" between men and women as its key definition. When feminists of color have challenged this universality, pointing out that "universal" equal rights have historically meant equal rights for white people, and insist on specificity and history as part of feminism, it is often met by popular feminism as an obstruction. In a similar move to the challenge to

FIGURE INTRO.4. "All Lives Matter" protest against Black Lives Matter, 2015.

the Black Lives Matter movement with "All Lives Matter," or the response to LGBTQ pride of "heterosexual pride," popular feminism insists that a universal gender identity must be the central category of analysis. This is a classic liberal move, denouncing specificity, insisting on a universal definition of identity—even as this "universality" typically signifies white, middle-class, cis-gendered, and heterosexual identity. In this way, popular feminism frequently refuses intersectionality, and often erases and devalues women of color, working-class women, trans women, and non-heteronormative women, even when it claims to include all women. The Women's March in 2017, as I discuss in the conclusion, is an example of popular feminism that makes that type of all-inclusive claim.

The "popular" of popular feminism is structured by this dynamic of inclusion and exclusion. But because of its indebtedness to corporate feminism and a desire to not alienate consumers, popular feminism also depends on affectively resisting the "mean" in mean girl cliques. Despite its exclusions, popular feminism is often an *accommodating* feminism, and in particular, accommodating men (even when this appears in ironic misandrist feminism). This accommodationist strategy is not just conducive to corporate expression; it exists in part in order to become *available* to corporate expression. Popular feminism thus also emanates from an affective space: historically, the visibility of feminism in the US media has predominantly been as angry, defiant, man-hating women. The current manifestation of popular feminism directly challenges this representation; while recognizing that gendered relations of power marginalize women, this critique is expressed in a friendly, safe way. Popular feminism is decidedly not angry—indeed, anger (at sexism, racism, patriarchy, abuse) seems to be an old-fashioned vestige, a ghost of feminism's past, one not suited to the popular media context of contemporary feminism. What we see today, as Gill puts it, is a "feminism that is actually encumbered by its desire not to be angry, not to be 'difficult', not to be 'humourless'"—a version that is implicitly "positioned against the figure of the 'feminist killjoy'" (Gill 2016b, 618).

In her book *The Promise of Happiness*, Sara Ahmed defines the feminist killjoy thus: "The feminist killjoy 'spoils' the happiness of others; she is a spoilsport because she refuses to convene, to assemble, or to meet up over happiness. In the thick sociality of everyday spaces, feminists are thus attributed as the origin of the bad feeling, as the ones who ruin the atmosphere" (2010, 65). Popular feminism is decidedly not a spoilsport, it is not the origin of bad feeling. We see this in its corporate-friendly expressions (because bad feelings are not good for marketing). We see this clearly in celebrity Emma Watson, who has become visible within popular feminism with her United Nations campaign "HeForShe," where she explicitly says that feminists need to invite men into a conversation about gender inequalities. We see this in the way that popular feminism is framed by heteronormativity and heterosexuality. To be clear, men *should* be in a conversation about gender inequalities. But popular feminism accommodates men through its heteronormativity, which is of course defined by gendered norms that already prioritize the logic of heterosexuality.

The Popular as Struggle

Finally, I theorize popular feminism through my third definition of the popular, as a terrain of struggle over meaning. As cultural theorist Stuart Hall famously said, "Popular culture is one of the sites where this struggle for and against a culture of the powerful is engaged: it is also the stake to be won or lost in that struggle.... It is the arena of consent and resistance" (1998, 453). The dynamic between consent and resistance is a key mobilizer within popular feminism, where it is privileged in an economy of visibility, and is firmly within the "culture of the powerful." This is a culture of racial and economic privilege. The most visible popular feminism is that within the arena of consent: it consents to heteronormativity, to the universality of whiteness, to dominant economic formations, to a trajectory of capitalist "success."

There are, of course, other feminisms that share some of the characteristics of media visibility and popularity but are positioned more within Hall's arena of resistance than consent: those that challenge and expose the whiteness of much of popular feminism; those that use the media visibility as a way to expose structural violence; those that are nonheteronormative; those that insist on intersectionality. Black Twitter, for example, as Caitlin Gunn (2015), Dayna Chatman (2017), André Brock (2012), and others have shown, has become a place for feminists of color to create campaigns for social justice. Many feminist blogs, such as *Black Girl Dangerous*, *Crunk Feminist Collective*, and *Feministing*, specifically critique the whiteness of much popular feminism and offer important intersectional analyses of gendered power relations in contemporary culture. There are popular feminist authors, such as Laurie Penny and Jessica Valenti, who write incisive critiques of gender and capitalism. In relation to these practices, popular feminism can be seen as a kind of backlash against feminism's goals of critiquing racism, capitalism, and patriarchy (and their deep relations). By commodifying and making feminism "safe," popular feminism resists structural critique.

The struggle between a consenting popular feminism and one that is more resistant became clearly evident in October 2017 in the United States, when multiple accusations of sexual harassment against Hollywood producer Harvey Weinstein were publicized; the Weinstein case mobilized, as is now well known, hundreds of other stories from women about harassment, which were manifest in the multimedia movement #MeToo (Kantor and Twohey 2017, n.p.).

As many have pointed out, the phrase "me too" was actually created in 2006 by an African American activist, Tarana Burke, a survivor of sexual assault, who wanted to share her story as a way to connect with other victims of sexual assault, especially women of color (Garcia 2017, n.p.). The fact that Burke, the originator of "me too," was largely eclipsed by the high-profile, mostly white female celebrities who came forward in the Weinstein (and Roger Ailes, and Matt Lauer, and what seems to be countless others) scandal is not insignificant. *Time* magazine's 2017 "Person of the Year" was named the "Silence Breakers," and the issue featured women who have come forward to expose sexual harassers and predators (Zacharek, Dockterman, and Sweetland Edwards 2017). Yet Burke, who created the movement, was inside the pages, not featured on the cover. The mainstream media has covered the #MeToo story expansively, which is an important move—but the stories are often about the powerful men who are accused, or the celebrity women who accuse them. Not surprisingly, there soon was a market for #MeToo, ranging from cookies to jewelry to clothing, as well as the emergence of new apps and other media technologies that attempt to document workplace sexual harassment.

In other words, while the public awareness of #MeToo has helped reveal how widespread and normative sexual harassment is, it is also more spectacularly focused on very visible public figures. This is not to dismiss the accusations in any way; rather, I want to point out that while "me too" existed in the early 2000s as a mechanism for building intersectional feminist community, it became spectacularly visible under the logics of popular feminism; this is the struggle of the popular. The #MeToo movement is expressed on those media platforms that easily lend themselves to commodification and simplification, those industries that provide platforms of visibility (entertainment, news media) already designed and scripted for *any* mode of spectacular spotlight. Some of the more spectacular #MeToo moments, such as when the celebrity components of the story distract us from systemic, structural sexism across all industries, can end up working against the calls for social change promised at its beginning, producing more and more visibility—and increasingly narrowing the discourses of that visibility in the process.

I argue that contemporary popular feminism reimagines and redirects what "empowerment" means for girls and women, and thus is restructuring feminist politics within neoliberal culture. Historically, feminisms have used "liberation" as a goal and specified this liberation as one from sexist and unequal social, political, and economic structures. Within popular feminism, empowerment is the central logic; with little to no specification as to what we want to empower women to do, popular feminism often restructures the politics of feminism to focus on the individual empowered woman. Here, the historical feminist politics of "the personal is the political" are often understood in the reverse, as "the political is the personal."

Why has popular feminism become popular now, in the twenty-first century? What are the various conditions that produce it in the current moment, that authorize its circulation? Popular feminism relies on other feminisms from the nineteenth and twentieth centuries for its gendered logics. Many of the issues popular feminism supports are not new: recognizing that women are hypersexualized and commodified in the media; identifying inequities in labor and the workplace; pointing out gendered asymmetries in individual self-esteem; and challenging the policing and regulation of the female body. The historical antecedents of popular feminism—such as antiracist movements, liberal feminism and women's liberation feminism, LGBTQ movements, third-wave feminist movements, and postfeminism—provide necessary conditions for a popular feminism to flourish in the current moment. Other feminist iterations and practices, such as intersectional feminism, queer feminism, and materialist feminism, also circulate and compete within an economy of visibility, which is organized around exclusion and inclusion. Yet popular feminism becomes the central feminism within an economy of visibility. Popular feminism is thus partly a residual movement, energized and authorized by decades of political organizing around identity issues, such as gender, race, and sexuality. But the popularity of popular feminism is also new and emergent— we see feminist slogans, messages, and practices in everyday spaces, on social media, and in afterschool programs. So what are the social, cultural, and economic conditions that need to be in place for popular feminism to flourish in this moment?

Perhaps most importantly, in order to emerge so forcefully, popular feminism needs a neoliberal capitalist context. Related to this, it needs digital media and its affordances, its commitment to capitalism, its expanded markets, its circulation capabilities. Digital media has afforded spaces and places for popular feminists to create media, voice their opinions, and launch businesses. These conditions have often been called "platform capitalism," implying the emptying or flattening out of the *content* of meaning, emphasizing instead the endless traffic and circulation of this content (see Srnicek 2016; Hearn 2017). These logics of visibility—composed of metrics, numbers, clicks, "likes," etcetera—form the social, cultural, and economic conditions for popular feminism, though the implications of these logics is not just for feminism, but also for social movements in general. The logics of platform capitalism emphasize metrics, numbers, "likes," and followers; given the predominance of digital media platforms that are predicated on the accumulation of numbers, where their business depends on these numbers, to make oneself visible or to express oneself is then also dependent on this kind of numerical accumulation. Jose van Dijck calls this the "popularity principle," where, despite differences among media platforms, these platforms are invested "in the same values or principles: popularity, hierarchical ranking, quick growth, large traffic volumes, fast turnovers, and personalized recommendations" (van Dijck 2013, n.p.).

And, as Brooke Erin Duffy (2017) details in her work about social media and aspirational labor, women largely populate many of the most visible genres of social media production, and digital media in general is crucial to the heightened visibility of popular feminism.[3] As Duffy theorizes, digital media encourages "aspirational labor," in which the successes of some women in digital spaces mobilize a general ethos where "everyone" can be creative and succeed (McRobbie 2016). The logic of aspirational labor depends on the popular feminist themes I examine in this book: self-esteem, confidence, and competence. This digital context, with its rapid circulation and loyalty to numerical accumulation, authorizes expressions and practices of popular feminism to an audience that has a wider reach than ever before. At the same time, these digital affordances also partly enable media to hyperbolize and bifurcate political positions, thus helping to generate a discursive climate of extreme views (such as misogyny).

More than any other historical influence, popular feminism emerges within the ongoing ethos and sensibility of postfeminism (Gill 2007). Postfeminism, as Rosalind Gill (2007), Angela McRobbie (2009), Diane Negra and Yvonne Tasker (2007), and others have argued, is dedicated to the recognition, and then repudiation, of feminism—and it is through this repudiation, an insistence that feminism is no longer needed as a politics, that women are empowered. Women, that is, are empowered within postfeminism precisely because feminism is seen as having done the political work needed to eradicate gender asymmetry.

In this way, postfeminism celebrates a kind of gendered "freedom" in which women are apparently free to become all they want to be. Women just have to be a "Girl Boss" or "Lean In" in order to overcome sexist history. Materially, what this means is that neoliberal values such as entrepreneurialism, individualism, and the expansion of capitalist markets are embraced and adopted by girls and women as a way to craft their selves.

These values are privileged within postfeminism, rather than feminist politics, which are seen are unproductive and obsolete. Postfeminism can be characterized as a set of ideas, elements, feelings, and emphases that operate as a kind of gendered neoliberalism. Importantly, the "post" in postfeminism is not necessarily temporal, as in a new "wave" after second- or third-wave Western feminism (Dosekun 2015). Rather, postfeminism and popular feminism are entangled together in contemporary media visibility. Postfeminism remains a dominant, visible iteration of feminism in culture, and is not displaced by popular feminism but rather bolstered by it. As Rosalind Gill points out, "New cultural trends do not simply displace older or existing ones. A momentarily visible resurgence of interest in feminism should not lead us to the false conclusion that antifeminist or postfeminist ideas no longer exist" (Gill 2016a, 2).

Yet, on the face of it, popular feminism seems quite distinct from postfeminism's disavowal of feminist politics. After all, popular feminism takes up the mantle of traditional feminist issues, pointing out that girls and women have experienced crises of gender in the twenty-first century, from low self-esteem to low numbers in leadership positions. Popular feminism asks: If the postfeminist claims of gender equality are actually true, why aren't there more female CEOs? Why are more women reporting sexual assault? Why is there such a discrepancy between women and men in technology fields? The early twenty-first century saw the emergence of a newly forged feminist avowal: popular feminism explicitly *embraces* feminist values and ideologies and is dedicated to recognizing that gender inequality still exists. Popular feminism recognizes the vulnerability of women in a sexist context, shifting away from the vague "girl power" slogan of postfeminism. The popular feminist recognition that vast gender inequities still organize our cultural, economic, and political worlds is important, and a necessary correction to the false optimism of postfeminism. Again, though, popular feminism in the current moment also shares great structural similarities with postfeminism (Gill 2016b). While postfeminism and popular feminism are oppositional on the surface, they are actually mutually sustaining. Indeed, the feminist visions that come into dominant view in the current moment are shaped by the same affective politics that shape postfeminism: entrepreneurial spirit, resilience, gumption.

The "feminist standpoint" that Nancy Hartsock theorized in 1983 was connected to a Marxist notion of a proletarian understanding of inequality—and is a perspective that emerges from struggle and collective achievement (Hartsock 1983). One doesn't just "have" a feminist standpoint simply because one is a woman, in other words. It is a political commitment, a struggle over power, an activist responsibility. There is no postfeminist or popular feminist standpoint; on the contrary, it is more a kind of attitude, a feminist weightlessness, "unencumbered by the need to have a position on anything" (Gill 2016b, 618). The success of postfeminism and popular feminism seems to begin and end with ease: you merely need to identify as female, but don't need to identify with the murky realms of gender's social construction, or with an identity that is unequal from the ground up. So despite this seeming contradiction, between disavowal and avowal of feminism, it does not necessarily mean that popular feminism critiques the roots of gender asymmetry; rather, popular feminism tinkers on the surface, embracing a palatable feminism, encouraging individual girls and women to just *be* empowered.

These discourses of post- and pop-feminist empowerment are intimately connected to cultural economies, where to be "empowered" is to be, as Angela McRobbie (2007) has pointed out, a better *economic* subject, not necessarily a better feminist subject. Post- and popular feminism utilize different subjectivities to become visible, but for both, visibility is paramount. For this, both post- and popular feminism require an economy of visibility.

Economies of Visibility

In *American Anatomies*, Robyn Wiegman (1995, 8) defined "economies of visibility" as "the epistemology of the visual that underlies both race and gender: that process of corporeal inscription that defines each as a binary, wholly visible affair." In this formulation, race and gender are defined in large part by their visual representation: they are easy to decipher and understand, their visible bodies, or "corporeal inscription," become the stuff of who, and what, they are. Wiegman traces this visual inscription of the body historically, in both the pre– and post–civil rights eras, and links the economy of visibility to the proliferation of cinema, television, and video and the representation of bodies as kinds of commodities. While surely media such as film and television continue to serve up bodies as narrative commodities, I'd like to extend Wiegman's definition to thinking about how economies of visibility work in an era of advanced capitalism and networked, multiple media platforms—and how these economies both create and validate popular feminism and popular misogyny. Within this mediated context, visibility becomes an end in itself, what is visible becomes what *is* (H. Gray 2013).

Feminist media studies scholars, critical race theorists, and cultural studies scholars have long been invested in studying the *politics* of visibility. The politics of visibility usually describes the process of making visible a political category (such as gender or race) that is and has been historically marginalized in the media, law, policy, and so on. This process involves what is simultaneously a category (visibility) and a qualifier (politics) that can articulate a political identity. Representation, or visibility, takes on a political valence. Here, the goal is that the coupling of "visibility" and "politics" can be productive of something, such as social change, that exceeds the visibility. "Politics," then, is a descriptor of the *practices* of visibility.

The politics of visibility has thus long been important for the marginalized, and continues to be. To demand visibility is to demand to be seen, to matter, to recognize oneself in dominant culture. As Nathaniel Frank has put it in relation to LGBTQ visibility, it is "the notion that increasing familiarity with marginalized groups is key to expanding respect for their rights" (Frank 2017, para. 1). The insistence of marginalized and disenfranchised communities—women, racial minorities, nonheteronormative communities, the working class—to be *seen* has been crucial to an understanding and an expansion of rights for these communities. So when, for example, civil rights activists mobilized to bring attention to the vast and varied racist practices of mid-twentieth-century US culture, it was to change those practices, to pursue social justice. When US media activists in the later part of the twentieth century challenged networks or other platforms to change representational practices in media in terms of race, gender, or sexuality, it was to change the way identities matter and are valued socially, politically, culturally. When social activists insist on calling attention to the "99%" of people who have the least amount of wealth in the world, as the Occupy movement did, they do so in an effort to change and disrupt wealth divisions and subsequent power relations. Of course, not all politics of visibility result in social change; the point here is that visibility is understood as leading to something, as part of a political struggle.

In the current environment, however, while the politics of visibility are still important and remain politically efficacious, *economies* of visibility increasingly structure not just our mediascapes but also our cultural and economic practices and daily lives. In the contemporary media and digital moment, media outlets and systems can easily absorb the visualization of basically any experience. Economies of visibility fundamentally shift politics of visibility so that visibility becomes *the end* rather than a means to an end. In this way, political categories such as race and gender have transformed their very logics from the inside out, so that the visibility of these categories is what matters, rather than the structural ground on and through which they are constructed. For example, wearing a T-shirt that says "This Is What a Feminist Looks Like" transmutes the political logic of what it means to be a feminist, as a political subjectivity invested in challenging gender inequities, into what a feminist *looks* like, her visual representation (even if the person wearing the T-shirt practices feminist politics). Visibility is thus restructured to stop functioning as a qualifier to politics. The T-shirt *is* the politics; the politics are contained within the visibility—visual representation becomes the beginning and the end of political action. Within this constraining framework of visibility, race and gender, as visibilities, are then apparently self-sufficient, absorbent, and therefore enough on their own. Identifying oneself as someone who looks like a feminist becomes sufficient political action. The identification, and announcement, of one's visibility is both the radical move and the end in itself (H. Gray 2013).[4] Economies of visibility do not describe a political process, but rather assume that visibility itself has been absorbed into the economy; indeed, that absorption *is* the political.

Here, it is useful to think about visibility in terms of the direction a spotlight takes, what a light focuses on. When discussing postfeminism, McRobbie relies on philosopher Gilles Deleuze's notion of luminosity to explain contemporary notions of empowerment, in which he describes visibilities not as objects of vision but rather as "forms of luminosity which are created by the light itself" (2009, 60). The "light" is composed of the conditions that make some objects seen and others unseen, and similarly, that make some bodies visible even as others are obscured. This is one of the moments when postfeminism and popular feminism overlap; for example, the popular feminist focus on confidence is directed toward those white middle-class women who are privileged enough to *expect* they are entitled to confidence. For McRobbie, the "light itself" is the conditions of contemporary neoliberal capitalism, which allow particular subjects and objects to be worthy of our vision.

FIGURE INTRO.5. "This Is What a Feminist Looks Like" T-shirt, 2016.

In other words, in the current moment of neoliberal capitalism and digital culture, the demand for a visibility *politics* competes with an *economization* of visibility. These demands for visibility are quite different; the goals and consequences of visibility transform when they are part of an economy of visibility. In fact, visibility itself is not necessarily the key logic in the contemporary moment but rather how visibility *is managed and controlled.* As Zeynep Gambetti says about the Gezi Park protests in Turkey, "The management of visibility controlled the signification of the event, pinning it to available structures without letting new meanings emerge" (Gambetti 2013, para. 1). The available structures for popular feminism's visibility in the current moment are usually those that are dominant centers of power: media companies, corporations, and the technology industries. In this sense, within the context of popular feminism, visibility often becomes synonymous with "trending," whether in the mainstream news media or on social media. To trend is a different process of visibility than to agitate to be seen in order to be granted basic rights. Trending is about recognition, and about making oneself available for normalization, as Herman Gray has argued; the visibility that fuels trending is a demand to be recognized in an attention economy (H. Gray 2013; Gambetti 2013). As Eunsong Kim has argued, "Trending is visibility granted by a closed, private corporation and their proprietary algorithms" (Kim 2016, para. 10). We are easily tempted to the popular and the luminous: we "like," we retweet, we repost, we encourage trending. Importantly, this does not supplant a politics of visibility; an economy of visibility does not simply produce a universal subject that is constructed by capitalist markets and circulation. It does signal, however, an acquiescence to a demand for a specific kind of visibility, one that is economized and bounded by corporate logics and desires.

To be clear: I'm not using "economy" as a mere metaphor. Rather, I adopt a more nuanced account of the logics and moralities of both economics and culture as a way to understand how identities are constructed within the economy of visibility, and to ask what is at stake in this kind of construction. For girls and women, adopting the logics and moralities of an economy of visibility means that despite the fact that popular feminism claims to be about empowerment, this kind of empowerment is often achieved through a focus on the visible body—precisely one of the aspects of patriarchy feminism has been fighting against for centuries. The visible body is also the commodifiable body.

All bodies are not commodifiable in the same way. For example, race, in the context of an economy of visibility, relies not only on the seen body but also on *how* this body is seen, so nonwhite and white bodies are mobilized differently. Again, the demands for visibility have different goals and consequences. An economy of visibility depends not only on the visible but also on a mechanism of surveillance: who is being watched and seen, and for what reason? An economy of visibility is thus dependent on the dynamic relationship of visibility and invisibility—and the boundaries between these are not always clear. Nonwhite people, nonheteronormative, nongender conforming individuals and communities, and the working class are subject to intense surveillance as a way to enforce social discipline; as such they are kept in a "state of consciousness and permanent visibility that assures the automatic functioning of power" (Foucault [1977] 1995, 201). Marginalized subjects, subjects of difference, are punished and disciplined precisely *when* the spotlight falls on them. Hypervisibility also functions as a figuration of difference, of threat, of terrorism. There are thus different ways to be visible; and visibility isn't always the solution. Visibility hides as it reveals. This not only frames the marginalized in discriminatory ways, it also works to render the complexities of intersectionality less visible, and does not attend to the spaces

FIGURE INTRO.6.
Making the invisible seen:
Transgender visibility.

Transgender

Day of Visibility

2016

#MoreThanVisibility

Be an Ally

that are created by those who do not "fit" within a popular feminist visible frame (Kim 2016).

The spotlight can also become the site of misogyny. Because an economy of visibility functions most effectively on a surface, rather than on a structural, level, for marginalized groups, to be "seen" has limitations. As critical race theorist Grace Hong has argued, "Visibility is not inclusion but surveillance" (Hong 2006, xxviii). When the borders and boundaries of visibility are economized, "inclusion" is about widening an already established set of norms. Thus, those who do not fit those norms because of difference become particularly vulnerable targets. We see this clearly with trans communities, who have recently occupied an ambivalent connection to visibility: on the one hand, it is crucial to be seen, to matter, as a non-gender-conforming community, one that has been hidden for so many years. But visibility can come at a cost at a moment when the visible is ever more primary, ever more difficult to move beyond. We witness this with the "bathroom bills" that have been recently passed in some US states, a series of legislations that define access to public facilities, specifically restrooms, for transgender individuals, and subjects them to extreme surveillance and violation. Trans activist and artist Reina Gossett argues that for trans women, "visibility is a pillar of criminalization, not a tenet of liberation" (Gossett cited in Kim 2016, para. 6). Within this context, Herman Gray's argument that visibility, a "proliferation of differences" in the media and cultural scapes, allows for structural racism to remain in place, is particularly important. Visibility is actually less powerful than invisibility in the maintenance of hegemonic structure, because visibility is more susceptible to critique (H. Gray 2013).

Yet economies define themselves as neutral. Crucially, economies are about individuals—consumers, buyers, sellers. In this definition, economies are seen in a way that validates capitalism, where production is invisible, and commodities, markets, and consumption are prioritized. Economies privilege and give value to the individual who can participate in that economy, and because they focus on individual bodies, they are by definition gendered, raced, and classed economies. Within the *politics* of visibility, bodies that are disenfranchised and marginalized are moved into the spotlight so as to highlight that disenfranchisement and marginalization. Within an economy of visibility, the *spotlight* on their bodies, their visibility, the number of views, is in fact its politics. This spotlight is literally designed for social media such as Instagram, Tumblr, and Snapchat.

Elements of an Economy of Visibility

What does it mean to "economize" visibility? Every economy is made up of different components. For example, as a basic concept, an economy relies on a space wherein forces of supply and demand operate, where buyers and sellers interact to trade or buy goods, where the value of products is deliberated, where consumers are identified, and where specific forms of labor and production occur. The spaces of supply and demand in an economy of visibility are largely mediated spaces—social media, television, film, digital media. These are the spaces where feminism becomes popular, viewed by millions of users, so that there is an opening of space to hear, think, and feel feminism. These are also the spaces that enable visibility of the body, that ask users to evaluate and judge the body, that function as spaces for public shaming. The spaces of an economy of visibility are networked spaces, interconnected nodes between and within multiple media platforms, and where profit is in some ways contingent on number of views.

In an economy of visibility, buyers and sellers interact to trade or buy goods—and within popular feminism, those "goods" are the themes I discuss in this book: self-esteem, confidence, competence. For example, the market here manifests in girl empowerment organizations, where girls who are the most visible in the media, such as white middle-class girls, are the ones seen as in need of being empowered because of issues of low self-esteem and self-confidence. As I discuss in chapter 2, many of these organizations, such as SPARK and AfricAid, use corporate, nonprofit, and governmental funds to form organizations. It also manifests in the form of the "girl effect" in international development discourse, where the girl is positioned as the prominent agent of social change, a heretofore unrecognized competent individual.[5]

The product in gendered economies of visibility is the body (most often the bodies of heteronormative cis-gendered women). Its value is constantly deliberated over, surveilled, evaluated, judged, and scrutinized through media discourses, law, and policy. We see this deliberation of value in misogynistic comments on social media, in campus rape culture, in conservative efforts to curb reproductive rights for women, in revenge porn, in slut and fat shaming. We also see it in popular feminist practices such as the "Love Your Body" discourses, corporate empowerment campaigns, and confidence organizations.

Consumers and producers are clearly identified in the economy of visibility. As with all economies, some are considered more valuable than others (though this does not mean that other sorts of consumers and producers don't exist). As I discuss in chapter 1, two of the most visible female consumers and producers in the contemporary economy of visibility are those that Anita Harris calls "Can-Do girls" and "At-Risk girls" (Harris 2003).[6] These two subject positions circulate with ease within an economy of visibility, where the Can-Do girl, typically white, middle-class, and entrepreneurial, embodies the themes of popular feminism: confident, empowered, entrepreneurial, filled with capacity. The Can-Do girl is positioned in opposition to the At-Risk girl—typically a girl of color or a working-class girl, and one who thus is seen as more susceptible to poverty, drugs, early pregnancy, and fewer career goals and ambitions. Visibility thus yields different gazes, or forms of surveillance, based on race and class. This constant surveillance, in turn, encourages girls' and women's participation in the circuits of media visibility. The demand for girls' and women's bodies, the economy of visibility's hunger for those bodies, endures from postfeminism to the current moment of popular feminism.

Within economies of visibility, there are markets. In the current environment, I see these markets as industries that are built around gendered consumers. These are industries that support and validate the Can-Do girl or invest in the At-Risk girl, that illuminate and make visible specific bodies over others, indeed, that create and sustain the demarcations between the Can-Do and the At-Risk girl. Some of these markets are more immaterial than material, focusing on confidence building, high self-esteem, and vague notions of empowerment. Others are markets that profit on skill sets such as coding that will ostensibly lead to confidence and empowerment.

And of course, in every economy, there is labor and work. In a gendered economy of visibility, there is a dominant presence of the emotional labor of femininity. In a context of neoliberal capitalism, as many have noted, the content and shape of work shifts, so that work becomes more and more about what Arlie Hochschild calls "emotional labor" (Hochschild 1983; see also Weeks 2011; Neff 2012; Gregg 2013; Baym 2015; Duffy 2017). Within dominant practices of neoliberal capitalism, work is more "insecure and casualized" (Gill and Pratt 2008), so that different kinds of labor emerge. In an economy of visibility, work and labor are primarily self-care and care work. This is in part because of labor shifts since the 1970s that Lisa Adkins (2001) describes as the "cultural feminization of work," in which, regardless of gender, more workers are expected to incorporate relational work into their routine practices. There are different definitions of self-care, and what it means to care for the self depends on cultural contexts such as institutionalized racism, conditions of poverty, and so on. Self-care, in a context of an economy of visibility, often involves precarious, informal modes of labor, in which girls and young women cultivate and acquire status as a form of currency, in order to make themselves marketable (Marwick 2013). Again, we see this on platforms such as Instagram, Twitter, and Tumblr, which become platforms for self-branding, as well as the places where self-care is both "proven" (through its visual statement) and also often monetized.

Within today's capitalism, specific girls and women are rendered visible only if they embody what McRobbie refers to as the "spectacularly feminine": "Women are actively engaged in the production of self. That is, it becomes increasingly difficult to function as a female subject without subjecting oneself to those technologies of self that are constitutive of the spectacularly feminine" (2009, 60). Here, McRobbie points to the tenuous connection between personal empowerment and visibility. Visibility can be the route to a kind of empowerment, but one that is "consummately and re-assuringly feminine," and that enables women to be, as Akane Kanai points out, "attributed with capacity, depending on their ability to articulate socially valued versions of femininity in these domains" (Kanai 2016, 18–19).

Kanai's point about the ways in which young women "may be attributed with capacity" depending on how well they can articulate and perform "socially valued versions of femininity" is key to the current moment of empowerment. Becoming visible and capacious—in media, law, policy, education, and so on—is necessary in this version of empowerment, but we need to think about how limits and parameters are drawn and maintained within popular feminism. Whose body can be a socially valued version of femininity within a popular feminist context? According to popular feminism, who is deemed worthy of empowering? And what are we empowering girls and women *to do*?

Within the context of neoliberal capitalism and its intense privileging of individual entrepreneurship and self-governance, contemporary discourses of empowerment stress the goal of becoming capable of governing oneself. In Barbara Cruikshank's (1999) work *The Will to Empower*, she thinks through the various ways that liberal democracies produce citizens who are capable of governing themselves, focusing particularly on the poor. She argues that in order for governments to motivate the poor to help themselves (thus abdicating state social responsibility), the poor had to be *known*: "Empowerment was planned to become, effortlessly, 'self-empowerment.' Expert reformers, private foundations, voluntary associations were and continue to be nongovernmental means of government" (Cruikshank 1999, 69). I see this "nongovernmental" means of government shaping gendered empowerment as well, though with different feminine bodies—white, heterosexual, middle-class—from Cruikshank's subjects. These subjects become known through economies of visibility, where they articulate a "socially valued version of femininity" and are thus justified as in need of empowerment. This is what Nikolas Rose (1999) theorized about the ways advanced liberalism is invested in "governing at a distance," where the onus of governing is on the individual, and empowerment is understood as *self*-empowerment. When girls and women are told to "be" confident and empowered, it is framed as an individual choice: they just need to believe it, and then they will become it. This confidence will help them become better economic subjects, without interrogating the broad economic context that encourages women and girls to not be confident in the first place.

Again, these are the elements that comprise an economy of visibility: supply and demand, buyers and sellers, and deliberation of value, products, consumers, and specific forms of labor and production. Though

I have laid them out here as separate elements, they are, importantly, deeply interrelated and intertwined. In other words, if the product in the economy of visibility is the feminine body, women and men are also the buyers; the consumers in this economy are also the products. The Can-Do and At-Risk girls can be conflated in the same girl, if one is empowered by her own choices, such as sexual choices, but the specific content of these choices place her At-Risk. The markets *for* girls, where girls are recognized as a key consumer demographic, exist alongside literal, much more malicious markets *in* girls, such as increasing numbers of girls and women who are sexually trafficked.[7] These components are not discrete but rather inform and constitute each other.

Economies of visibility can illuminate the importance of feminism to a larger public. To be sure, the increasing public awareness of feminism is important and has political meaning. Yet the popular feminist practices that are most visible are often those that "articulate socially valued versions of femininity," or what Mia McKenzie (2013, n.p.) has called White Feminism™, a description of the way that "white women put their own needs and well-being above black women everyday and call it 'feminism.'" This book is my attempt to position some of these different versions of feminism in relation to each other, and to offer a conjunctural analysis of the capitalist context that sustains and values some feminisms over others, a context that enables some women to be luminous and to have spectacular visibility, while others are obscured and eclipsed.

Popular Misogyny

The economic goal of empowerment, sustained by the economy of visibility, is a key logic of popular feminism: the size and reach of a contemporary economic market for both feminist paraphernalia and ideology is staggering. Available across various media platforms, this popular feminism often takes on the quality of a spectacle-based neoliberal set of commodities that offer inflections on the meaning of "popular" at each destination. Again, though, it is unproductive to simply dismiss popular feminism as just another branding exercise that serves to accumulate capital. Rather, what *is* productive, and what this book aims to develop, is a critical examination of the interlocution of feminism and misogyny in popular culture. In order to ferret out the mechanics and stakes within which popular feminism operates, we need to examine the simultaneous popularity of misogyny. Popular misogyny is expressed more as a norm, invisible, commonplace. Girls and women are hypervisible because they are so often understood as bodies. Boys and men are less conducive to spectacular visibility because they aren't conceived of as bodies in the same way. Masculine desire is regularly displayed in the media, but it is not marked as *masculine* but rather the norm. The result is that popular misogyny lives in widespread sentiments that "boys will be boys" when they commit sexual violence, and in media representations of heteronormativity. It is bolstered through anonymity online, where rape and death threats become routine. Masculinities are not so urgently, so violently, demanded as femininities in economies of visibility.

Despite this, popular misogyny also circulates in an economy of visibility, perhaps now, in the twenty-first century, more than ever before. The technological affordances of social media have authorized popular misogynistic expressions in a similar manner as popular feminism—the audience is wider, the circulation happens on many interconnected networks with relative ease, and the broader cultural political context, symbolized by the election of Trump, as well as other extreme-right successes around the world, endorses an aggressive, defensive popular misogyny. Yet while popular feminism instantiates primarily as visibility, popular misogyny is not only expressed in an economy of visibility but is also reified into institutions and structures.

While forms of misogyny, of course, existed before popular feminism's recent rise, *Empowered* contends with how, and in what ways, misogyny has altered its media tactics and tropes in response to popular feminism. Popular feminism and popular misogyny are engaged in a constant dynamic, one that continuously shapes and reshapes not only feminism but also patriarchy. While we can think of the ways that popular feminism uses media and networks to (ironically) restructure feminism to be focused on the individual rather than collective politics, misogyny also transfigures patriarchy in this moment. In the contemporary context, patriarchy is perceived to be threatened in specific ways by feminism, in which the "injuries" dealt to masculinity and whiteness are seen as in need of repair and recuperation. While some of the forms of popular misogyny I discuss in this book are brutally vicious and violent, others are more conventional acts of objectification. And while misogyny takes different forms, in the following pages I mainly examine those forms that borrow from a heteronormative playbook in order to enact rage and vitriol, and those that wage demands on women's bodies based on the entitlements promised by heteronormativity.

Like popular feminism, popular misogyny takes on a range of forms, from live-tweeting sexual assault and rape cases to an increase in death and rape threats expressed on social media platforms toward women who either identify as feminists (such as Jessica Valenti or Mikki Kendall) or those who enter into previously male-dominated professions such as game development and commentary (such as Anita Sarkeesian or Brianna Wu) to revenge-porn websites to a rise in men's rights organizations to an increase in global sex trafficking of women and girls. While economies of visibility frame much of contemporary popular culture, popular feminism and popular misogyny are positioned in different ways within these economies. Popular misogyny, while seemingly present in all areas of social and cultural life, is not spectacularly visible in the way popular feminism is. But like popular feminism, popular misogynistic practices exist along a continuum. While the men's rights activism of websites such as Return of Kings, with its unapologetic hatred of women that informs all of its writing, is an important part of popular misogyny, so too are the more moderate voices of other men's rights organizations, such as the National Coalition for Men and their efforts to change policy on custody and paternal rights. And, despite the increasing visibility of popular feminism, popular misogyny seems to have more and more success in inserting itself in policy and legal discourse, where the legacy of patriarchy legitimates misogynistic arguments as common sense, allowing for the conversion of misogynistic ideas into action with terrible efficiency. We see this insertion of popular misogyny in the vast number of anti-abortion bills and laws that have been proposed and passed in the United States since 2008; in the continued disparity between men and women who work in the technology industry; in the ways that the first woman to be a major party's nominee for US president, Hillary Clinton, is objectified and devalued because of her gender. We see it in the election of Donald Trump as president of the United States.

Popular misogyny isn't openly embraced or even often given headlines— at least not in a way that *acknowledges* it as misogyny. When misogynistic acts become visible, it is often by emphasizing outlier individuals, who, if they are white men, are often characterized as mentally ill, such as Elliot Rodger, the twenty-two-year-old man who killed six people and wounded thirteen others in Santa Barbara, California, in 2014. Rodger documented

FIGURE
INTRO.7.
A men's rights
organization's
attempt to re-
route the mes-
sage of popular
feminism: "Stop
violence against
women but not
against men."

his rage against women online and apparently went on the rampage because women rejected him sexually, yet dominant media sources described his issues with depression and mental illness as the reason for the rampage. Much media representation of misogyny is framed in such a way, with a focus on anomalous individuals, thus consciously or unconsciously ignoring and obscuring the deeply embedded networked aspect of popular misogyny.[8]

A networked misogyny means that the concept itself is constantly moving from one node to another, emerging in different spaces, with varied manifestations. Popular misogyny cannot be characterized in the same way as popular feminism, which because of its heightened visibility in the contemporary moment often has concrete, material representations. For me, to confront popular misogyny means to confront the notion that patriarchy itself needs to be assessed differently than it ever has been before; it is not just a discrete group of organizations, or roles, or spaces, but rather, we must see it as *networked* (Banet-Weiser and Miltner 2015). Both are networked movements, finding expression in nodes ranging from social media to global meet-ups to fashion to neomasculine boot camps. Through this dynamic, both feminism and misogyny are reimagined, take new forms, and have a variety of effects. This is how networks work: they allow for different spaces of expression simultaneously in that they function through rapid and asynchronous communication; they decentralize power even as they remain loyal to hegemonic institutions (Castells 2007, 2012). Again, we see this norm in the election of an unapologetic misogynist as president of the United States, in federal policy deliberations on health care that include only male representatives, in the continuing disparity in wages between men and women (not to mention wage disparities between white people and people of color).

Popular misogyny is also an ongoing recuperative project. Despite the fact that misogyny has long existed as a norm in policy, culture, economics, and the political realm, in the current moment there is an overt claim that masculinity, and more generally, patriarchy, are under threat. Popular misogyny is often expressed as a need to take something "back"—such as patriarchy—from the greedy hands of women and feminists. We see this palpably in the increasing visibility of the extreme right across the globe. While the racist ideologies of the extreme right have often been correctly identified as white nationalism, the extreme right has always also run on an overtly misogynistic agenda; as Matthew Lyons points out, "Harassing and defaming women isn't just a tactic; it also serves the alt-right's broader agenda and long-term vision for society" (2016, para. 8). Again, a key logic of the extreme right is recuperation: men's rights organizations in digital culture are filled with proclamations about how women and feminists have not only destroyed society but emasculated it. As Corey Savage, writing on the men's activist website Return of Kings, puts it: "We have been robbed of our lives as we've been trained from childhood to serve a matriarchal system with 'tolerance' and 'equality' as our religion" (Savage 2017, para. 29). Like popular feminism, much of the logic of popular misogyny revolves around twinned discourses of capacity and injury. Expressions of popular misogyny often rely upon the idea that men have been *injured* by women: men are seen to be denied rights because women have gained them; men are no longer confident because women are more confident; men have lost jobs and power because women have entered into previously male-dominated realms, regardless of how slowly. Men's rights organizations and other forms of popular misogyny dedicate themselves to restoring the *capacity* of men, the restoration and recuperation of a traditional heteronormative masculinity and of patriarchy itself. This often is seen as a backlash to popular feminism, and surely it is that. But it is also more than that, as backlash implies a linear direction—misogyny lashes "back" at feminism. In contrast, popular misogyny lashes out in all directions, finding expression in obvious, and not so obvious, ways.

To consider the "popular" in popular misogyny, then, is to take account of the way it refuses to sit still. It may not always emerge in recognizable forms, but it is nearly impossible to escape it. It exists along a continuum, where at the radical end, such as the extreme right, it is often disparaged by the status quo (at least superficially). But when misogyny is extreme and read as an anomaly, as an unfortunate expression of a few deranged individuals, this works to validate and render invisible the other, less obvious ways it works as a norm. Thus, contemporary expressions of popular misogyny are seen *not* as structural but as the anomalous expressions of individuals responding to feminism. If misogyny were acknowledged as a social, political, economic, and cultural structure, then it could be subjected to criticism and challenged in a way that individual expressions, often dismissed as anomalous and insignificant, cannot be. And even when it is considered, as it sometimes is, as a movement, it is minimized as a kind of autonomous force, the "fringe," rather than a condensed version of structural expression. The networked nature of popular feminism and popular misogyny allows for this kind of restructuring, as networks are inherently flexible, reprogrammable, and infinitely expandable. That is, this confrontation with patriarchy in the contemporary moment returns us to the familiar, the ongoing—the various microaggressions we confront, the presumptions of male privilege—but those familiar problems are now equipped with digital tools, such as online comments sections and social media sites. This networked misogyny is similar to the way J. K. Gibson-Graham (2006) described feminism as "analogically" rather than institutionally organized. Different misogynies across networks, in other words, inform each other, constitute each other, are related to each other.

This networked continuum is the backdrop for all expressions of misogyny, whether that be the extreme right, a political norm, a labor practice, or a backlash against popular feminism. I examine many of these popular misogynistic expressions throughout this book; there are some examples, such as the UN Women campaign and the "don't mancriminate" campaign I analyze in chapter 1, where there is a clear and obvious response, a backlash, from popular misogyny. There are others, such as the pick-up artist industry I examine in chapter 3, that present as a recuperative project, aiming to restore sexual authority to men. And still there are others, such as the toxic geek masculinity context that is the subject of chapter 4, that consider the encroachment of women in the technology industries as an injury to masculinity.

Bad Romance: Popular Feminism and Popular Misogyny

Empowered seeks to make sense of the constellation of popular feminist expressions, ideologies, practices, activism, and commodity objects through a range of texts, cultural practices, and organizations, as well as the misogynistic responses to them. Clearly, popular misogyny does not neatly map onto historical movements of feminism. Popular misogyny is not a movement; it is a deeply embedded networked context, one that structures not only the material world of law, policy, and regulation but also identity, affect, and sexuality. Among other things, it is a reactive response to popular feminism; a waging of battle, a call to arms. This does not end with one round; both feminism and misogyny are continually restructured through this dynamic.

The spectacle of popular feminism is part of the way that popular misogyny maintains an invisibility, even as it is becoming more difficult in a contemporary media climate to remain invisible. Herman Gray's critique of visibility, and what he calls the continuing "investment in the cultural politics of representation for the liberal subject of identity," is crucial here (H. Gray 2013, 772). Gray questions what visibility might mean as a political practice in an era of a shift from *race* to *difference.* Gray's focus is on race, specifically African American identity, but I want to think about what this also means for gendered identity. The cultural conditions that made it important to demand visibility in the first place—not enough representation, representation that is highly stereotypical, institutionalized sexism—have shifted in an age of popular feminism and popular misogyny, so that the demand *looks* different. Rather, the demand for visibility as something that is not coupled with a political project is becoming more and more paramount. As popular feminism makes increasing demands for visibility, the political project of popular misogyny continues on more powerfully as a less visible, structuring force. To be clear: the visibility of popular feminism has been in large part about making what is hidden, routinized, and normalized about popular misogyny more public, displayed, and explicit.

The luminosity that spotlights some feminisms, and feminine bodies, over others also garners a misogynistic reaction. The digital context for a contemporary economy of visibility is also one that enables and validates what Jack Bratich (2011) has called "affective divergence." Bratich, as well as scholars such as Mark Andrejevic (2002), Beth Kolko, Lisa Nakamura, Gilbert Rodman (2013), and others, argue that along with the more positive implications of convergence culture, we also need to take account of the ways in which our new technologies and networked publics enable a *divergence*: cultures of judgment, aggression, and violence. As Bratich argues, "We are in the midst of a media fueled popularization of bullies, a convergence of micro-violence perhaps comprising a cultural will-to-humiliation" (Bratich 2011, 66). It might be the case that the visibility of popular feminism, no matter how commodified or banal, allows for an opening of space and mind to think about broader opposition to structural sexism and racism. But popular misogyny performs a similar function, and opens up spaces and opportunities for a more systematic attack on women and women's rights—it is the context for a "popularization of bullies, a convergence of micro-violence" that coalesces in a neutralization of antagonism.

Indeed, the "cultural will-to-humiliation" is what makes contemporary popular misogyny a *shifted* set of discourses and practices from previous historical moments. Popular misogyny is a constellation of a "popularization of bullies," present not only online but offline as well. This is the wider political and popular context for the most recent crisis in masculinity: networked misogyny operates as a way to consolidate a "cultural will-to-humiliation" that promises the restoration of male privilege, prerogative, and rightful ownership of economic, cultural, and political spaces (Bratich 2011).

This restoration of male privilege is the logical crux of the mirroring effect I see between popular feminism and popular misogyny. Indeed, in the contemporary US context of the Donald Trump administration, the federal government is organized around white male injury. For example, Cynthia Young (forthcoming) argues that civil rights rhetoric has been appropriated in the United States by a contemporary white identity politics: "Civil rights rhetoric helps express a form of whiteness that is both racist and avowedly antiracist, a form of whiteness that simultaneously claims to be disadvantaged and uniquely empowered to 'take the country back.'" (Young, forthcoming). Young argues that a confluence of factors—including the attacks of September 11, 2001; wars in Iraq and Afghanistan; the global economic collapse in 2007–8; and the election of Barack Obama—have "combined with significant cultural shifts [and] have contributed to the re-making of white identity as uniquely vulnerable and victimized in the contemporary moment." The reimagining of white Americans after 9/11 as victims of global terror has partly enabled a reactionary identity politics, one that promises to "take America back," and that has reached its most grotesque incarnation to date in the rise of Donald Trump as the president of the United States, with his campaign promise to "make America great again." Echoing Young, Nicholas Confessore (2016, n.p.), in the *New York Times*, points out that Trump's popularity among white people who feel disenfranchised has a number of origin points as well: "The resentment among whites feels both old and distinctly of this moment."

As Young (forthcoming) incisively argues, "taking America back" and "making it great again" is both overtly and covertly about whiteness; immigration and people of color predominantly *cause* the apparent threat to America, as this "imagined victimhood" is also crafted as a response to the predicted demographic demise of white Americans of European descent, who will be a statistical minority by the middle of the century. This whiteness identity builds on America's history of racism, and at the same time excludes the experiences of other claims of the present-day burdens of that racism.

Young's argument about whiteness extends to masculinity as well. Indeed, this is how the funhouse mirror of popular feminism and popular misogyny works: the injuries caused by centuries of structural racism and sexism are turned on their head so that it is white men who feel these injuries most deeply in the contemporary moment. This white masculine identity denies structural racism, seeing white individuals as uniquely injured. Needless to say, not all white middle-class men feel that they are victims, and not all extrapolate their sense of individual victimization onto the victimization of the American nation. However, this context— that white men are under threat through a kind of reverse racism, or sexism, positions men as those who are being discriminated against.

One of the persistent questions I ask in this book is thus one about structure: Who feels entitled—and is rewarded—for taking up social space in public? How is this space distributed? Who does the spotlight shine its light on? This question is partly about digital spaces, but it also encompasses more than that. Clearly, the affordances of technology contribute to a misogyny that is both networked and popular. But a focus on these particular *facets* of the problem of misogyny blinds us to the larger problem of misogyny itself. When we seek to understand popular misogyny by seeing it as a manifestation of digital culture, we can then write it off as merely a negative effect of technology. Instead, I argue that we need to see it for what it is: a manifestation of neoliberalism, a consolidation of the logic of neoliberal violence. Neoliberalism and popular misogyny are just as interconnected as neoliberalism and popular feminism, despite a general mediated discourse that positions popular misogyny as an outlier, a deviation from the culturally acceptable norms of traditional masculinity. Neoliberalism, however, produces not only ideology but also violence, and it is a structuring force that is both popular and networked.

In the following chapters, I explore the relationship between popular feminism and popular misogyny. In each chapter, I examine what I feel to be one of the major themes that shape this relationship: shame, confidence, competence, and, finally, rage. Using these themes as an optic, in each chapter I attempt to take account of the networked nature of popular feminism and popular misogyny, and argue that these networks, circulating in an economy of visibility, allow for a deeper understanding of the relationship between the two: sometimes it is mirroring, sometimes appropriation, sometimes backlash, sometimes explicit violence. This book is my attempt to make sense of this interrelated dynamic between popular feminism and popular misogyny; the way the two movements are conjunctural even as they are asymmetrical, intersecting in their various patterns of actions and expressions, echoing each other in complex and contradictory ways. This means challenging the normalization, and the sheer *popularity,* of popular misogyny, and not shrugging it off as an inevitable expression of boys being boys. It also means recognizing—and mobilizing—the ambivalence of popular feminism, and parsing through the way in which the "popular" of popular feminism means that it doesn't sit still; it is a struggle over meaning, a way to imagine a different future.

ONE. THE FUNHOUSE MIRROR

It doesn't matter what they say. I mean, yes, I kick like a girl, and I swim like a girl, and I walk like a girl, and I wake up in the morning like a girl because I am a girl. And that is not something that I should be ashamed of, so I'm going to do it, anyway. — ALWAYS, #LikeAGirl

Always, the feminine hygiene company, debuted their #LikeAGirl campaign in the summer of 2014. The campaign was directed by Lauren Greenfield, better known for her monographs *Girl Culture* and *THIN*, and for her critically acclaimed documentary *Queen of Versailles*; she is deeply invested in girl culture, both publicly and politically. The campaign's website sports the tagline "Fighting to Empower Girls Everywhere"; the company has formed partnerships with UNESCO, as part of their Global Puberty Education program, as well as the Lean In Foundation and the Girl Scouts.

The #LikeAGirl ad begins with Greenfield posing as the director of a video shoot, asking a group of young women, in their late teens and early twenties, to "show me what it looks like to run like a girl." From the beginning of the ad, the focus is on the female body itself—bodies that move, throw, run. As the ad continues, the young women answer Greenfield with caricature. They run in exaggerated movements, flailing their arms, fussing with their hair. They run slowly, inefficiently, unfocused and un-trained. Follow-up questions—"show me what it looks like to fight like a girl" and "to throw like a girl"—find similar results: flailing arms, embarrassed laughter, clearly ineffectual body movements. The ad then cuts to text: "We then asked young girls the same questions." The ad returns to Greenfield with a group of younger girls: one identifies as ten years old; others look even younger. In contrast to the women in the ad, the young girls respond earnestly, forcefully; they run, fight, and throw with strength and confidence. One young girl, when asked what it means to run like a girl, says, "It means run as fast as you can." The ad then cuts again to text: "When did doing something like a girl become an insult?" The implication is clear: the answer to this question comes with the gap in ages between the two groups. Doing things "like a girl" becomes an insult somewhere during adolescence. The tone of the ad then changes, offering more empowered responses. A young woman is asked, "What advice do you have to girls who are told you run like a girl, hit like a girl, throw like a girl, swim like a girl?" She answers, "Keep doing it 'cuz it's working. If somebody else says that running like a girl, or kicking like a girl, or shooting like a girl is something that you shouldn't be doing, that's their problem. Because if you're still scoring, and you're still getting to the ball on time, and you're still being first, you're doing it right." The ad ends with a final screen of text: "Let's make #LikeAGirl mean amazing things. Join us to champion girls' confidence at always.com." The intention is clear: Always wants to intervene in the early onset of what some have called the gendered confidence gap (where boys and men are more confident than girls and women in their everyday lives) before it crystallizes into a full-blown crisis (Kay and Shipman 2014b).

Always and its #LikeAGirl campaign are part of a constellation of recent corporate players invested in resolving what they deem a "girl crisis"—namely, "plummeting self-esteem and confidence"—through ads and campaigns that encourage empowerment for girls and young women. These corporate campaigns are an increasingly common form of corporate social responsibility, in which the company's efforts are not attached to a particular political goal—such as fair trade or environmentalism—but rather to the more diffuse realm of gendered subjectivity. Of course, companies such as Always have massive advertising budgets, so campaigns such as #LikeAGirl can be highly produced and distributed, and have an already established presence within an economy of visibility. Ex-

FIGURE 1.1. Always, #LikeAGirl campaign, 2015.

amples of popular feminism such as this campaign are privileged within this economy, as advertising, of course, has media visibility as its central logic. While the Always campaign gained considerable visibility throughout 2014, it wasn't until a shortened version aired during the Super Bowl, the professional US football championship game, in February 2015, that the campaign became even more widely visible. The Super Bowl is one of the most watched live sports broadcasts in the United States, and because of the wide audience, companies compete by creating remarkably expensive ads to be shown during the show. Adobe ranked Always' #LikeAGirl the top digital campaign of the Super Bowl, based on mentions in social media (Friedman 2015), and it was broadly noted that this was the first time a feminine care product was advertised during the Super Bowl. The Super Bowl is notorious for its male-targeted ads, though the landscape has been changing in recent years as women viewers have been recognized as an important consumer demographic. The Super Bowl has also been recognized as an exemplar in a changing advertising landscape, where companies are shifting advertising tactics to appeal to women. Indeed, during the Super Bowl in 2017, the car company Audi explicitly referenced the gendered pay gap as part of their ad. Rather than use idealized versions of women cleaning the house, taking care of children, and so on, companies such as Procter & Gamble (the parent company of Always) and Audi are now selling products based on messages of female empowerment (see also Zeisler 2016).

Always' #LikeAGirl campaign is a compelling example of the increasing prominence of girls' confidence within advertising and corporate campaigns. By asking viewers to "join" them in championing girls' confidence, Always positions itself as part of a broader empowerment movement, itself supported by popular feminism. As I argued in the introduction, popular feminism is feminism that marshals the "popular" in various ways: it is expressed and practiced on multiple media platforms, it attracts other like-minded groups and individuals, and it manifests in a terrain of struggle, with competing demands for power. While there are different forms of popular feminism, there are some, such as expensive ad campaigns, that are more easily circulated within an economy of visibility, a context that is particularly amenable to corporate media campaigns. That is, Always, like every company, needs to sell products in order to survive—and feminine hygiene products no less. Thus popular feminist ads are connected to an aspirational notion of consumerism and are a part of a broader brand culture; indeed, popular feminist ads are an important way that popular feminism itself is branded.

The Always campaign offers one iteration of popular feminism and female empowerment; throughout this book I'll explore some of the different versions of empowerment supported by popular feminism. Popular feminism exists along a continuum, and thus the definition of empowerment that is marshaled at any given point on that continuum will also have different dimensions and definitions. As I'll detail throughout this book, popular feminist explorations and affirmations circulate in and across multiple media platforms with ease and frequency, creating a frenetic landscape of feminist discourse. There are significant differences within and between feminisms and their goals, and they can't be generalized. Within popular feminism, that is, there are varied goals under the broad rubric of empowerment: intersectional feminism, corporate feminism, feminist consumption, and so on.

In this chapter, I examine the economy of visibility that supports popular feminism and popular misogyny. The economy of visibility is validated and affirmed within neoliberal capitalism, which is dedicated to seeking out new markets and brands in all facets of life. Here, I discuss the branding of popular feminism and popular misogyny. Of course, popular feminist and popular misogynist brands did not simply emerge in the twenty-first century but are instead connected to historical processes of branding politics (Arviddson 2006; Hearn 2008; Banet-Weiser 2012).

In the twenty-first century, both girls and women use popular feminism to construct themselves as empowered entrepreneurs, and popular feminism becomes a platform for economic success. At the same time, there are many heterosexual men who seem to find themselves in a masculinity crisis—a crisis that is often blamed on those same empowered entrepreneurial women, as well as on global economic recession. This crisis often manifests in popular misogyny. Like the Always ad that laments the plummeting self-esteem in adolescent girls, the market for self-esteem has recognized men and boys as consumers as well, positioning men as incurring injuries due to low self-esteem. For example, men's rights organizations have had a heightened visibility over the last few decades largely because of online communication (which allows people to connect more easily), and often focus on building self-esteem and confidence. This focus is manifest in visual campaigns that mirror popular feminist campaigns, marshaling the themes of popular feminism—such as self-esteem, confidence, and competence—and applying these themes to themselves. Like much of popular feminism, these campaigns purport to challenge existing social relations; I argue that this mirroring effect is that of a funhouse mirror, in which politics and bodies are distorted and transfigured so that men—heterosexual, white men—are the ones who appear to be injured by widespread inequities and structural disparities. Men's rights campaigns are often framed as a route to return to the way things "should be" between men and women (before those angry, pesky feminists got in the way).

Thus, at the heart of confidence and empowerment campaigns for both women and men is the dual dynamic of injury and capacity: women respond to the injuries caused by centuries of being undervalued as citizens and overvalued as objectified bodies. Men, in turn, call out this injury, and claim that in the current moment, it is men who are injured—by a series of wounds caused by women and feminists. Both popular feminist and popular misogynistic campaigns seek to demonstrate individual capacity as a way to suture this wound, to overcome this injury.

This dual dynamic of injury and capacity characterizes how popular feminism and popular misogyny function in the current moment. To think through the ways in which this dynamic functions, I'll first discuss the ways that popular feminism has been harnessed for marketing and advertising purposes, as a way to construct a popular feminist brand. I use the space of advertising and its representations and discourses as a kind of heuristic guide, a way of tracing the trajectory of the residual and emergent iterations of feminism and misogyny. A primary mode of address in popular feminist advertising is what I call *sentimental earnestness*. A similarly earnest mode of address is used in campaigns created by men's rights organizations; in both media forms, earnestness works to shore up popular feminism and popular misogyny. The intense conviction that propels earnestness is, not surprisingly, different for popular feminism and popular misogyny, but in both, earnestness frames and shapes how and in what ways women and men are both injured and infused with capacity.

Sentimental earnestness is both a central logic in popular feminism and a mode of address that can be thought of, in advertising industry lingo, as a "unique selling position"; sentimental earnestness is a distinct mechanism that connects certain feminist messages to particular products. The sentimental earnestness of popular feminism seems, first and foremost, recuperative: this manifestation of feminism sees girls and women as being "in crisis"—a crisis due to insecurity, or a lack of self-confidence, or a lack of leadership, among other things. Indeed, postfeminism is in some ways blamed for being complicit with the perpetuation of this crisis, because postfeminism is partly a response to what was considered a kind of hand-wringing feminist discourse that positioned women as victims.

Popular feminism, in many ways, is a return to earnestness, a return to a focus on gendered injuries, by centering on the cultural, economic, and political injuries women experience by living in sexist societies. Yet it is also distinct in the way it marshals entrepreneurialism and feminine capacity as a response to these injuries. I argue that the qualifier to feminism, the "popular" of popular feminism, and the sentimental earnestness that is the dominant form of address in popular feminist ads, do important cultural work in shoring up a particular feminine/feminist subject. Popular feminism harnesses feminist politics to an economic context, even if this harnessing is one of avowal and recuperation with popular feminism.

Popular Feminist Advertising

The 1990s witnessed the emergence of a particular "crisis in girls" (Hains 2012). This "crisis" was ostensibly caused by widespread exclusion of girls from math and science programs in schools, rising numbers of white middle-class girls with eating disorders and other body-image issues, and reports of general low self-confidence that, depending on how you listened, emerged from the erosion of the traditional nuclear family or from media representations of hypersexualized teenagers who wore their skirts too high and their shirts too low. This new crisis was broadly lamented, by parents and politicians and reporters, and also detailed in research reports, including, in 1991, the influential American Association of University Women report, *Shortchanging Girls, Shortchanging America*, which connected girls' low self-esteem and confidence to the low success of girls in science and math (Hains 2012). This report, as well as subsequent others, stimulated a national conversation and response, including renewed efforts to encourage girls to enter science, technology, engineering, and math (STEM) fields, educational programs focusing on body image and bullying practices at schools, and changes in public policy so that girls were included as valuable citizens (Hains 2012; Projansky 2014; Hasinoff 2015).

Yet, while girls experience a crisis in confidence, there is a simultaneous link made between girls and power—namely, the power to consume. This power manifested, starting in the 1990s, with the slogan "girl power," and the industry that grew rapidly to capitalize on it (Banet-Weiser 2007; Negra and Tasker 2007; McRobbie 2009). Girl power proved a potent means to sell clothing, sports, and young adult literature (among other things). As important, girl power is not simply a commodity in its own right but also refers to girls as powerful consumers, who represent a primary market (where girls have their own income), a market of influencers (where girls influence their parents' consumer choices), and a future market (where girls' consumer loyalty is cultivated as future customers) (McNeal 1992; Banet-Weiser 2007).

The simultaneous positioning of girls as "in crisis" (and therefore in need of empowerment) and as valuable consumers, has helped to create a *market* for empowerment. The power of girls has, for much of recent history and in innumerable ways, been legislated against, policed, and regulated. Thus, our very recent association of girls with power—and indeed, even celebration of the fact that girls could be powerful—is innovative and even radical. However, that celebration should not be taken at face value. That is, when we celebrate girl power, which girl are we actually celebrating? It is clear that she belongs to a particular race and class—typically white and wealthy enough to purchase the latest trends and a smart phone—and thus has the economic and cultural privilege required to access power.[1]

Alongside the efforts to empower girls through external mechanisms—policy, education, consumption practices—there has also been a mandate to "empower oneself," especially in the context of neoliberal capitalism and the privileging of the entrepreneur as the identity to aspire to. This dual dynamic, of empowering women through external mechanisms and the neoliberal imperative to empower oneself, forms the crux of the current "confidence movement," which aims to inspire self-confidence in girls and women (Gill and Orgad 2015). While there are different definitions of what "confidence" means for the confidence movement (as I argue in chapter 3), much of the "confidence problem" is located squarely on the body and in one's self-image. And the "solution" to this problem is often found in branding and advertising, which have harnessed the goal of self-confidence and attached it to products (Zeisler 2016). As the Always ad campaign emphasizes, girls are widely believed to have plummeting self-confidence in adolescence and young adulthood, so Always and other companies have targeted this demographic with messages that focus on self-love, self-esteem, and body positivity.

These messages of self-love, self-esteem, and body positivity are delivered primarily without irony. While irony has long been a trope within all forms of advertising, with consumer audiences hailed as being in on the joke, much of the sentimental earnestness of popular feminist ads tells us the opposite: *this is not a joke.* Girls and women are in crisis, a crisis of confidence, and we (Always or Nike or Dove) are here to fix it. In this way, popular feminism is recuperative, one that importantly insists that terms and concepts such as "sexism," often considered old-fashioned and stuffy, are still alive and kicking. Here, we see a shift from "girl power" and a move toward vulnerability as a selling point. Popular feminist advertising uses an affective mode of address—sentiment, hurt, anger, loss—to signal both that a gendered crisis exists, and that there is a solution. The solution is often tied to consumption, and circulates within an economy of visibility, where feminist "products" have a heightened presence.

The solution here, however, is not only to purchase certain products that will lead to a certain kind of self-empowerment. Such faith in the power of the product is surely part of it—these are advertising campaigns, and they build their brands by attracting consumers, after all—but the sentimentally earnest mode of address also aims to educate. These popular feminist ads take pride in pointing out the confidence and self-esteem gap in women so that they can overcome it, and become more competitive in school and the workforce. Thus, much of popular feminist advertising seems to fulfill a starkly economic function, where feminist politics are folded into neoliberal logics and rerouted toward individualism. While some elements of a feminist critique are maintained in this folding, the focus on individual women rather than a collective politics thus also functions as a disavowal.

Popular feminist ads feature statistics about the lack of girls and women in STEM fields, offer emotional and powerful narratives critiquing stereotypes about girls' abilities, and dramatize the dilemmas of the "confidence gap," all while also advertising a given product or a company. In this way, they are a far cry from the hypersexualized, objectifying ads of postfeminism. Indeed, I believe that these ads represent a fundamental shift in the neoliberal economy's deployment of feminist politics and principles. Here, we see an embrace of what Catherine Rottenberg (2014) calls "neoliberal feminism," where feminism is shifted toward the individual, but is not vacated of politics. As I argue in the next chapter, a self-esteem industry has emerged around girls and women and the issue of self-confidence—an industry that includes self-help books, educational programs, and corporate empowerment campaigns (Banet-Weiser 2014). The logic of these different efforts to build confidence in girls implies that if the crisis in confidence is "resolved" during adolescence and young adulthood, women will be better able to "lean in" and feel more adequate in the workplace. This trajectory, then, has an ultimate goal: to ensure that women are better, more confident economic subjects. Using the twinned tropes of capacity and injury, popular feminist ads tap into highly visible neoliberal logics, and are mobilized in part by the economy of visibility in which they circulate.

While the bulk of popular feminism's ads have emerged in the twenty-first century, one of the important early campaigns came in 1992, when the Nike corporation created what became an impactful ad campaign that specifically positioned sports as a route to empowerment for girls and women. The ad campaign, "If You Let Me Play," created before hashtags existed, first appeared as a print ad. The campaign consisted of several different images of girls playing sports or engaging in physical activity, with text that reads in part, "And one day when you're out in the world running, feet flying dogs barking smiles grinning, you'll hear those immortal words calling, calling inside your head *Oh you run like a girl* and you will say shout scream whisper call back Yes. *What exactly did you think I was?*" (Nike 1992).

The campaign expanded to television in 1995, a key medium in an economy of visibility. The ads in the campaign tap into the discourses of injury and capacity that consistently circulate in this economy, highlighting the different ways girls have been injured simply because they are girls. The ads then highlight sports as the way to stimulate and mobilize capacity in girls and women. One ad begins with a series of shots of girls repeating the phrase "If you let me play sports . . ." and then cuts to a series of other girls completing this sentence in varied ways: "I will have more self-confidence," "I will be 60 percent less likely to have breast cancer," "I will have less depression," "I will be more likely to leave a man who beats me," and finally, "I will be strong" (Nike 1995). With this campaign, Nike inaugurated the beginning of corporate efforts to associate sports with self-confidence, strength, and empowerment for girls and women. While in 1972, the US government passed the amendment Title IX, which states that no one can be excluded from participation or subjected to discrimination within education based on sex, it wasn't until two decades later that corporations began to use the amendment as a marketing campaign (Cooky and McDonald 2005).

In the first half of the 1990s, Nike was expert with this kind of marketing, and can be understood as an early participant in what Rosalind Gill and Shani Orgad (2015) call the contemporary "confidence (cult)ure."[2] Nike has continued to be an important player in girls' empowerment organizations, and the company's ad campaigns have continued to circulate in an economy of visibility using the tropes of injury and capacity. As I detail in chapter 3, Nike has now partnered with the World Bank and the UN to form the "Girl Effect" campaign to advocate for girls' education in poverty-stricken areas of the Global South, focusing explicitly on girls' capacity for entrepreneurship and economic potential. But their "If You Let Me Play" campaign set the standard for sentimental earnestness as a mode of address: the ad is emotionally powerful, with young girls stating facts about breast cancer, domestic abuse, and self-confidence. It also set the tone for popular feminism's marshaling of injury and capacity as twinned discourses in an economy of visibility.

That same standard has endured for more than two decades, and sentimental earnestness continues to shape much of popular feminist advertising. Around the same time as the Always #LikeAGirl campaign emerged, another girls' empowerment campaign, CoverGirl's #GirlsCan, was aired on multiple media platforms. Like Always' #LikeAGirl, Cover-

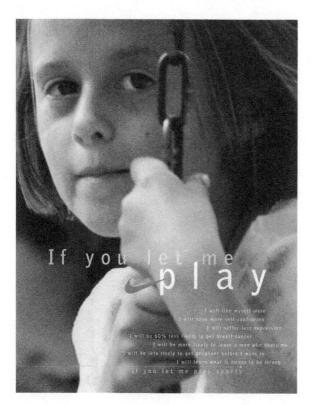

FIGURE 1.2.

Nike, "If You Let Me Play" campaign, 1995.

Girl's #GirlsCan also debuted in a very visible space, the closing ceremonies of the Winter Olympic Games in Sochi. The CoverGirl ad features celebrities such as Queen Latifah, Katy Perry, Janelle Monáe, and Sofia Vergara. The narrative of the ad is simple, and begins with Ellen DeGeneres (a spokesperson for CoverGirl) boldly stating, "Girls can't. Sometimes you hear it, more often you feel it." The narrative that "girls can't" quickly gives way to a counternarrative—that "girls *can.*" Each of these celebrities forcefully contradicts cultural stereotypes about girls and women using their own success as evidence. Queen Latifah looks into the camera and says, "I heard that girls couldn't rap. I rap. Girls couldn't own their own businesses? I own my own business" (CoverGirl 2014). Pink insists that girls can rock, Janelle Monáe points out that girls can dance "crazy." DeGeneres offers this overly vague and broadly ambitious advice: "I've learned you just have to be yourself." Like Always' #LikeAGirl, the CoverGirl ad is custom-made for social media with the already established hashtag. The ad ends with the traditional CoverGirl tagline: "Easy, Breezy, Beautiful."

FIGURE 1.3.
CoverGirl,
#GirlsCan cam-
paign, Becky G,
2015.

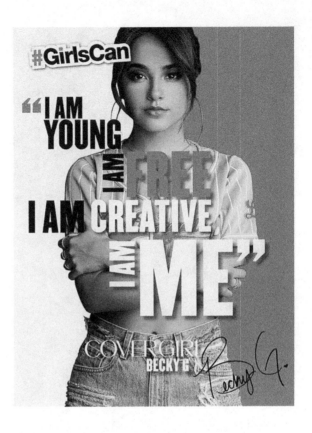

The ad was generally well-received; *Adweek's* David Griner (2014) praised it, claiming, "Instead of simply celebrating their beauty, the Procter & Gamble brand creates a candid and compelling rallying cry for female empowerment." Of course, all of the women who are depicted in the ad *are* relatively conventionally beautiful, and most are celebrities who are highly visible. Indeed, the CoverGirl ad is a telling example of what moves into the spotlight in an economy of visibility: this economy necessarily privileges beauty and the body. Even the unnamed hockey player in the ad dramatically removes her helmet to reveal long blond hair and striking blue eyes. In other words, I would amend Griner's statement to say that it is not "instead of" but *through* a celebration of beauty that Procter & Gamble creates a rallying cry for female empowerment—this is precisely the kind of popular feminism that circulates with ease within an economy of visibility. The continued focus on physical beauty as a pipeline to empowerment belies the generality of "girls can," as it is *specific* girls who can. Like the Always ad, #GirlsCan also visually focuses on the body, depicting women singing, dancing, playing sports, as the route to empowerment, even as it also implies that confidence is something unrelated to the body. After all, CoverGirl is a powerful cosmetics company; as such, it is by definition committed to an ideal of physical beauty.

Both Always and CoverGirl are not only attempting to recognize the importance of building confidence in girls but also obviously tapping into a consumer audience of girls and women as users of feminine hygiene products and makeup. Kimberly Taylor, a marketing professor at Florida International University, says about these ads, "There is a recognition that if you continue to show these images that really don't fit who your consumers are anymore, they will go somewhere else" (Taylor, cited in Berman 2015, n.p.), thus implying that girls want to see empowering images of themselves in the media. This is an important goal, and Taylor is absolutely right: Always is concerned about their consumers (as is CoverGirl). The message of these companies is clear: both emphasize that girls and women should be what Anita Harris (2004a) has called "Can-Do girls" (indeed, that is the tagline of the CoverGirl ad); "can-do" here means to be economically empowered. All of the women who "can" in the CoverGirl ad are clear examples of economic success—they are successful business women, television personalities, pop music stars, and professional athletes. Success here is understood as what has typically been understood as *masculine* success: it is about making money and becoming famous (especially if it is doing what you love). Success is also measured by visibility— the more an ad circulates across media platforms, and the more there is an emphasis on the "Can-Do" girl, the more visible the ad will be.

Again, the popular feminist messages that become the most visible in an economy of visibility are those that reflect "neoliberal feminism" (Rottenberg 2014). The ads begin with a focus on the injury women experience as a result of living in a sexist world, and then move to the hopeful message of women's capacity. "Capacity" here has a neoliberal inflection: there is no critique of the ways that capitalist success might be due to the divisions of labor required by capitalism itself; rather, it is up to individual women to believe that they "can." The messages of these ads place the responsibility on the young women who are the products' consumers. There is an absence of collectivity in these ads, and there is no gesture toward empowerment through solidarity, no critique of structural barriers. Rather, girls and women individually need to lean in, be confident, to stop thinking "I can't." This relieves institutions of the burden of having to grapple with their own gendered asymmetries and restructure them. And in so doing, the message that "girls can," as important as it is, remains another iteration in an economy of visibility, as an end in itself rather than a route to dismantling asymmetries of power. As Ellen DeGeneres says in the CoverGirl ad, "Just be yourself"—a self that is committed to and celebrates neoliberal capitalist success, which is in turn a structure that is designed with, and only functions through, vast inequalities across gender, race, and class.

The Always and CoverGirl campaigns identify a lack of confidence in girls and women, and then offer a way to address this lack by mirroring the behavior of the women in the ads (and building their brands in the process). While the Always campaign is more complex, in both of these campaigns, and others like them, the solution is merely telling oneself, convincing oneself, to *be* confident. As the woman in the Always ad says, "I am a girl . . . that's not something I should be ashamed of, so I'm going to do it anyway." Ellen DeGeneres implores us to "just be ourselves." The message of these ads assumes that self-confidence is attainable for all women; it is within our grasp, we just need to reach for it. And importantly, self-confidence can be *seen*; in an economy of visibility, it is articulated through the strong, earnest body. This body is one who has been injured but has the capacity to overcome these injuries because she is a girl.

The Mirroring of Popular Misogyny

Perhaps one of the most volatile cultural arenas for the dynamic relationship of popular feminism and popular misogyny is within rape culture. Rape, like the many forms of exploitation and violence suffered disproportionately by women, has long been a feminist issue, and has emerged in various ways depending on the historical moment.[3] A postfeminist framing of date rape thus used women's confidence and agency as a way to redirect blame away from men and toward women; women were blamed for "allowing" rape to occur (see Roiphe 2014). Within the era of popular feminism, however, "rape culture" began to be increasingly used as a term for feminists and other media commentators to describe not only high school and college campuses but other more public spaces, such as newsrooms, corporations, and sports. Though feminists have long used the term and concept "rape culture" (indeed, a feminist documentary in 1975 was titled *Rape Culture*), it began to circulate with frequency in the popular media in the first decade of the twenty-first century. Rather than a niche feminist issue, invoking rape culture has become much more normative within the mainstream media, much like popular feminism itself. Rape culture has been seen as rampant on college campuses, where studies have interviewed men age eighteen to twenty-five who said that they "did not consider it rape if the woman was too drunk to know what is going on" (Edwards, Bradshaw, and Hinsz 2014, n.p.). It is a widely cited statistic (although a contested one) that one in four women on college campuses is sexually assaulted (Ziering and Dick 2015). A crucial component of popular feminism has been to call attention to rape culture, to reveal its pervasive and normative presence.[4]

Thus, in what initially is a reversal of a postfeminist framing of rape as something for which women should be held responsible, a popular feminist frame of rape culture directs the blame once again toward men's actions. Yet this produces a *reaction* by popular misogyny, one that insists yet again on the sexual agency of women as the primary issue rather than the violence of men. For example, men's rights organizations contest statistics about rape, arguing that women are blaming men for their bad decisions. While men's rights organizations cover a range of topics, and some are more moderate in tone and accusation than others, the focus of all of them are the particular injuries that *men* experience—usually at the hand of feminism. Indeed, men's rights organizations claim that the "real" victims of gender discrimination are not women but men. Society, according to these organizations, has ignored the suffering of men and instead takes them for granted (Blake 2015). Men's rights organizations insist that the injuries incurred by men, from custody rights to job security to sexual rejection, need to be addressed in order for traditional masculinity to be restored. Specifically in the context of rape culture, it is *women's* sexual agency that is the problem, not the fact that men rape women. An article detailing the career of Warren Farrell, considered to be the father of the men's rights movement, states "that female sexual power was eclipsing any societal advantages that men might have. 'The powerful woman doesn't feel the effect of her secretary's miniskirt power, cleavage power and flirtation power,' [Farrell] wrote. 'Men do.' And thanks to feminism, he argued, when women felt ill-treated they could now more easily pursue sexual-harassment or date rape charges—a notion that carries strong currency among today's men's rights activists" (Blake 2015, n.p.). Indeed, according to this reasoning, in an era of popular feminism, the

FIGURE 1.4.
WAVAW Rape
Crisis Centre,
Vancouver,
Canada, "Don't Be
That Guy" cam-
paign, 2013.

insistence that rape culture *exists at all* is an affront to men. The logic here is that women are sexual subjects—and their sexual subjectivity automatically results in the emasculation of men. If women are sexually desiring subjects, then, according to this logic, rape culture *cannot* exist as women are always in control of consent. Again, men are the ones injured by this control women apparently have, and are thus the "real" victims of contemporary sexual politics. This fundamental disagreement over even acknowledging that rape culture exists as a culture, rather than discrete acts, is a central issue for not only postfeminism but also men's rights organizations. The goal of these organizations, then, is to restore men's capacity, for jobs, for control, for just being "men."

FIGURE 1.5. Edmonton Men's Rights Organization, "Don't Be That Girl" campaign, 2013.

The discourses of injury and capacity that structure the dynamic between popular feminism and popular misogyny were at work in a series of men's rights campaigns between 2013 and 2016. These ads directly responded to popular feminist efforts to bring awareness to the prevalence of rape culture. For example, in 2013 a Canadian rape-awareness group, Battered Women's Support Services (BWSS), created a series of posters, "Don't Be That Guy," described as a "behavioral marketing campaign [that] sends the message that sex without consent is sexual assault" (Chambers 2016, n.p.). The visual campaign was aimed at men between eighteen and twenty-five years old, as a way to ask men "to take responsibility for their behavior" (Chambers 2016, n.p.). One ad depicts a group of men and women at a bar, with the focus on a woman smiling and talking to two men as she holds a martini. The text reads, "Just Because She's Drinking . . . Doesn't Mean She Wants Sex." Another ad depicts a white woman passed out face down on a couch, her listless hand loosely holding a spilled glass of wine. The text here reads, "Just Because She Isn't Saying No . . . Doesn't Mean She's Saying Yes." These posters, along with two others on the same theme, were placed in restrooms in Vancouver's bar district; they embody the sentimental earnestness mode of address discussed earlier.

A short time later, a similar series of ads began to appear across social media. The campaign mirrored the rape-awareness campaign in almost every aspect, including using the same images. But its intentions were the opposite. Created by a men's rights organization in Canada, Men's Rights Edmonton, the campaign was titled "Don't Be That Girl." The text accompanying these images read, "Just Because You Regret a One Night Stand... Doesn't Mean It Wasn't Consensual." The campaign, of course, was both a parody and a criticism of the "Don't Be That Guy" series, and was aimed at what Men's Rights Edmonton called a "different type of criminal: women who make false rape accusations" (Men's Rights Edmonton, quoted in Straughan 2013a, n.p.). The campaign received widespread media coverage, most of which was critical, and described the group as blaming the victim and apologizing for rapists.

For Men's Rights Edmonton, however, those criticisms were irrelevant, because the logic behind the posters obviates the category of rapist altogether. Rather, the campaign focuses on the injuries experienced by men because of feminist rantings about rape culture—men are not rapists, here, but are rather falsely accused. And because these are *false* accusations of rape, then no rape occurred, therefore the BWSS campaign is built on faulty logic. Indeed, in this frame, rape culture is entirely imaginary on the part of feminists, and in order to restore men's capacity to be masculine, feminists need to be taken down. Again, the tropes of injury and capacity are those with traction in the economy of visibility, and Men's Rights Edmonton competes for visibility with popular feminism on these grounds. Aside from the posters, which were plastered in bar bathrooms in Edmonton, the organization's website also featured this logic. On the website, for example, is a video titled "Don't Be that Lying Feminist," from one of the site's frequent commentators, Karen Straughan (whose online identity is "Girl Writes What"). Straughan painstakingly demolishes feminist responses to the campaign, arguing that feminists fail to distinguish between victims and nonvictims, and thus cast all women as victims with ulterior motives. Describing those women who make false claims of rape, she says, "For the malicious false accuser who does it to get revenge, or to get the edge in a custody battle, the rape kit would be no different from a pap smear or a pelvic exam, something that women submit to on a regular basis" (Straughan 2013b, n.p.). Again, this recalls a postfeminist framing of date rape, which insists that if women are sexual agents, then they should be in control of their consent. It also emphasizes that it is men who are injured here, by the "malicious false accuser." Straughan implies that women who accuse men of rape do so for ulterior motives—regret, bad sex, or even revenge. The fact that a spokesperson for the campaign is a woman is a familiar tactic within men's rights organizations, in which a woman who supports such organizations apparently offers empirical evidence for the facticity, the logic, of the arguments made against women. The "Don't Be That Girl" campaign also calls out the earnestness of popular feminism's attention to rape culture, and indeed takes it further to accuse rape victims of making false accusations.

Other men's rights campaigns similarly call out the sentimental earnestness of popular feminist campaigns by mirroring them, visually and textually, but with parody. The United Nations Entity for Gender Equality and the Empowerment of Women (otherwise known as "UN Women") created a campaign in 2013 to call attention to the way in which search engines, and Google in particular, use the autocomplete feature to talk about women in painfully pointed ways. Representatives for UN Women typed phrases into a Google search, for example, "women shouldn't" and "women cannot"; the auto responses that came up onscreen were painful, to say the least: "women shouldn't vote," "women shouldn't have rights," and "women shouldn't work." Some were quite violent, such as the "women need" example: "women need to be put in their place" and "women need to be controlled." Using the global advertising firm Ogilvy and Mather Dubai, UN Women created a visual campaign featuring a series of posters with the faces of a variety of women, each with a search bar covering her mouth, with the search results listed underneath.[5]

A year after this campaign launched, an online magazine hosted by a company in India, *MaggCom*, created its own campaign: "Don't Mancriminate." The campaign again mirrors the UN Women's campaign almost exactly, using faces of different men (including celebrities), with a text bar covering the men's mouths. Rather than use Google's autocomplete, this campaign takes popular feminist exhortations for gender equality and turns them on their head, suggesting that it is men who suffer from inequities. One poster features the actor Elijah Wood, with text covering Wood's mouth: "It's a Man's World . . . Bullshit." Under this, the text reads, "I don't get free drinks. I don't get free entry. I don't get sympathy." Another ad has the text "You Want Gender Equality? Take It" covering the man's mouth, with the text below reading "I don't have to hold the door. I don't have to hold the bags. I don't have to give my seat." The "Don't Mancriminate"

FIGURE 1.6. UN Women, "The Autocomplete Truth" campaign, 2013.

campaign signals that it is *women* who are privileged in the world, and, as if that weren't bad enough, those women are ungrateful for all of the various things that men have given up for them. Indeed, the awkwardly worded tagline implies discrimination against men, angrily pointing out all the suffering of men for the apparent sacrifices they have made for women.

The Funhouse Mirror

In the "Don't Mancriminate" campaign, *MaggCom* uses a similar strategy as Men's Rights Edmonton, in which the campaigns mock and mirror the popular feminist campaigns in order to point out their apparently faulty logic. What also emerges, of course, is the sheer ludicrousness of the comparison made by both of these men's rights efforts—as if the import behind the message that "women need to be controlled" is on par with the whiny declaration "I don't have to hold the bags." But this is how the funhouse mirror works: it contorts and distorts the realities of systemic sexism so that this reality somehow works in favor of popular misogyny, as a way to address male injuries. These distortions work via tone. It is clear that these men's rights responses are a parody, a joke. This parody creates a distraction from the rampant frequency of rape and sexist abuse. It directs our attention elsewhere, belittling the problem itself. Indeed, this is a familiar tactic for groups in power, and shares a powerful similarity with the "injuries" of whiteness. The sentiment behind "Don't Mancriminate" is paralleled to that behind "reverse racism," an accusation made by white people when they feel as if their "rightful" position—in college admission or jobs—is taken by a person of color. Within this logic, an equal playing field is assumed between asymmetrical groups—men and women, whites and nonwhites. Popular misogyny doesn't deny this asymmetry, but it views it as a historical relic. That is, discrimination may have existed in the past, but today, the scales have tipped. Apparently, we live in a period of equality; if anything, it is the women who have all the power.

But, the logic of popular misogyny continues, some people—read: women, nonwhites—can't seem to appreciate all of their benefits. Pesky feminists and activists continue to demand more and more equality. Thus, men, and white men in particular, who continue to hold positions of power, who continue to enjoy benefit and privilege because of their race and gender, who continue to be validated and protected by institutionalized sexism and racism, are ironically the ones in our contemporary moment who are "injured." The continued activism for the rights for and cultural value of women and nonwhite people is understood by dominant groups as a series of repeated injuries. It signals, according to the logic of popular misogyny, an unfair protectionism. Because women have achieved equality with men, why then should they be protected? This insistence on an equal playing field is crucial to the logic of neoliberalism, as it was for liberalism in years past. The individual, not gendered or raced but merely a "person," is the key subject in this logic. If all individuals are equal, there is no need for specificity of identity; indeed, insisting on this very specificity is precisely what is causing the injury.

We see this in the logic of "Don't Be *That Girl*" as well as in the challenges by white people to the Black Lives Matter movement that *All* Lives Matter. Alicia Garza, Opal Tometi, and Patrisse Cullors, the creators of the Black Lives Matter movement, have eloquently explained the reasons why it is crucial to recognize that black lives matter in particular: it is a movement that calls attention to the ways in which black people have been deprived of their rights and dignity, the ways that state violence specifically targets black people, and the fact that 50 percent of incarcerated individuals are black people: "The fact is that the lives of Black people—not ALL people—exist within these conditions is a consequence of state violence" (Garza n.d., n.p.). Relatedly, to argue that women are responsible for being raped is to assume that they don't exist within the conditions of patriarchy. Again, this is the distortion of the funhouse mirror, the dynamic of popular feminism and popular misogyny, in which widespread gender and racial inequities are transfigured to become the source of injury for white men. Protection of rights for those who are disenfranchised—any kind of protection, regardless of how ineffective—is understood by men's rights organizations as the source of their injury, a protection that disrupts the equal playing field, and reverts it to one that is yet again unequal—but this time, it is white men who are disadvantaged.

The idea of "mirroring" is based on recognizing the power of the visual—to mirror is to reflect, to look back. Not surprisingly, mirroring is a central mechanism in an economy of visibility. As I discussed in the introduction, contemporary neoliberal culture nurtures an economy of visibility as opposed to a politics of visibility. The politics of visibility assumes that making visible a marginalized identity, that calling attention to discrimination based on gender or race, can hopefully prompt social change. While the politics of visibility is still vital in the contemporary moment—

we merely need to see the importance of Black Lives Matter to understand this—it is economies of visibility that increasingly structure our cultural practices and our everyday lives. Within an economy of visibility, the political indicates the absorption of visibility into the economy; specific identities are deemed irrelevant and thus are not acknowledged (H. Gray 2013).

Men's rights organizations operate within an economy of visibility; these organizations take the issues that popular feminism is centered around, such as confidence and empowerment, and mirror them in a way that distorts and transforms the target of confidence and empowerment so that it is men (and particularly white men) who suffer, not women. Part of the supposed injury felt by men within popular misogyny is their emasculation by women, specifically feminists. Emasculation is understood in a variety of ways, including labor, work and "breadwinner" status, and sexual agency and domination. Here, the feminine sexual agency so celebrated within postfeminism is cast within a zero-sum framework, so that as women are hired for a job, or acquire more sexual agency or erotic capital, those gains always come at the expense of men. Contemporary men's rights organizations do not deny women's agency; while clearly sexual objectification of women is still a central logic within all realms of social and cultural life, this objectification clashes with an increasingly recognized sexual subjectivity of women. Indeed, Rosalind Gill argues that a key element of a "postfeminist sensibility" is the celebration of this sexual agency, in which we see a shift from "sex object to sexually desiring subject" (Gill 2007, 151). Casting women as sex objects in media, culture, and politics has been a powerful mechanism of control, because to be objectified, as Laura Mulvey ([1975] 1989) wrote long ago, is to be transfigured into a *thing* to be looked at, gazed upon. However, when the gaze is returned, the status of object is disrupted, and it is harder to manage the control over a sexual subject. This dynamic, between women as sexual objects and women as sexual agents, is the funhouse mirroring effect, where the politics are distorted and shaped to serve the purpose of popular misogyny. Popular misogyny, that is, uses the concept of women as sexually desiring subjects, as sexual agents, as a way to justify practices that end up solidifying misogyny. The idea that women are sexually desiring subjects doesn't give women more sexual agency within popular misogyny; rather, the idea of women as sexual agents is exploited by popular misogyny to rationalize rape culture. An industry has emerged to regain control of the gaze, and to reimagine and reframe women as objects—and as the cause of injury. In other words, women (and especially feminists) pose a threat to men within the logics of popular misogyny, precisely because of the perceived *power* that women have. Popular misogyny is distinct in the contemporary moment because it acknowledges that women are not merely objects (even those women whom misogynists might still wish were mere objects), so a response is needed to contain this perceived feminine power.

Indeed, men's rights organizations often mobilize to action based on the perceived threat that women pose to their positions of masculinity. This mobilization is enabled by the economy of visibility that is the context for the dynamic relationship between popular feminism and popular misogyny. Marshaling the tropes of injury and capacity, popular feminism and popular misogyny engage in a battle for dominance in the economy of visibility, with popular misogyny expressing itself in a defensive, reactive mode. This reaction takes shape, as I detail in the following chapters, in death threats, "doxing" (revealing personal information online), online harassment, public shaming, and "revenge porn." Within an economy of visibility, the expressions of popular feminism often begin and end with visibility, yet these expressions garner a hostile, often violent, reaction from popular misogyny.

TWO. SHAME

Love Yourself and Be Humiliated

Just as television news was devolving into a modern coliseum, the internet came along and compounded this culture of shame and vitriol. Remember: The story of my affair was not broken by The Washington Post, The New York Times or the networks, but online by the Drudge Report. The comments on television and online were excruciating. I ceased being a three-dimensional person. Instead I became a whore, a bimbo, a slut and worse. Just days after the story broke, Fox asked its viewers to vote on this pressing question: Is Monica Lewinsky an "average girl" or a "young tramp looking for thrills"? — MONICA LEWINSKY, 2017

In March 2015, after years of self-imposed absence from public view, Monica Lewinsky gave a TED talk called "The Price of Shame." For the first time since the scandal with then president Bill Clinton, seventeen years earlier, Lewinsky decided to share her experience—as "patient zero of losing a personal reputation on a global scale almost instantaneously" (Lewinsky 2015). She then compared the cultural, social, and technological context of 1998 with that of 2015. Today's numerous media platforms—all digital and incestuously networked—allow for what Lewinsky argues is an unprecedented taking of people's private words and images and making them public: "public without consent, public without context, public without compassion" (Lewinsky 2015). In this way, she argues, contemporary online culture "traffics in shame." We have created, in short, what Nicolaus Mills calls "the politics of humiliation" (Mills 2017).

Lewinsky is adamant about the incentive that drives this culture of humiliation: it is incredibly profitable. She argues that the "price of shame" is not measured in terms of victims of public humiliation, often women, people of color, and those who are not heteronormative. Rather, the price measures the profit of those who prey on them (not the victims): "This invasion of others is a raw material, efficiently and ruthlessly mined, packaged, and sold at a profit. A marketplace has emerged, where public humiliation is a commodity, and shame is an industry. How is the money made? Clicks. The more shame, the more clicks. The more clicks, the more advertising dollars" (Lewinsky 2015). In a more recent op-ed piece for the *New York Times*, Lewinsky (2017) concretizes her claim with a specific example: Roger Ailes, the former president of Fox News, died in May 2017 after being ousted from the network as a result of numerous sexual harassment claims. As Lewinsky persuasively argues, Ailes became president of Fox News just two years before the Clinton affair, and "took the story of the affair and the trial that followed and made certain his anchors hammered it ceaselessly, 24 hours a day. . . . It worked like magic: The story hooked viewers and made them Fox loyalists. For the past 15 years, Fox News has been the No. 1 news station; last year the network made about $2.3 billion" (Lewinsky 2017, n.p.). Publicly shaming women is indeed a big business.

In the following chapter, I examine how online trafficking in shame shapes and frames the relationship between popular feminism and popular misogyny. Part of popular feminism has been an emphasis on loving one's body, and resisting cultural and social norms about idealized feminine bodies. Yet, while body positivity is important, it also maintains a visual focus on the feminine body. In turn, part of popular misogyny has been precisely to shame the feminine body, constantly regulating and disciplining women's bodies as a way to assert masculine dominance. I also argue, following Lewinsky, that networked media provides the fertile ground for the proliferation of popular misogyny—even as it also provides the context for the circulation of popular feminism.

As Lewinsky points out, the technologies of the early twenty-first century have allowed for new practices of looking, and shifted ways of seeing[1]—as well as allowing new markets and industries to emerge. The economy of visibility that I analyze in this book is one of multiple perspectives; the desire for visibility, or what Herman Gray (2013) calls the process of being "subject(ed) to recognition," indicates a move toward seeing visibility as an end in itself, where what is visible becomes what *is*. The multiple perspectives that are enabled by social media enhance this dynamic, with new media platforms for visibly witnessing and shaming bodies seemingly cropping up every day. Social media sites such as Facebook, Twitter, Instagram, Snapchat, and Yik Yak certainly have multiple functions, but shaming, especially of women's bodies, seems to be a practice that they all share, if not encourage. In particular, these kinds of media platforms have been utilized, in a startling variety of ways, as instruments of popular misogyny.

But these same media platforms also are the ground for popular feminism. The economy of visibility that nurtures the practice of online shaming also authorizes a countermovement of loving one's body, insisting on healthy self-esteem for girls and women. The discourses of feminine self-esteem that circulate within an economy of visibility are primarily those that focus on the visible body, where girls and women are entreated to love their bodies, to have self-confidence, to reject low self-esteem. However, the power, and the danger, of our insistence on self-esteem are revealed further when we consider its flip side. Revenge porn and online harassment are practices that utilize techniques such as slut shaming, fat shaming, sexual humiliation, and threats of sexual violence to publicly shame women online. But what is the effect of this kind of shame supposed to be? Misogynistic public shaming is *just* about humiliation; in many ways, it is about rendering one's target unable to act, to disable their agency. As Danielle Keats Citron (2014) and others have detailed, the shame and humiliation that is part of online harassment has as a goal the prevention of action: relationships are destroyed, jobs vanish, lives are lost. However, engaging in humiliating women who have "wronged" men (either as a culture or individually) is also about bolstering men's own sense of action or agency; this is the way popular misogyny uses the concepts of popular feminism to its own ends, in a distorted political expression. Again, this is the "blood sport" of misogynistic shaming: it is literally about the pleasure of watching others suffer. It is "revenge" masked as a warped kind of justice. And, like other expressions of popular feminism and popular misogyny, the twinned discourses of self-esteem and shaming utilize the tropes of injury and capacity as a central logic: the capacity of women to "love their body" apparently injures men's sense of self-esteem (because in the body positivity discourse, women don't need men to affirm their bodies), and shaming is seen as the conduit to restoring masculine capacity. The neoliberal individualism of popular feminism, despite being about capacity and injury, also renders popular feminism *in*capable of adequately responding to the violence of popular misogyny.

In a circular way, the reaction to online shaming, by educators, lawmakers, and others, is to encourage girls and women to have "healthy self-esteem" and to "love their bodies." The message, sometimes explicit, sometimes implicit, is that if we love our bodies we won't make suspect sexual choices. We will thus solve the problem endemic to this economy of visibility not by actually confronting the vicious misogyny at the heart of that economy but by making its potential victims upright and unbesmirchable. Yet the conventions that shape what it actually means to be unbesmirchable are predominantly those that conform to dominant racial, classed, and heterosexual gender norms, again reaffirming visibility as a politics on its own. In an economy of visibility, visibility is an end in itself, and the "Love Your Body" movement plays into this in the way that visibility turns its lens on the individual girl or woman. As Myra Mendible puts it, "Shame as commodity spectacle is most productive (and profitable) when projected on media-worthy objects, on bodies that matter enough to merit attention" (2016, 3). In this way, the visible "Love Your Body" movement is less concerned with the technological ways that specific female sexualities are policed, or the way that this kind of policing is embedded within an online culture that encourages popular misogyny. Shame thus becomes a self-discipline, predicated on a desire *not* to be shamed. Online, the threat of public shaming is always there, lurking in the background; someone, it seems, is always waiting to shame you.

Here, I examine the entwined relationship between gendered self-esteem and misogynistic public shaming, as iterations of popular feminism and popular misogyny. This relationship takes form within, indeed is conditioned by, an economy of visibility. I argue that the threat of public shaming shapes the popular feminism of the current moment, as well as the way that feminists talk about, and the way popular culture focuses on, body positivity and healthy self-esteem: these popular feminist practices ask for affirmation from an anonymous, diffused public, with the full knowledge that public shaming is potentially a result. Public shaming is a key disciplinary mechanism of popular misogyny, enabled by the accessibility of digital media platforms and the way these platforms offer an opportunity to shame bodies to a wide audience (and often anonymously).

Indeed, the broader context for an economy of visibility is digital culture, which also frames popular feminism and popular misogyny as networked movements that move across and within multiple media platforms. The mechanisms of self-esteem and shame play important roles in both popular feminism and popular misogyny. For popular feminism, to practically *encourage* shaming is a form of self-discipline, a sort of hazing, if you will: Can you emerge from it? Can you love your body in a culture that says you should hate it? If you can, then you can become a digital life, your own brand, your own industry. Like hazing, the request for affirmation is about building armor, like requesting admission to an elite sorority, except the request—and one's vulnerability—is extended to a vast audience of strangers, and finds purchase in an economy of visibility. Shame is thus the constitutive flip side of self-esteem, and both are a gateway into digital media existence today; we can enter the gates of digital media existence only by going through one of them. Only when one "asks" to be shamed can one *become* a digital identity, such as when girls and young women upload videos to YouTube asking, "Am I pretty or ugly?" (as I discuss later in this chapter).

Exposing oneself to public shaming is literally the cost of doing business within a digital world. To not only "put yourself out there" but to do it with the explicit request for affirmation and judgment becomes a ritual of digital identity: how durable are you? The market for self-esteem tells the online-savvy girls and women who participate that by buying into this market, one can usurp the social media platforms that are both the source of shame and the means for making shame public. The message is that by believing in yourself publicly, you can overcome the haters. But the reality is far less transparent. The way that self-esteem becomes legible as a response to shame is by becoming part of the *discourse* of shame; shame is positioned as a threat or danger to one's self-esteem, therefore it functions as a disciplinary mechanism in perpetuity, there is no point where it might end.

This chapter thus investigates shame as a mobilizing dynamic in both popular feminism and popular misogyny. Jon Ronson (2015, n.p.), writing about the use of social media as a public shaming mechanism, states, "The great thing about social media was how it gave a voice to voiceless people. We are now turning it into a surveillance society where the smartest way to survive is to go back to being voiceless." The idea of social media as a context for the voiceless, what danah boyd (2010) has called a "networked public," is key to the shape of popular feminism as a networked movement. Shaming tactics in popular misogyny disrupt this network; by shaming individual bodies of women and thus encouraging women and girls to remove themselves from social media to avoid this, popular misogyny challenges the possibility of feminist community. The public shaming of women's bodies has been a regulatory practice for centuries, in which the sexual subjectivities of women, especially women of color, have been judged and policed in all realms of life, from the mundanities of the domestic realm to the street and the workplace to the abstract realm of law and public policy. And, as Ronson (2015) points out, this is intensified in social media, where it is not only one's reputation at stake but also often one's livelihood.

But Ronson doesn't analyze how these stakes are deeply gendered. In Ronson's book *So You've Been Publicly Shamed*, he details several stories of public shaming, from the revelation of plagiarism of author Jonah Lehrer to the publicist Justine Sacco's racist tweet in 2013 to the tweeting of two men overheard making sexual jokes at a technology conference. As Ronson argues, the reputation of these individuals (as well as others in the book) was forever damaged by public shaming. However, what Ronson fails to consider in his book are the ways in which publicly shaming a woman is profoundly different from shaming a man. Shaming, in any form, is a mechanism of power designed to humiliate. And while certainly men are shamed as well, there is clearly a gendered difference in both the quantity and the content of shaming that occurs, not only in the contemporary moment but also historically. Ronson does not comment on this gendered dynamic—even when his anecdotes constantly reveal its influence. For example, Hank, the man who was fired for making sexual jokes at a technology conference after a woman, Adria Richards, who was sitting behind him, tweeted about it, was contacted by men's rights activists after apologizing to Richards. These men's rights bloggers told him that his apology "revealed him to be a man with 'a complete lack of backbone'" (Ronson 2016, 119). A 4Chan thread about Richards was created at the same time, where people made comments like "Let's crucify this cunt" and "Cut out her uterus with an xacto knife" (Ronson 2016, 120). As Ronson details, people sent Richards photoshopped images of her face superimposed onto the bodies of pornography actors. On Facebook someone wrote, "Fuck that bitch make her pay make her obey" (Ronson 2016, 120). While Ronson offered these details, he doesn't engage them as gendered differences in how men and women are shamed—telling a man to "be more of a man" by standing up to a woman accuser is strikingly different from rape and death threats made to a woman. Mendible, writing about how race figures into a politics of shame, argues that when whites feel that they are no longer in control, "shame entrepreneurs offer a panacea for what ails an anxious hierarchy: a means to tighten the reins on designated others and a way to assuage bruised egos and 'restore psychological comfort for the group'" (2016, 8). In a similar way, when men feel that they are no longer in control, they shame women through the fact that *they are women* as a "means to tighten the reins on designated others and a way to assuage bruised egos."

Shame thus "works to maintain fundamental social divisions and antagonisms"; it functions to regulate and police the gendered body. The dominant public response to women who have been publicly shamed or humiliated through revenge porn and online harassment has been the familiar tactic of blaming the victim: don't take nude photos of yourself; don't act in "slutty" ways. Here, the only way to avoid shame is to not be present. If "putting yourself out there" is the means to make yourself legible in a digital world, media refusal means to shut oneself off from the market (Portwood-Stacer 2013). Media refusal is also the refusal to participate in an economy of visibility, where visibility is self-sufficient and an end in itself. It means, in this context, to render oneself invisible.

Love Your Body . . . or Else

In January 2016, *Time* magazine featured a cover story with the title "Barbie's Got a New Body" (Dockterman 2016).[2] The article detailed the recent release by the Mattel toy company of three new body shapes for "the world's best-selling doll": tall, petite, and curvy. As reporter Eliana Dockterman points out about this "historic change," "They'll all be called Barbie, but it's the curvy one—with meat on her thighs and a protruding tummy and behind—that marks the most startling change to the most infamous body in the world" (Dockterman 2016, n.p.). There are clear reasons Mattel would release new body shapes at this particular historical moment, not least of which is that sales of Barbie have been dropping radically for years, especially in the context of other companies releasing more "realistic" dolls for girls (such as Disney's Elsa, from the movie *Frozen*). Another reason is more difficult to measure, but perhaps more significant: an explosion of popular feminist messages about healthy self-esteem and the fact that popular feminism has gone mainstream. In tweets and Instagram pics, on Tumblr pages and Facebook posts, and on other media platforms, girls and women are endlessly exhorted to be "confident," which is centered as a key logic for one to "love their bodies."

The popular feminist mandate to be confident (which I discuss at length in chapter 3) is in part a response to generations of relentless messages about what the ideal of femininity is, what girls and women should look like. The standard of beauty that was long ago called the "tyranny of slenderness" (Chernin 1994) has become even more tyrannical in the contemporary moment, in part because of the dramatic increase in images of the body that circulate, endlessly and abundantly, through social media. It is these images of the idealized feminine body that clutter the economy of visibility; indeed, even as Mattel is lauding their new body shapes for Barbie, the traditional Barbie is not referred to as "curvy," "tall," or "petite," but simply as "Barbie." This maintains an idealized feminine body not only as the norm, but as the visible norm.

Yet even as the average US teenage girl is flooded with images of the "perfect" female body, she is also inundated with what seems like the opposite of that "perfection": exhortations that she should love herself for who she is. A key element of contemporary popular feminism is self-confidence; the imperative that women and girls be "confident," especially in their bodies, is relentlessly circulated on media platforms. Women's magazines such as *InStyle* and *Elle* have featured confidence as the key topic of issues: *Elle*'s issue from December 2014 is titled "The Confidence Issue: A Smart Woman's Guide to Self-Belief," featuring Kim Kardashian on the cover; *InStyle*'s issue from February 2016 features a glowering Jennifer Lopez on the cover, with the featured headline "Love Your Body: Even When Nothing Seems to Flatter." And the Internet is both taking its cues from and in turn influencing the grocery store checkout aisle. We have seen a dramatic increase in social media campaigns to be confident and to "love your body," ranging from #GirlsCan to #SpeakBeautiful to #RealBeauty (see Elias, Gill, and Scharff 2017). These campaigns trade on the dynamic relationship of injury and capacity that circulate so well in an economy of visibility, where the injury of narrow, idealized feminine body image is circulated but then countered with the apparent capacity of all women to "love their bodies" and be self-confident. But the injury here is not primarily inflicted on women by society; rather, low self-confidence is *self*-injury, and the biggest injury to women is that which they bring on themselves by not "loving their body" (Favaro 2017). As Laura Favaro argues in her study of user forums for women's magazines, women often embrace the neoliberal impulse to see society and systemic sexism as a problem they can solve just by overcoming it: "Low self-esteem and feelings of vulnerability are translated into notions of insufficient personal drive, effort and responsibility for her own life" (Favaro 2017, 212).

In other words, as Rosalind Gill and Shani Orgad (2015) have argued, for women and girls, to be self-confident is the new mandate of our time, and one that is an individual achievement rather than a recognition of structural gender asymmetries. It has been articulated as a crucial part of building one's career, health campaigns, and educational programs, and is the key logic of "Love Your Body" campaigns (King 2006; Elias, Gill, and Scharff 2017). As Ana Sofia Elias, Rosalind Gill, and Christina Scharff (2017) point out, the discourses that shape the "Love Your Body" exhortation trace the various mechanisms—institutional, emotional, physical— that work to maintain dominant systems of power. The notion that you should "love your body" positions confidence as the route to self-esteem, which is in turn positioned as fundamentally about feeling positive about one's body and a form of feminist politics in and of itself.

Within the rise of "Love Your Body" discourses, among the most visible are perhaps corporate campaigns such as Special K's "Own It," which depicts women of various ages, body sizes, and ability celebrating their bodies, with the ad's climax featuring a woman looking into a mirror and having the mirror shatter (along with, apparently, society's conventions), and Dove's Campaign for Real Beauty, which features a series of short videos distributed online, most of which focus on how women are their own worst critics when it comes to their bodies. However, other, less highly produced and corporate-backed examples have spread beyond media and into everything from self-help books to school health interventions (such as nutrition classes and antibullying workshops) to training programs designed to help girls and women (such as nonprofit organizations that offer classes on how to gain self-confidence). As Gill and Elias (2014, 21) argue, "These messages urging girls and women to 'love your body' are affirmative, familiarly feminist exhortations to believe in ourselves, feel confident and attractive 'at any size,' to 'remember' that we are 'incredible.' They instruct young women that 'the power is in your hands.'"

FIGURE 2.1. *Elle UK* magazine, "The Confidence Issue," 2014.

If we understand confidence to be a "mandate of our time," we need to think through what it means to mandate confidence in, and on, the body (Gill and Orgad 2015). A mandate is typically an official order, one that implies (sometimes explicitly, other times implicitly) severe consequences if one does not comply. And indeed, a mandate of the economy of visibility is that one's body is circulating in a visible way, as a body that one "loves." What are the consequences for women if they do not "love" their bodies? I argue here that shame is the primary consequence, so that shame becomes a tool of self-discipline: we can find reasons to be ashamed of our bodies everywhere, from the endless perkiness of Victoria's Secret window displays to the endless criticisms of message boards. Therefore, the only response is that we must "love" our bodies. Yet the key to shaming as self-discipline is an emphasis on the "self"—it is the responsibility of individual women and girls to love their bodies, regardless of how much, and how often, culture tells us we should hate them. This is in keeping with a broader neoliberal context that privileges the economy of visibility and its emphasis on the individual self.

FIGURE 2.2.

InStyle magazine, "Love Your Body" issue, 2016.

To be clear, part of "Love Your Body" discourses is a critique of the ways in which the beauty industry has portrayed women—indeed, has *injured* women. In fact, one of the largest corporate campaigns involved is Dove's Self-Esteem Fund, and Dove is, of course, a huge player in the beauty industry. This kind of contradiction is typical of popular feminism, where often the "Love Your Body" messages challenge not only the point of the beauty industry's constant quest to encourage one to buy products through shaming of the body but also that for-profit corporations often depend on this kind of cycle of shame consumption. This is the central logic of the injury/capacity dynamic that is emphasized in an economy of visibility; like many other logics within neoliberal capitalism, injury is presented only to have a resolution at hand, most often found within individual capacities. Additionally, the injury itself is often framed as an individual one, brought on by oneself—if you *don't* love your body, that's because you aren't confident enough. The "Love Your Body" discourses are, at least in part, an attempt to respond to earlier feminist critiques

FIGURE 2.3. Dove, "Movement for Self-Esteem" ad, 2017.

of the media and the beauty industry. "Love Your Body" discourses challenge these image ideals by insisting that women should be confident in their bodies regardless of whether they "fit" into a conventional beauty ideal. Thus, in many ways, the "Love Your Body" discourses are to be celebrated. These campaigns can make concrete what seem to be abstractions of feminism, and can offer one way for women to feel better about their bodies, to overcome the injury of socially and culturally dominant norms of femininity. Indeed, they are particularly powerful because of the way they seem to interrupt the hostile judgment and surveillance of women's bodies that has become almost entirely normative in contemporary culture.

Of course, the quest for self-esteem is not a contemporary phenomenon, though it manifests in different ways in the present moment of social media. Like advertising in general, the contemporary market for self-esteem needs a concept of the therapeutic as a way to articulate its aims and goals. Eva Illouz (2008, 3), in *Saving the Modern Soul*, analyzes the concept of the "therapeutic" in contemporary culture, and argues, "The therapeutic is a site within which we invent ourselves as individuals, with wants, needs, and desires to be known, categorized, and controlled for the sake of freedom." The gendered nature of being "self-made" continues in this vein, and indeed, is exacerbated by advanced capitalism's expansion of markets into intimate and personal realms. As Illouz has argued, the "large industrial machine of emotions management" is also enabled by the entrepreneurial focus of neoliberalism, and reflects neoliberal ideologies of the individual: as in any other business, the business of the "self" must be approached with an entrepreneurial spirit, one that seeks personal empowerment, confidence, and self-esteem (Illouz 2008). For women and girls, the business of the self has largely meant focusing on personal attitude adjustment rather than on a broader culture and politics of gender asymmetry. Again, within the economy of visibility, the injury of low self-esteem is seen as something that is an individual problem, one of "not believing in yourself" or "listening to haters." This in turn positions individual *capacity to* believe in oneself as the resolution to low self-esteem, rather than look to structural sexism, which provides the context for low self-esteem in the first place.

Miki McGee (2005) characterizes this shift in focus of self-help as moving to a cultural notion of the self as "art," a constant project to work on and improve. This cultural notion, however, is tied to the neoliberal imperative to "govern the self" and to think of it as a brand or a commodity, which then overwrites the possible benefits of thinking of the self as a "work of art." As McGee points out, "Instead, in its most recent iterations, the ideal of life as a work of art turns out to be not an alternative but rather a trap: a model perfectly suited to the conditions of advanced capitalism, where the intimate sphere becomes a site of ongoing and tireless production, a design studio for reinventing one's most marketable self. Through this emphasis on the aesthetic, the impulse toward individual self-determination—a value that has long served as a catalyst for progressive social change—has been harnessed in the service of accelerated consumption and production" (McGee 2005, 22).

As McGee argues, the practice of self-help transforms into an *industry* for self-help, and the ways to achieve self-esteem (and other forms of inner happiness and individual mental health) are understood through the framework of consumption. Advertising, marketing, and branding have of course long been a central logic to what T. J. Jackson Lears calls a "therapeutic ethos," encouraging consumers to buy products as a form of therapy (Lears 1983). McGee, however, points to the ways in which self-determination is newly understood as a capitalist industry.

The notion that work on the self in the intimate sphere becomes a "design studio for reinventing one's most marketable self" continues to have currency in the first part of the twenty-first century, especially in gendered terms. This is reflected in reality television makeover shows, the increasing normalization of professions such as "life coaches" and "love coaches," and the practice of self-branding (Ouellette and Hay 2008; Weber 2009; Hearn 2010; Bratich 2011; Banet-Weiser 2012; Hochschild 2012; Sender 2012). In the contemporary moment, self-help continues to have a different focus on girls' and women's bodies; it encourages women and girls to "love your body" and have a "healthy" self-esteem. It is popular feminism, with its shifted focus on personal empowerment, that emerges as a context for the industry of self-help and the route to healthy self-esteem. The focus of gendered self-help for women and girls in the twenty-first-century United States is about a market-inspired notion of self-esteem that focuses on normative feminine bodies and consumption practices that allow access to that normative body.

Girls and the "Problem" of Self-Esteem

Indeed, popular feminism is the broad context for one mediated iteration of the "Love Your Body" discourse, the popular video genre of "Am I Pretty?" videos on YouTube, where girls upload videos of themselves in the midst of their everyday lives, asking viewers to evaluate their physical appearance.[3] As I have argued, these videos tap into multiple dimensions of a networked popular feminism: the girls who post these videos are using technology to "put themselves out there"; by asking anonymous users to evaluate their physical appearance, they suggest they are self-confident enough to risk the injury of rejection; and YouTube is a central media mechanism in an economy of visibility, a digital site that depends on the visual circulation of media productions (Banet-Weiser 2014).

One of the most enduring videos in this genre, titled simply "Am I Pretty or Ugly?" (2010), begins with a young white girl looking into a webcam, saying, "I just wanted to make a random video to ask if I'm ugly or not. . . . A lot of people say I'm ugly and I think I'm ugly and fat. My friends who are girls—say 'Oh you're so beautiful.' . . . and I'm like 'Shut up, I'm not beautiful.'" The video, posted in 2010, received over 7 million views by 2014, and generated thousands of comments. Many of the comments referred to the girl's seemingly obvious lack of self-esteem, or responded to negative comments that were posted about the poster's physical appearance. For example, one commenter said, "I feel sick reading these comments it doesn't matter why this girl posted this video and yes she is pretty but why people feel the need to right horrible messages

FIGURE 2.4. "Am I Pretty or Ugly?," YouTube, 2013.

about her disgusts me she's probably only about 12 and people seem to think its okay to judge her [on] her appearances and call her ugly. Its sick and its bullying and people can have low self esteem, self harm and attempt suicide because of comments like this stop hate comments and just leave her alone until you want to say something nice." Another commenter offered maternal advice: "Just be yourself and at your age, don't worry about it. At this time in your life, these insecurities are normal. I have 2 daughters one is your age and one is older. Worry about being a nice person and your education and not what others think about you. If you have a lot of friends just be happy and listen to them, if they're true friends they won't steer you wrong." And yet another chimed in with "You should not care what people think just be yourself your beautiful no matter what."

But those affirming quotes were an attempt to quell the dominant tone of the comment section, which was not nearly as generous. Again, frequent comments stated that the young girl was indeed "ugly"; another repeated criticism was that she was an "attention whore." One typical example out of many is from a commenter who said, "ugly as fuck. if you want attention talk to a therapist." Most comments, like the ones listed above, referred (either positively or negatively) to the girl's sense of self, instructing the girl who posted the video to "just be yourself," and "don't worry about what others think," or, conversely, to feel shame and to "talk to a therapist."

This video is remarkable in part for how unremarkable it is. As Douglas Quenqua (2014) points out, a YouTube search for "Am I Pretty?" turns up more than 23,000 results. While most have been posted between 2013 and 2016, some videos were posted as early as 2009. The increase in the number of videos has quickly captured the attention of the US mainstream press and the blogosphere, covering what some have called a "new genre" of YouTube videos. Experts, ranging from educators to media pundits to parents, weighed in on how these videos ostensibly expressed the self-esteem problem of young girls in the United States (E. Gray 2012; Restauri 2012; Rochman 2012; Smith 2012). Because so many of the comments on these videos are negative and body shaming, the videos have been highlighted as a particularly destructive YouTube genre, and parents and educators even asked the site to take them down because they were seen as so damaging to girls' self-esteem.

The very existence of this "new genre" of YouTube videos is frequently explained away as a symbol of young girls' dwindling self-esteem in the contemporary moment, an expression of "body image anxieties" that is enabled in a heightened way in digital spaces.[4] While self-esteem issues may be part of a general normative context of being an adolescent, the videos need to be contextualized within hegemonic gender construction, including the popular feminist environment I detail in this book that centers on a specific concept of confidence and empowerment. This popular feminist context authorizes self-esteem to emerge not just as a personal issue but also as a lucrative market that targets young, middle-class girls as its consumers.

Indeed, these videos explicitly engage in the twinned discourses of injury and capacity: the girls who post the videos state their potential injury of low self-esteem—"Am I Pretty?"—while also exercising their capacity to use technology to "put themselves out there." For example, in the video referenced above, the young girl ends the post with these words: "So, leave me a comment below telling me if I'm pretty or ugly. Simple as that." There is actually nothing simple about these videos. Clearly, the fact that these videos became a national news story means that they are not, in fact, simple: the "Am I Pretty?" videos tell us something more complicated about the way in which specific girls are positioned in public culture, within a context of popular feminism. The videos are in the same family as the late 1990s website hotornot.com, which asked users to rate women as "hot" or "not." However, the "Am I Pretty?" videos are products of a more mainstream popular feminism: the videos are posted by the girls themselves, not by users or webmasters, the request for validation comes from the individual girl. The attention these videos have generated taps into several intertwined cultural and political discourses for young, middle-class girls in the United States, yet for the most part the focus of this attention has been explicitly directed to the apparent self-esteem "problem" for young girls.

The professionals who comment on the "Am I Pretty?" videos are no doubt correct: the videos represent a new, technological form of an old practice of both surveilling girls and then shaming them for not embodying cultural and conventional physical ideals. Young, white, middle-class girls in the United States have often been recognized as a demographic who are overly concerned with their own physical appearance and with the judgment of others, and as such have been subject to surveillance by peers, popular culture, and parents (among others). This culture of surveillance is complex and often marshals shaming as a disciplinary device: peer culture, celebrity culture, and norms of femininity routinely survey and discipline girls through increasingly elaborate systems of normative evaluation (found in both offline and online spaces). And girls frequently post images of themselves on evaluative social media sites (such as Facebook, Instagram, and Tumblr) that encourage users to "like," "heart," or otherwise approve of a girl's appearance and performance.

In this way, the "Am I Pretty?" video genre is positioned within the "Love Your Body" discourse. Indeed, the question asked by the posters perhaps provides part of the impetus for "loving one's body" in the first place. "Love Your Body" discourse insists that one shouldn't need to ask if one is pretty, yet the whole notion that there must be an *imperative* to love one's body indicates a latent injury to self-esteem. The body shaming that is expressed through the comments on "Am I Pretty?" videos provides a motivation to realize one's capacity to love oneself. Like many other popular feminist expressions, the injury experienced by individual girls who post "Am I Pretty?" videos differs by race and class—as does the capacity to overcome this injury. For middle-class white girls, self-esteem is a "hot" commodity (indeed, one that trades on a cultural definition of "hotness"). A whole industry has been built around it: there are best-selling books, seminars, and classes about "mean girls" and bullying; eating disorders continue to be a problem for young girls; popular culture is constantly regaling the latest efforts by female celebrities to conform to an idealized feminine body; and there are numerous nonprofit organizations, as well as corporate and federal programs, that have emerged with a focus on girls' self-esteem. From self-help literature with titles such as *200 Ways to Raise a Girl's Self-Esteem: An Indispensable Guide for Parents, Teachers, and Other Concerned Caregivers* (Glennon 1999), *I'm Gonna Like Me: Letting Off a Little Self-Esteem* (Curtis and Cornell 2007), and *Girls on Track: A Parent's Guide to Inspiring Our Daughters to Achieve a Lifetime of Self-Esteem and Respect* (Barker 2004) to more scholarly books such as *School Girls: Young Women, Self-Esteem, and the Confidence Gap* (Orenstein 1995), *The Lolita Effect: The Media Sexualization of Young Girls and What We Can Do about It* (Durham 2008), and *The Purity Myth: How America's Obsession with Virginity Is Hurting Young Women* (Valenti 2010), it seems clear that girls' self-esteem in the early twenty-first century is a remarkably brandable commodity (see Banet-Weiser 2012, esp. ch. 1).

The injury that results in low self-esteem for white middle-class girls, however, is one that circulates easily within an economy of visibility, which privileges the whiteness of popular feminism. Surely it is the case that working-class girls and girls of color are subject to injuries of low self-esteem issues given that the cultures in which they live are structured by institutionalized racism; yet the focus on them is different and is typically about their status as "at risk" in social, economic, and cultural terms (Harris 2004a; Gilman 2012). The popular feminism that most clearly circulates in an economy of visibility privileges the white middle-class girls who fit the category of the "Can-Do" girl—potentially empowered, entrepreneurial, and media savvy (Harris 2004a). As I discussed in the introduction, the negative inverse to the Can-Do girls are the At-Risk girls, who are often girls of color and working-class girls. The At-Risk girls do not demonstrate the same potential as the Can-Do girls; they are, after all, already "at risk." It is the Can-Do girl who has been scripted as a national "problem"; her body has been the site of public national investment, cultivated and imagined as a future citizen, an investment circulated in an economy of visibility. In contrast, the At-Risk girl is always already at risk because of her raced and classed body.

The injuries of low self-esteem would be confounded if they were considered within, say, a racist context that already positions girls of color as marginalized, or within an economic context within which large numbers of girls of color are disenfranchised. Yet a public and political view on these issues comes into focus when large numbers of white middle-class girls are seen to have been injured by these issues—it is then that the capacity to overcome this injury becomes a central element of popular feminism. Importantly, these two categories of girls are not discrete; rather, they are mutually constitutive. The positioning of white middle-class girls as Can-Do girls is paramount to the way in which more vulnerable girl populations, because of racism and socioeconomic divisions, are situated and understood as "at risk." The Can-Do girl becomes visible in an economy of visibility while the At-Risk girl is eclipsed. As R. Danielle Egan argues about the regulation imposed on the sexual practices of middle-class girls, "The white bourgeois body has been conceptualized as pure, hygienic, and emblematic of restraint and rationality; and the middle- and upper-class child the embodiment of innocence, purity, and the bright future of the class, race, and nation" (2013, 82). In this way, white middle-class girls are hypervisible (in a way other girls are not) but also are constantly harnessed for a host of ideological campaigns because of that visibility, including an increase in abstinence-only education, hypersexualization in media programs, and the backlash against women's rights in the United States.

Shame, Online Harassment, and Popular Misogyny

On any given day, one can go to a popular feminist website, such as *Jezebel, Feministing, Black Girl Dangerous, Feminist Current,* and read about yet another instance in which a woman was harassed online. This "call out" culture is an important part of the networked media context of popular feminism, one of the varied ways to combat the injuries women experience when harassed online. The reason for the harassment varies—it could be because one was tweeting a feminist sentiment, or because one posted a selfie on Instagram, or because one wrote a long-form essay about, well, online harassment, in a blog. Online harassment comes in different forms and has different expressions: it can be a version of virtual catcalling in which a woman's body is scrutinized (and often criticized); it can be explicitly violent, as a rape or a death threat; or it can be "doxing," the release of personal information about a woman, such as her phone number, address, or other confidential information. In her book *Hate Crimes in Cyberspace* (2014), Danielle Keats Citron defines "cyber harassment" as anything that "involves threats of violence, privacy invasions, reputation-harming lies, calls for strangers to physically harm victims, and technological attacks" (3). The Internet, Citron argues, exponentially expands the audience for harassment, because the architecture of the web "extends the life of destructive posts" (4). As Citron points out, 70 percent of online harassment is targeted at women, and women of color are disproportionately harassed. Most online harassment of women involves sexual comments or threats of sexual violence, such as rape and sexual assault, as well as shaming of sexual practices and photos. The stunning frequency of harassment online is not just due to scattered instances of bored boys behaving badly. It is a manifestation of a popular misogyny that has grown alongside the growth of popular feminism. Like popular feminism, popular misogyny is networked, a node in an interconnected network of misogynistic practices, in part a reaction to the popular circulation and embrace of feminism (Banet-Weiser and Miltner 2015).

All forms of feminisms have historically incurred backlash, efforts to dismantle and delegitimize its varied politics. One common justification offered by men for misogynistic practices—though, of course, they do not characterize these practices as misogynistic—is that they have been wronged by women in some way: women have taken "their" jobs; they have emasculated them; they have encroached on sacred masculine spaces; they have refused sexual advances or broken off relationships. Men, according to this logic, have suffered *the* authentic injury—to their masculinity. They have been made to feel shame in being a man. A particularly stark example of this involved the feminist blogger/reporter Lindy West. West writes for popular feminist blogs such as *Jezebel*, as well as more mainstream outlets such as GQ and the *Guardian*; she often writes about feminist issues such as rape culture, body image, and fat shaming. In the summer of 2013, West wrote about rape culture, and suggested that male comedians should not use rape as a joke. Predictably, in a context of popular feminism and popular misogyny, men responded to this comment with violent and vitriolic messages, focusing especially on West's body: a typical response was "No one would want to rape that fat, disgusting mess" (West 2015, n.p.). As West herself details in a segment on the radio program *This American Life*, these kinds of messages are more or less normative. But then one commenter decided to create a Twitter account of West's deceased father, and used that account to continue to fat shame and humiliate her. West responded to this user by writing a post in *Jezebel*, and surprisingly, the man emailed her and apologized, and agreed to dialogue with West on *This American Life*. When she asked him why he would do such a personal, painful thing, he said he became angry with her because she seemed comfortable in her body, a body that was considered heavy by conventional standards. He was also heavy, and did not feel comfortable; in his words, "When you talked about being proud of who you are and where you are and where you're going, that kind of stoked that anger that I had" (*This American Life* 2015). When West asked him specifically if the anger he felt was because she was a woman, he replied, "Definitely. Women are being more forthright in their writing. You know, they're not—there isn't a sense of timidity to when they speak or when they write. They're saying it loud." He then went on to say he felt threatened by this. This is a remarkable, and unique, example of a misogynist admitting to his misogyny because he felt emasculated by a woman only because she was self-confident.

Many men take no part in such self-pity and feelings of emasculation by women, and many support a variety of feminisms. Other men are perhaps ambivalent about feminism but nurse their wounds in private, without lashing out in violent ways. And then there is a group of men who respond to their purported injuries by publicly shaming women. As with popular feminism, here injury is deeply entwined with capacity, manifested in the capacity for online violence and harassment. As we have seen, shame operates as a disciplining mechanism. Within the context of popular misogyny, the public shaming of women—of their bodies, their sexual practices, their personal histories, their politics—has become a normative tool for expressing an imagined injustice. This injustice can be specific and personal, such as a girlfriend breaking up with a man, or more diffused, such as the affront apparently felt when a woman takes up space in what was previously a masculine realm, either through voice, body, or political sentiment.[5]

Revenge Porn

"Revenge porn" refers to the uploading of explicit images and videos of women onto websites and message boards, mostly by ex-lovers, without the consent of the photographed subject. While there are a few men whose images and videos are uploaded, 90 percent of revenge porn victims are women (Citron 2014, 17; Chemaly 2016). The content is often accompanied by identifying information, anything from the woman's name and address to the name of her employer to links to social networking profiles.

Perhaps the best-known revenge porn Web site is Isanyoneup.com. This website was founded by Hunter Moore in 2010, and was taken down in 2014. Moore, who once described himself on Twitter as a "professional life ruiner," conceived of the website as a space where disgruntled exes could enact a form of revenge against their former lovers and partners. This "revenge" primarily involved users sending Moore submissions of nude photos of their former partners, almost always obtained without consent. Almost immediately after Isanyoneup.com went live, Moore began to receive twenty to thirty submissions per day. When posting nude images that others sent him, even without the consent of the subjects, Moore was able to elide Section 230 of the Communications Decency Act, which prevents website owners from being held liable for content other users post (e.g., Dickson 2014). There is, in other words, no adequate legal structure that protects the (mostly) women who end up on the site (Citron 2014). At its height, in November 2011, Isanyoneup.com was receiving 30 million page views per month (Dickson 2014). By April 2014, the website was finally shut down following an FBI investigation because many of the images had been illegally obtained, but not before creating a model for other online spaces to devote time and space to revenge porn.

Sites such as Isanyoneup.com multiply their means of shaming; they not only post the names, images, and personal information of nonconsenting victims, thus shaming and humiliating them in a public space, but also encourage victim blaming and shaming by implying that it is the subject's "fault" for having taken these pictures in the first place. Moore himself engages in this kind of shaming: he claims that anyone who ends up on his site is there "due to their own poor judgment" (Dickson 2014, n.p.). He earned money from the site every month because, in his words, the individuals in the nude photos had made "bad decisions," thus shifting responsibility for the hacking to the women themselves (Citron 2014). This theme of "poor judgment" was the focus of the news media when the site was shut down—after Hunter had been charged with aiding and abetting hacking and with aggravated identity theft. This victim blaming works, in a familiar way, to inhibit victims from coming forward; as Matthew Goldstein (2015, n.p.), writing in the New York Times, points out, "It's not clear just how widespread revenge porn is. Victims are often unwilling to come forward out of fear of bringing more attention to the videos and photos. Advocates also say that some victims are reluctant to pursue legal action because they blame themselves and worry that a jury will not be sympathetic."

Since the arrest of Moore and the shuttering of Isanyoneup.com, anti-revenge porn laws have been passed in thirty-four states in the United

States. In 2012, revenge porn victim Holly Jacobs began the "End Revenge Porn" campaign, which is a hub of information where victims can receive information about their cases, get referrals for legal counsel, and so on (see Cyber Civil Rights Initiative n.d.). As Citron (2014) points out, current legal procedures are inadequate for addressing cybercrimes because of the diffused and unregulated nature of the Internet. The difficulty in fighting these cases, as well as the way that the structure of the Internet enables popular misogyny, allows for misogynistic shaming to become normative, an expected element of having a digital presence. Again, popular misogyny circulates within an economy of visibility in many of the same ways that popular feminism does; the popular feminist and misogynistic expressions and practices that become most visible are those that resonate and validate already existing norms within neoliberal gender relations.

As misogynistic shaming becomes increasingly normative and expected, we see other forms emerging. In August 2014, sexually explicit private photographs were stolen from the phones and cloud accounts of celebrities such as Jennifer Lawrence and Kate Upton, and then posted to anonymous image boards such as AnonIB and 4Chan, as well as uploaded to file-sharing services such as Reddit. This particular hacking episode became known as "The Fappening," the title the subreddit used on the open-source site Reddit (Marwick 2017).[6] As Amanda Marcotte (2014) has pointed out, the hackers who stole and then posted these photos were most likely doing it for "bragging rights"; since they did it anonymously to avoid prosecution, they garnered no money but rather a particular kind of fame within the popular misogyny landscape. As Marcotte argues, "This violation gives us a peek into a sick but thriving subculture, or really series of subcultures, of men who are excited by the idea of violating a woman against her will and who get together in online spaces to swap ideas on how to do this, tell bragging stories about violating women, and sharing the photographic evidence of their violations. They're doing this not for fame or fortune, but because they loathe women and want to use sex and sexuality to hurt and punish women, often just for existing" (2014, para. 3).

Though different from revenge porn, which purportedly has a specific intent against individual women for wronging specific men, this kind of violation is also about publicly shaming and humiliating women, to engage in the "blood sport" of shame. "The Fappening" is also about control through shaming but in a more general sense, as it serves as a broad warning to all women that their private sexual lives can be made public; as Marcotte points out, "The men in these groups really do believe they are *entitled* to own and control female bodies" (2014, para. 10).

Loving One's Body in a Context of Shame

Actress Jennifer Lawrence was the most prominent celebrity violated in "The Fappening," and was outspoken in her response. She argued that it was not a "scandal" but a sex crime, and a personal violation. Indeed, she turned the discourse of shame on its head, claiming, "Anybody who looked at those pictures, you're perpetuating a sexual offense. You should cower with shame. Even people who I know and love say, 'Oh, yeah, I looked at the pictures.' I don't want to get mad, but at the same time I'm thinking, I didn't tell you that you could look at my naked body" (Kashner 2014, n.p.). Lawrence is an actress who is often identified as a celebrity feminist; as such she is part of popular feminism. Yet her boldness in calling the hacking of her nude photos a sex crime also reveals the failings of popular feminism, which wasn't able to generate a forceful response. At the same time, however, her response is also an example of the benefits of popular feminism: that it has become so popular that specific women with privilege—of race, or socio-economic class—can speak out without repercussion.

This example is telling in how it reveals both the strengths and limitations of a popular feminism that depends on both an economy of visibility and a broader ideological context of neoliberalism. Ultimately, in becoming not only visible but spectacular, popular feminism in an economy of visibility constitutes a restructuring of feminist politics as often about flexible *popularity* and creating better economic subjects. It is predicated on its ability not only to engineer a market for feminist-inspired consumer goods but also to create a newly acceptable "feminist" subjectivity that is hyperfeminine and heterosexual, often white, and, most importantly, invested in the desire to become a corporatized, consumable (popular) body. Rather than denying the necessity of feminist politics, this form of popular feminism makes a feminist subjectivity readily available, visible, and digestible for desiring consumers. This is why Lawrence's powerful statement that posting nude photos without consent is a sexual violation can be "heard" only so loudly. It is not that celebrity feminism, or popular feminist fashion, or feminist hashtag activism is vacated of political meaning. But while there are similarities between feminist political practice that insists upon a structural critique of patriarchy and gender discrimination, and popular feminist exhortations for women and girls to just "be beautiful the way you are!," there are also differences.

Importantly, the capacities of girls and women encouraged and celebrated by popular feminism are not objectionable in and of themselves, but the injuries that mobilize these capacities are those that are easily circulated in an economy of visibility: body image issues, lack of self-esteem, and self-confidence issues. If popular feminism in an economy of visibility focuses on the gendered injuries that can become the most visibly circulated, then other injuries—due, say, to racism, transphobia, homophobia, and so on— are rendered less visible. The capacity to overcome these injuries is also something validated by the economy of visibility: love your body, believe that you are beautiful, just be confident. Popular feminism *is* feminism, but it also engages in what Lauren Berlant (2008, 2) calls a "love affair with conventionality," where women continue to perform heterofemininity in very particular yet general ways "in the hope that better love will happen someday." This love affair is almost always heterosexual, and is overly ambitious yet nonspecific: it engages women as future-oriented, prescribing behavior that validates conventional and accepted gender norms, even with the knowledge that these norms will continue to marginalize women (Berlant 2008). While popular feminism taps into desire and yearning and thinking beyond the often stifling norms of sexual and gendered difference, it does so through a spectacular visibility. When this version of popular feminism is offered up by a beautiful celebrity, or through a highly produced ad, it becomes visible in heightened ways.

Popular misogyny similarly trades on the spectacularly visible. As I've discussed in this chapter, one form of public shaming in contemporary digital culture is through posting a video, tweet, or image of a woman or girl, without her permission, as a way to make it visible to a vast public in order to police and regulate women's (often sexual) behaviors. The economy of visibility is not simply a backdrop for the practice of public shaming, it is absolutely *necessary* for the practice to exist. Like popular feminism, the popular misogynistic practice of public shaming focuses on individuals—specifically, individual women who have apparently injured either specific men (the impetus for revenge porn, for example) or masculine identity in general (the impetus for fat shaming or slut shaming). Public shaming is used as a way to recuperate masculine identity, to realize the capacity of masculinity. The popular feminist mandates for self-confidence and high self-esteem become part of this dynamic: the relationship between feeling good about oneself and negative public judgment is constitutive. The quest for self-esteem, as when a girl posts a video on YouTube and asks an anonymous public if she is "pretty or not," demands a particular risk on the part of the video poster, it requires opening oneself up to be shamed.

Loving one's body, or asking online users to evaluate your physical appearance, is framed by popular feminism as an affirmation, a way of "putting oneself out there." "Putting oneself out there" in online spaces is a key mechanism of the economy of visibility, in which visibility is framed as a conduit to empowerment. The girls and women who are supposedly empowered within the economy of visibility are primarily those who can afford, due to race and class identity, to have a "love affair with conventionality"; this empowerment through visibility is primarily one that validates a version of the feminine body. And this visibility is given substance in part *because* it risks misogyny in the form of surveillance, judgment, and shame. Popular feminism's encouragement of self-esteem is important, but it also relies upon the economy of visibility that endorses popular feminism for its expression. It doesn't question the ways that an economy of visibility is also the route for the circulation of popular misogyny, through similar tropes of individual injury and capacity. Understanding and explaining popular feminism in terms of individual self-esteem or loving one's body denies how an economy of visibility functions as a distraction from the various ways in which the bodies of girls and women are under different sorts of threats institutionally and legally.

On one level, efforts that encourage girls to feel self-possessed in a climate that works assiduously, and continuously, to position girls as inferior and lacking in a male-dominated culture is crucial in order to voice opinion, concerns, and challenges to a male-dominated culture. But on another level, individual self-esteem or loving one's body indicates a different kind of effort, one that encourages girls to *attend* to a male-dominated culture, not to challenge or disrupt it. Unsurprisingly, popular feminism claims to be committed to the first goal. Yet it is impossible to overlook the fact that self-possession is acquired only in the contemporary moment through careful attention to the second.

In the contemporary moment, when girls are seen as newly empowered through digital technology, and when girls use digital technology in increasing numbers, it is tempting to understand the rise of popular feminism as proof that girls have more power and more choices. Indeed, we are aware of these choices precisely because they are expressed and circulated within an economy of visibility. As I discuss in chapter 4, that interpretation is especially tempting in the realm of technology, where girls and women have long been marginalized. But the popular feminist market for self-esteem and the neoliberal contexts that authorize this market also work in the current moment to contain girls and women through this very market. Self-esteem promises a kind of empowerment through the body, but the body is precisely the thing under threat in the current moment. An economy of visibility encourages women and girls to think of themselves as "worthy" of media visibility, a worth that is then reduced to individual problems of self-esteem, or loving one's body. This question of "worth," in turn, validates and normalizes a visual culture of misogynistic public shaming.

We need to see the "Love Your Body" call as part of a popular feminist landscape that is systematically restructuring feminist politics and praxis, where making it "popular" is also about making it safer and more legible for a corporate and neoliberal culture—and importantly, making it *visible*. In particular, one way that popular feminism and the "Love Your Body" movement becomes visible is by shying away from structural critique of patriarchy and engaging instead primarily with individuals; that is, the particular body of each girl or woman. This is an important first step, but it doesn't engage in a critique of the broader context that creates the conditions (and the choices) that encourage women to hate their bodies in the first place. It also does not critique the way popular feminisms circulate in an economy of visibility, where they are shaped by priorities that are about individuals more than collectivities, and are more about individual self-reflection than structural critique.

THREE. CONFIDENCE
The Con Game

Sexism: a system for deciding whose confidence is warranted; whose is not.
Sexism: a confidence system. — SARA AHMED, *Losing Confidence*, 2016

If there is a common theme among different iterations of popular feminism, it is clearly "confidence." The theme of confidence circulates in an economy of visibility with remarkable ease and reach: there are thousands of Instagram posts on female self-confidence; hundreds of Tumblr pages dedicated to inspirational messages imploring women and girls to be more confident; and blogs, best-selling books, web pages, and infomercials all promising the key to achieving confidence. In the previous chapter, I examined some of the ways in which the *body* figures as central in the struggle for confidence for both men and women, in which shame over the body and/or sexual choices is positioned as the key factor in plummeting self-esteem. In this chapter, I explore the networked relationship between popular feminism and popular misogyny as this relationship is negotiated and struggled over through the frame of self-confidence.

"Confidence," of course, means different things. Within popular feminism, the frame of confidence is typically about economic confidence, a confidence in being economically successful within a capitalist context. It is this definition of female confidence that circulates easily in an economy of visibility; in this chapter, I look at some popular feminist practices of confidence and argue that their neoliberal vision focusing on the self—and particularly on the self as confident and assured—is offered as the panacea for gendered wage gaps, exploitative labor, and the "glass ceiling" itself. However, at the same time that women are experiencing a crisis of confidence, men are also reportedly suffering from a lack of self-confidence, both economically and personally. Within popular feminism and popular misogyny, confidence is understood and positioned as a set of skills one must learn and master. While popular feminism positions confidence as a skill to be learned so that women can be more successful in life (and success here is primarily defined as financial success, or success in the workplace), popular misogyny positions masculine confidence as not only about economic confidence but also, and urgently, about *sexual confidence*. The lack of self-confidence for men is often understood as an explicit reaction to self-confident women; the injury to men in terms of self-confidence is apparently caused explicitly by women.

A central element of the dynamic between popular feminism and popular misogyny is an investment in confidence as both injury (a loss of confidence) and a capacity (a recuperation of confidence), although this is expressed differently within popular feminism than within popular misogyny. I argue here, however, following Sara Ahmed (2016), that we have *too much confidence* in the power of confidence. Confidence is positioned as the primary, if not the only, resolution to gendered inequalities, and it is a resolution that depends on individual men and women, not on social and cultural structure. A key component of popular feminism has been confidence campaigns for girls and women, ranging from the formal campaigns of organizations, policy makers, and corporations to educational programs to hashtag activism. These confidence campaigns claim their goal to be helping girls and women *achieve* economic confidence.

The efforts to instill confidence within women have not gone unchallenged, however; in the contemporary moment, men claim to be losing both economic and sexual confidence precisely because of these newly confident women. Confidence, within the call-and-response dynamic of popular feminism and popular misogyny, is in scarce supply: if women have it, it apparently means they are taking it *away* from men. In the following pages, I explore these different gendered definitions of confidence, and argue that confidence, for both popular feminism and popular misogyny, is offered as a more or less empty resolution that is more about individual attitudes than challenging structured inequities. Confidence, in this context, is an individual personality trait that circulates with ease in an economy of visibility, so that it becomes an end in itself, an aspiration without context or history.

But what does "confidence" actually mean? Is it the same as "self-esteem"? Certainly the two share a similarity, especially in the way that they are positioned within popular feminism and popular misogyny. Within psychological debates about the differences between the two, self-esteem is usually positioned as an internal value, a feeling of self-worth. Confidence, on the other hand, is tied to *action*, an external quality that one works to achieve (Kay and Shipman 2014a). While high self-esteem is often connected to confidence, they are separate affective qualities: one can be confident in some areas while also having a feeling of low self-worth. Self-esteem is understood as an internal battle with oneself, while confidence is about *mastery*—it takes practice, determination, and resilience (Kay and Shipman 2014a).

There are resources marketed to help women achieve this mastery. While these resources vary widely, from memoirs to self-help books to podcasts to corporate training seminars to organizations dedicated to female confidence, self-confidence as an individual personality trait is a theme that runs through all of them. Perhaps the best-known of these resources emerged in March 2013, when Sheryl Sandberg's now famous (or infamous, depending on your perspective) book *Lean In: Women, Work, and the Will to Lead* hit the bookshelves and generated an immediate media frenzy. The work is part memoir and part feminist philosophy (or, as she would likely characterize it, "a call to arms"). There are many criticisms of Sandberg's work, and the ways in which the advice in the book is relevant only for those in racial- and class-based positions of privilege that make it possible to "lean in" in the first place (see Rottenberg 2014). Here, I'd like to focus on a small but revealing aspect of Sandberg's argument: throughout the book she tries to convince her readers that the reason for the deep gender asymmetries in the workplace is what she calls "the leadership ambition gap" (Sandberg 2013, 15). This argument finds dialogue with another best-selling book, Katty Kay and Claire Shipman's *The Confidence Code: The Science and Art of Self-Assurance—What Women Should Know* (2014a), which, like *Lean In*, also mainly addressed women in high-powered fields, and argued that the most important reason women were failing to become CEOs or otherwise advancing their careers was an "acute lack of confidence" (Kay and Shipman 2014b, para. 4). The authors argue that "success, it turns out, correlates just as closely with confidence as with competence"; however, the "good news is that with work, confidence can be acquired" (Kay and Shipman 2014b, para. 13). *Work* is the key here: women need to work to acquire confidence, so that they will be more confident *at work*. Here, entrepreneurialism and capitalist accomplishment are the only routes to feminist political identity. Sandberg's feminism is a conflation of gender equality with the ethics of capitalist production and participation. Feminism, it seems, is nowhere if it isn't leaning in, eager for capitalist success.

Of course, despite neoliberal proclamations for expanding markets and ever-increasing roles for entrepreneurs, for every entrepreneur who "makes it," whether that be a Silicon Valley start-up, a beauty vlogger, an Instagram model, or a YouTube star, there are thousands who do not achieve economic success. The gendered labor that is necessary for an entrepreneurial ethos is what Brooke Erin Duffy has called "aspirational labor," which she defines as "a highly gendered form of (mostly) uncompensated work that 1) amateur participants believe has the potential to 'pay off' in terms of future economic and social capital; and 2) that keeps female content creators immersed in the public circulation of commodities" (Duffy 2015, para. 6). Aspirational labor relies on, among other things, confidence—confidence that the work will eventually pay off. The sheer irrationality of this confidence in a contracting economy that is deeply disproportional in terms of who actually "makes it" does not, then, disrupt or harm the discourse of confidence. Rather, confidence sustains neoliberal capitalism: all one has to do is work on *confidence*, and mastery and success will apparently follow. Indeed, in the twenty-first century, confidence is a condition of both neoliberal capitalism and popular feminism.

Sandberg is perhaps the most visible of popular feminist memoirists, but there have been many other memoirs that have explained gendered labor inequalities—at least for those women who are sufficiently white and sufficiently wealthy to have the opportunity for a high-paying career—in terms of women's lack of confidence. Nina DiSesa (2008), the first female chairwoman at a major advertising company, wrote *Seducing the Boys Club*, which advised women to primarily act like men as much as possible, except when they should rely on their "feminine wiles" to seduce and manipulate their male counterparts. Sophia Amoruso (2015), founder and CEO of online clothing outlet Nasty Gal, wrote *#GirlBoss*, which is intended to be an inspirational ode to girls and women to overcome obstacles—including a lack of confidence.[1]

All of these memoirs are guides for women to become better economic subjects; they are part of popular feminism to be sure, and like much of popular feminism, these books hinge on confidence as the solution to gender inequality. The books recognize gendered inequality in the workforce as a specific injury, but rather than point to patriarchal structural forces for this inequality, the authors offer advice on how to join the existing structure and become an entrepreneurial feminist through one's individual capacity in the form of confidence.

Indeed, lack of self-confidence is offered as the key reason for inequality within *neoliberal capitalism*, not patriarchy. Here, confidence organizations also focus on the popular feminist dynamic of injury and capacity. And, while these organizations often do focus on self-love and self-care, their primary focus is on how women feel inadequate in the workplace, as *economic* subjects. Many empowerment organizations emphasize that lack of confidence is the primary reason women cannot move forward in their careers. Rather than focus on structural issues, such as divisions of labor in the workplace, inadequate support for maternity and childcare, and ingrained ideologies that continue to privilege men as more rational, capable leaders, empowerment organizations ask women to find it in *themselves* to just "be" more confident. It is the mandate to *just be* confident, rather than a focus on the context that encourages women to lack self-confidence, that becomes visible in an economy of visibility (Gill and Orgad 2015). Certainly, confidence campaigns recognize the injury women experience when they are told they are less than, weaker than, men. However, these campaigns typically respond with calling for feminine capacity to simply overcome this context and be confident.

There is a similar dynamic in campaigns to restore self-confidence in heterosexual men. For example, one apparent reason for a heterosexual, masculine crisis of confidence is located in the spaces of work and career, where a hegemonic construction of men as breadwinners has been disrupted by global economic recession and a subsequent loss of employment for many. This crisis of masculinity often manifests in a particular heterosexual masculine crisis of confidence: a lack of sexual confidence, or a lack of erotic capital (Hakim 2011). Similar to popular feminism's perspective on confidence, sexual confidence, in the context of popular misogyny, is also about learning a skill set. Indeed, as I discuss later in this chapter, an entire industry has emerged to train men to be "masters" in picking up women. Within the frame of popular misogyny, masculine sexual confidence is expressed by manipulating women by using specific skills to seduce them into sexual activity.

Crucial to this exploration is the slippery slope between confidence and being "conned." I don't think we should ignore the etymology of a con game or a con artist. Confidence is defined as having trust in oneself, feeling certain about a truth. A con artist is, in contrast, someone who is adept at manipulating that truth, that certainty; of course, the "con" stems from confidence. A confidence *game* is one in which a person swindles or robs another person after gaining their confidence. Confidence in this moment is positioned, by both popular feminism and popular misogyny, as a commodity—and, like all commodities, it receives its value from scarcity. Within popular feminism and popular misogyny, both men and women are seen to lack confidence. The lack of confidence that men (often white, cis-gendered, heterosexual men) feel in themselves is frequently blamed on an "overconfidence" in women (Ahmed 2016). This overconfidence is apparently enabled by popular feminism, and is in turn a confidence that is accessed by white, cis-gendered, heterosexual women. Confidence is positioned as a zero-sum game, so that if women have it, that ownership comes at the expense of men—and the goal is to take it away, to take it "back," from women. The lack of sexual confidence apparently experienced by men is a reflection of a crisis of masculinity, in which feminists and women have robbed men of their "natural" sexual superiority, and drastic steps need to be taken to regain it. These steps are found within a variety of spaces and industries, all devoted to teaching men how to regain confidence. "Confidence" here means the ability to seduce a woman, any woman—and again, it is something that has been taken away precisely because of women's sexual confidence.

Confidence in an Economy of Visibility: Confidence Organizations and the Marshaling of Injury and Capacity

In the United States, hundreds of organizations that have the empowerment of girls as a goal have been founded since the 1990s.[2] The *source* of empowerment varies widely between these organizations. Some, like SPARK (Sexualization Protest: Action, Resistance, Knowledge), aim to empower girls to challenge hypersexualization in the media; others, such as the Confidence Coalition, see empowerment as emanating from self-confidence. The goal of more development-oriented organizations such as AfricAid is to improve the lives of girls through education, with the belief that knowledge is the most potent source of empowerment. Despite this variety, the definition shared by nearly all of these organizations denotes a transference of power, a flow from the powerful to the disempowered, here recognized as girls. For some organizations, such as SPARK and the Confidence Coalition, empowerment involves the girls themselves with a focus on shaping these girls to be confident leaders, imbuing them along the way with high self-esteem and a healthy body image. For others, such as AfricAid and other NGOs, the mechanism of empowerment targets donors rather than imagined subjects, positioning girls (especially in the Global South) as beneficiaries: though these girls have been victims of poverty and poor education, the narrative goes, we now have the chance to transform them into "human capital investments" (Switzer 2013, 347). Yet other organizations focus on educating girls in particular skills, including filmmaking and writing, and on basic training in STEM fields.

Needless to say, confidence is an admirable goal, especially for girls living in a sexist and racist world. And yet, the means of achieving these goals are as problematic as the goals are worthwhile. That is, a popular feminist construction of confidence is one that is expressed within an economy of visibility, in which the idea of "confidence" is self-absorbent, enough on its own. Confidence is something that women need to just try to have—and if they cannot attain it, it is their own failing. Aspirational messages, confidence pledges, social media memes with inspirational messages such as "Wear confidence like makeup" and "Confidence is the best accessory a girl can have," and so on are widely distributed through media, easily absorbed and disseminated.

For example, one organization, the Confidence Coalition, was founded by the Kappa Delta sorority, and professes to be dedicated to what they call the "confidence movement" that "encourages women and girls to stand up to peer pressure and media stereotypes, say no to risky behavior and abusive relationships, and put an end to relational aggression, such as bullying—on the playground and in the office" ("About" n.d., n.p.). One of the ways the organization builds confidence is by asking girls and women to take a "confidence pledge" by the Confidence Coalition. These pledges are divided into three age groups: Collegians, Women, and Girls. Each

FIGURE 3.1.
"Confidence: Wear
It Like Makeup,"
Tumblr, 2017.

pledge, however, is the same, with a few different word choices. All begin with the simple "Today, I pledge to be more confident in myself and my abilities." For Collegians and women, the following three pledges are the same: "I pledge to be forgiving and generous to myself and others"; "I will not attempt to sabotage anyone else's self-confidence"; and "I will have the confidence to stand up to myself and others." The pledge for girls is written in simpler language: "I will love myself the way I am. I don't need to be anyone but ME!" and "I will accept others for who they are." All three pledges end with "By joining with others, I will make the world a better place for all women and girls. I will encourage confidence in myself, my friends, my family and others" ("Sign the Pledge" n.d., n.p.).

While certainly self-confidence is an important goal, this organization (which is actually a coalition of individuals, NGOs, and companies) relies primarily on conventional feminine routines, activities, and identities as activist practices. In many ways, empowerment is something that we actualize as individuals in our own lives. But when empowerment and confidence are part of an industry, this transforms confidence into a commodity, an empty mandate that is accessible only to those who are able to consume it, to merely fill themselves with confidence. The pledges, which all begin with "I" and only superficially acknowledge institutionalized gender politics and other structural problems, place the burden of confidence on individual girls and women, while sidestepping the social mechanisms and structures that encourage girls and women to have a lack of confidence in the first place. Even the pledge to "join with others" is followed with "I will encourage confidence in myself, my friends, my family and others." This positions "confidence" as both a choice and commodity—girls and women just need to buy, and to buy into, confidence, and then apparently it will happen. The various activities endorsed by the Confidence Coalition are typically undertaken individually; success—measured in terms of self-confidence—is also an individual accomplishment. The problem with this kind of commodification is that confidence, understood and expressed within a popular feminist sensibility and a context of capitalist marketability, becomes a practice that *absorbs*—rather than energizes or mobilizes—politics. It functions well within an economy of visibility, where it recognizes the injury to women and girls in terms of a lack of self-confidence, and then positions the capacity to overcome this injury as an individual achievement, an attitude adjustment. When popular feminist confidence is created and organized within an economy of visibility, there are only particular narrative frames that support it; confidence as an aspirational pledge that individual girls say to themselves every morning is part of this dominant narrative. Feminist collective politics, incisive critiques of structural racism—these narratives don't become as visible, and are thus often eclipsed by a norm that defines confidence as a choice and a commodity.

For example, the SPARK (Sexualization Protest: Action, Resistance, Knowledge) organization focuses its efforts on feminist issues, especially the sexualization of girls.[3] SPARK has an explicitly feminist mission. The stated goal of the organization is to encourage collective feminist activism for girls. On the organization's website, for example, there are suggestions on how to be an activist and how to improve one's self-esteem. Some of these suggestions are in many ways similar to the Confidence pledges from the Confidence Coalition, such as visiting toy stores and marking sexist toys with a Post-it note reading "You've been SPARKed!," and disconnecting from gossip, dancing in one's room, and stating "It's okay to be weird." Yet, unlike the Confidence Coalition, SPARK does more to operationalize their stated missions in terms of social change. For example, SPARK's Change .org petition in 2012 to convince *Seventeen* magazine to stop using photoshopped models was widely covered in mainstream news, including the *New York Times* (Dwyer 2012) and the *Washington Post* (vanden Heuvel

FIGURE 3.2. SPARK activism at Toys"R"Us, 2011.

2012). The petition worked, and *Seventeen* ceased using photoshopped models in their fashion layouts (Hu 2012). Convincing a national fashion magazine to halt a practice that is key to the beauty industry that supports them in order to challenge unrealistic and idealized representations of female beauty is an impressive accomplishment.

Yet, because SPARK's activism is circulated primarily through and within an economy of visibility that supports a particular version of popular feminism, it was shaped in a familiar narrative, and was transformed from a collective action to efforts that are more individual and thus more easily commodified (as the founders of SPARK openly acknowledge). Again, this is how the economy of visibility works; feminist expressions that do not exceed much beyond their own visibility are privileged over those that require more engaged contemplation. Feminist expressions that are corporate-friendly and palatable to a wide audience are given visibility in this economy. It is not that the popular feminist mandate of confidence is vacant of political meaning, but when this mandate is structured by an economy of visibility, it becomes difficult (and often even impossible) for the *potential* of confidence to overrun the prescribed pathways of this economy. SPARK avoids the more obvious manifestation of this problem because it taps into contemporary iterations of empowerment and confidence. Yet because SPARK becomes legible within an economy of visibility, its politics are transfigured to this logic, where the campaign itself is reduced to an easily circulated narrative. SPARK's *Seventeen* magazine campaign is clearly meant to highlight the ways in which idealized standards of female beauty exclude most women, and is an important message. But the focus on beauty also instantiates that girls' power is located in their physicality, in their bodies; as such, the organization is working against its own higher goals, and furthering the problematic emphasis on a girl's power as located in that which is visible.

SPARK is aware of the problems of this narrow definition of confidence, and the burdens of the female body that is commodified and made visible. When the *Seventeen* story was covered by the national news, it was told as a narrative of a brave white girl, Julia Bluhm, all of fourteen years old, who started the petition against *Seventeen*, and who prevailed against all odds to convince a behemoth publishing company to change their routine editorial procedures. The role SPARK played in this story, as the organization that created the campaign against *Seventeen*, was rarely mentioned; the mobilization efforts of an organization and the labor of an entire team of people was distilled into a narrative about one heroic and successful girl. Indeed, the founders of SPARK wrote explicitly about this problem in an article: "Julia and her teammates came to understand that it was not insignificant that this global media revolution was attributed to a thin, White, soft-spoken, articulate, middle-class girl from a small town in Maine. In protesting the sexualising, 'perfection'-inducing digital wand of Photoshop, Julia's body was turned into a safe canvas upon which to project our desires for 'Everygirl'—a squeaky clean 'average' girl whose desire for her friends in ballet class not to stress about their weight seemed empathic and sweet, fitting into accepted norms of femininity" (Edell, Brown, and Tolman 2013, 280).

As Dana Edell, Lyn Mikel Brown, and Deborah Tolman point out, the media's narrative of the SPARK campaign was transfigured from one of collective activism to one of an individual act of self-empowerment. Even when the SPARK founders called attention to the way their organization was being positioned in the media, the narrative was maintained. Within an economy of visibility, the feminist goals of SPARK are legible only when articulated by the "safe canvas" of an individual girl because that is the image that is most easily visible. In another article, Tolman points out that the actual story of SPARK's campaign, a collective action of angry girls seeking to overturn the status quo, is "dangerous"; this story emphasizes not only collectivity and overt feminist politics but *anger*, and is not easily subsumed into the current brand of neoliberal feminism (Tolman 2012; Rottenberg 2014, 419). By contrast, the story of a lone hero working to change the establishment, the archetypical David versus Goliath tale, is the perfect fit for popular feminism within an economy of visibility. It is precisely the kind of narrative that validates the newly confident girl as a marketable subject, while also normalizing the individual entrepreneur as the person who succeeds in the economy of visibility and the market of empowerment it supports. The way in which SPARK is positioned within cultural and social discourse as advocating the "right" kind of activism and empowerment normalizes a popular feminist neoliberal female subject. In other words, while SPARK may be self-reflective about the way the media individualizes its politics, the organization is nonetheless part of a particular economy of visibility. Thus, media frames that are legitimated and validated within an economy of visibility are those that turn their focus on individual empowerment, and then work to erase SPARK's more overtly feminist goals of girls working collectively to protest systemic discrimination.

Teen Vogue is another example of how a narrative about women's confidence gains purchase in an economy of visibility, albeit from a slightly different perspective. Women's magazines such as *Cosmopolitan* and *Elle* have jumped on the confidence bandwagon in recent years, with whole issues devoted to women's confidence, such as *Elle*'s "Confidence Issue: A Smart Woman's Guide to Self-Belief" in 2014. Of course, women's magazines have long trafficked in issues of confidence; they are often guidebooks for how to be more confident in a conventional, heteronormative, racialized way (Currie 1999; McRobbie 2004; Favaro 2017). *Teen Vogue*, an offshoot from *Vogue*, emerged in 2004 with other publications aimed at teenage girls, such as *Teen Cosmo* and *Teen People*. In 2016, with the appointment of new editor Elaine Welteroth, *Teen Vogue* reimagined its focus, so alongside the typical teen magazine fare such as fashion and relationships, the magazine began publishing more overtly political, and often feminist, articles. In December 2016, reporter Lauren Duca (2016) published an article titled "Donald Trump Is Gaslighting America," suggesting that Trump was engaging in psychological manipulation of the American people. The article quickly went viral on social media, and the mainstream press picked up on it as well, with NPR (Folkenflik 2016), the *New York Times* (North 2016), the *Atlantic* (Gilbert 2016), and the *Guardian* (Parkinson 2016), among others, running op-ed pieces on both the article and the magazine itself. *Teen Vogue* has continued in this spirit, publishing articles about trans identity, reproductive rights, and the Black Lives Matter movement, among other political issues.

Yet *Teen Vogue* is also an example of how powerful the economy of visibility is in creating and framing narratives about women. The SPARK example demonstrates how the story of an individual is more legible in this economy than the story of feminist collectivity. In a similar fashion, when Duca's article on Trump and gaslighting emerged, media outlets (and individuals using those outlets) immediately tried to reframe the story as "inappropriate" for *Teen Vogue*, because teenage girls apparently have limited roles, and expressing thoughtful, incisive critiques of a known misogynist who happens to the president-elect of the United States is not one of them. As Sophie Gilbert, writing in the *Atlantic*, commented, those who circulated the article often did so with an incredulous tone, "seeming surprised that a teen-oriented magazine was publishing incisive political coverage rather than makeup tutorials or One Direction interviews" (Gilbert 2016, para. 1). The media coverage of the article was expressed predominantly in this way, framing the article and others in *Teen Vogue* as "unlikely" and inappropriate for teenage girls. Within an economy of visibility, popular feminism is more likely to be found in vague aspirational expressions, affirming body positivity and self-confidence—the sort of material usually covered by newly popular feminist-inspired women's magazines. The political turn of *Teen Vogue* disrupts this narrative, and challenges why specific stories become visible while others are obscured. Not surprisingly, the response by popular misogyny is to diminish the magazine through a reminder that teenage girls are not supposed to be interested in politics, but only in makeup and boy bands.

This clash of narratives, or apparent cognitive dissonance about the fact that women and girls are politically engaged, was captured in an on-air interview with Duca by Fox News' conservative host Tucker Carlson, in which after repeated interruptions by Carlson, Duca said, "You're actually being a partisan hack that's just attacking me ad nauseam and not allowing me to speak" (Feldman 2016, para. 5). This was a powerful moment, where Duca reminded viewers not only of the misogyny that framed her interview but also of the normative practice of not allowing women to speak—especially about politics. Because Fox News is part of the economy of visibility,

Carlson rejoined by reminding viewers that women and girls have a specific heteronormative feminine role in this economy: "You should stick to the thigh-high boots. You're better at that" (Feldman 2016, para. 8). While Duca points out the injuries women experience in a sexist culture, where they are so often attacked and not heard, Carlson offers a familiar framing of capacity in response: stick to dominant disciplinary practices of femininity, don't overstep into realms where women don't belong.

Duca and Carlson's conversation reflects the injury/capacity dynamic that circulates so easily within an economy of visibility. Duca reminds Carlson of the injury of sexism, where women are constantly interrupted and often literally silenced (not to mention the interview was based on her article about Trump gaslighting the nation, and makes a connection to a long history of men gaslighting women). In response, Carlson attempts to regain masculine capacity by belittling Duca precisely because she is a woman. Even when popular feminists such as Duca attempt to harness visibility (gained through *Teen Vogue*) as a politics, the logics of the economy of visibility constrain and regulate those politics. This clash of meanings about gendered injury and capacity mark the difference between a popular feminism that circulates within an economy of visibility, and those other feminisms, such as intersectional feminism or queer feminism, that don't have a clear pathway or visible narrative within this economy. In other words, even if feminisms engage the politics of visibility, such as SPARK or *Teen Vogue*, the discursive move is to reposition these politics within an economy of visibility, where collective feminist politics represented in a petition campaign or an investigative journalist reporting on rampant misogyny are reframed to conform with the structures of this economy: safe, palatable, friendly, and normative.

Even structural issues such as global poverty are subject to the constraints and logics of an economy of visibility, where the visibility of poverty, the circulation of its image, becomes its politics. For example, alongside organizations such as SPARK and Confidence Coalition, which hope to empower primarily middle-class white girls of the Global North through confidence and self-esteem, a number of nonprofit organizations have emerged to help provide resources for those girls who are seen as victims of poverty and poor education, especially in the Global South. The movement to target girls in this campaign is part of a global campaign by Nike and the World Health Organization called the "Girl Effect," which recognizes and thus distributes resources to girls as the agents of social

GIRLS ARE THE MOST POWERFUL FORCE FOR CHANGE ON THE PLANET.
WELCOME TO THE GIRL EFFECT.

EXPLORE. DISCOVER.
TAKE WHAT YOU NEED...

G
THE GIRL EFFECT

FIGURE 3.3. "Girl Effect" ad, 2014.

change. Now that NGOS and multinational corporations alike highlight the "Girl Effect" as key to contemporary social and economic change, girls living with the local manifestations of global poverty are seen to be particularly worthy of investment.[4]

Consider, for example, the empowerment organization AfricAid. The tagline of this nonprofit is "Reach Teach Empower"; its mission statement declares its dedication to supporting "girls' education in Africa in order to provide young women with the opportunity to transform their own lives and the futures of their communities" ("Mission and Vision" n.d., n.p.). The primary aim of the organization is to generate educational scholarships, with the specific aim "to empower African girls to be leaders." The organization's website follows a conventional humanitarian aesthetic, with pictures of smiling young African girls at school and at play, as well as an embedded video demonstrating one particular effort of the organization—to start a school in Tanzania. The text is inspirational, asking viewers to "learn more about our projects helping to educate and empower thousands of girls across Tanzania," and to "find out how you can get involved and become a champion for girls' education" ("Welcome to AfricAid" n.d.). While the organization clearly has good intentions, the images and text that describe their goals resonate with imperialist discourse about "saving the other" through imposing Western norms and standards. Indeed, AfricAid and the "Girl Effect" continues a focus on women in development within neoliberalism; as Inderpal Grewal points out about human rights discourse in the late twentieth century: "Women outside the West, in human rights discourses, were represented as objects of charity and care by the West but could become subjects who could participate in the global economy and become global citizens; this was the 'third-world' victim who had become a global subject" (Grewal 2005, 130).

The goals of AfricAid, though important, follow many other nonprofit organizations; the organization follows, like many others, a similar model to UNICEF, where individual girls are "sponsored" for a small amount of money per day. This UNICEF feel has proven to function well in an economy of visibility, where the visibility of particular kinds of humanitarianism offers a Western narrative about girls and women as "objects of charity" (Grewal 2005; Brough 2012; Chouliaraki 2013). The website includes a merchandise page, where items made by girls—everything from knitted tea cozies to bowls made from discarded bottle caps—are sold, with profits going to girls' education. These artifacts, both visual and material, are sold with the "intent of bringing distant, 'real' human suffering closer to the American public-as-donor—just close enough so that one could possess the image, as evidence of their philanthropic contribution" (Brough 2012, 178). In the case of AfricAid, the beneficiaries of the philanthropy are girls living in global poverty, and as such, the girls who are the recipients of the 'empowerment' the organization promises are framed in such a way that they are worthy of donor's sympathy—and their donations.

But it is not only a humanitarian and imperialist aesthetic that is embodied by empowerment organizations such as AfricAid. The focus of SPARK and the Confidence Coalition is built on the same fundamental concept that mobilizes organizations like AfricAid; all of these organizations rely on the contrast between the *current* state of girls—their injuries—and what *could* happen—their exceptional capacity (Koffman and Gill 2013). With confidence organizations such as SPARK and the Confidence Coalition, the focus is primarily on individual self-esteem and body image, and with the development organizations that address girls in the Global South, the focus is on conditions of poverty. Within this frame, the "Girl Effect," and the organizations that mobilize this discourse, position girls, especially those in the Global South, as not only the key to international development

FIGURE 3.4. "Girl Effect" and *Lean In* author Sheryl Sandberg, 2013.

Girl Effect ✅
@girleffect

Follow ⌄

.@sherylsandberg talks exclusively to @NiNyampinga journalist Nicole about education, tech and female empowerment:
bit.ly/2rbjKXa

❝ It's never too early to lean in. We really want to encourage all girls not just to participate but to lean. And know inside that you can do it.

- Sheryl Sandberg

8:32 AM - 22 May 2017 from City of London, London

but also the embodiment of the future neoliberal subject. While the girls who are the intended audience of SPARK and the Confidence Coalition are seen as always already neoliberal subjects, who just need the self-confidence to realize their potential, girls in the Global South are seen as *potential* neoliberal subjects, hindered by poverty and patriarchy; they merely have to be harnessed by development organizations in order to realize their self-empowerment. An economy of visibility is necessary for this harnessing, where images of girls in the Global South are abundant, tapping into both a popular feminist and a neoliberal entrepreneurial narrative; indeed, Koffman and Gill (2013) point out that development initiatives such as the "Girl Effect" portray girls in poverty as "already entrepreneurial" because they have *had* to be resourceful: "Poverty, it seems, can be celebrated for the entrepreneurial capacities it stimulates" (90).

These confidence organizations, though having different goals, exemplify the twinned discourses of injury and capacity upon which popular feminism depends. The Confidence Coalition and SPARK highlight the injury incurred by girls living in a society that values them primarily through their bodies, but because they circulate in an economy of visibility, the capacity of girls to overcome injury is also framed through their bodies. The girls who are targeted in these organizations are Can-Do girls (Harris

2003), who are savvy, entrepreneurial, and need guidance to realize their capacity. Girl empowerment organizations dedicated to eradicating global poverty, however, target At-Risk girls (Harris 2003). As such, they understand and capitalize on the ways in which poverty is a gendered injury, and they support and validate the empowered, confident feminine subject. It is a girl's capacity to be entrepreneurial that is the focus of these organizations, in which an investment in girls as agents of social change is warranted insofar as the return on investment is financial growth (Grewal 2005; Switzer 2013). Bodies here become Return On Investments in a popular feminist economy of visibility.

Confidence Is Not Just for Women: Men's Rights Organizations and Seduction Communities

If confidence is commodified within an economy of visibility, it follows the logic of other capitalist commodities: it receives value because of its scarcity. And, again, within the funhouse mirror of popular feminism and popular misogyny, confidence is understood within a zero-sum frame: if women have it, or are trying to achieve it, then it is at the expense of men's confidence. As women are implored through empowerment organizations and popular feminist memoirs to lean in and "just be" more confident, this is seen as a threat to men's "natural" confidence, which is often expressed as a relationship between work and sexual confidence. If women *lack* confidence simply because they are women, men have *lost* confidence sexually and in the workplace because of the efforts of popular feminism. Indeed, confidence for popular misogyny is a kind of "call to arms," an aggressive, reactive series of campaigns directed specifically at popular feminism.

Amid the economic crisis that dawned in 2007 and swept the globe in 2008, Bruce Springsteen produced *Wrecking Ball*, an album dedicated to documenting the ravages of contemporary global capitalism and corporate greed. When asked about the anger that seems to emanate from this album, Springsteen replied, "I think our politics come out of psychology. And psychology of course comes out of your formative years. I grew up in a house where my mother was the primary breadwinner, and my father struggled to find work. I saw that that was deeply painful, and created a crisis of masculinity, let's say. And that was something that was unrepairable. Lack of work creates a loss of self. Work creates an enormous sense of self" (Springsteen 2012; see also Remnick 2012).

The "crisis in masculinity" that Springsteen saw in his father occurred in the 1960s and '70s, when the artist was a boy in seaside New Jersey. As I've argued, however, the crisis of gender is ongoing: it doesn't have a single beginning, and is never completely resolved. Rather, tactics and strategies in social, economic, and political realms emerge in different historical moments to address whatever the current manifestations of crisis might be. Yet those manifestations are expressions and practices of specific historical moments, and as such are merely the tip of a far-reaching iceberg. In twenty-first-century United States, the context for manifestations of a crisis in masculinity consists of American mythologies of rugged individualism, stoicism, and persistence, which have shaped the symbolic construction of the white male blue-collar worker as the quintessential American man, the self-made individual who perseveres under hardship, who sees every crisis as an opportunity.

Springsteen's *Wrecking Ball* addresses a contemporary economic crisis, one which Diane Negra and Yvonne Tasker (2014) have detailed in their work on "gendering the recession." The Great Recession of 2007–8 challenged hegemonic masculinity, therefore creating an enormous need on the part of men to reassert that masculinity. Being male—or more accurately—being the right kind of male, is at the symbolic heart of Western national identities; keeping that symbolic heart beating involves, not surprisingly, the devaluation of women. Indeed, as in most historical crises of masculinity, women and their accomplishments are often found to be blameworthy. We need only look to post–World War II American culture, when women in the workforce were widely understood as the reason for the crisis in masculinity experienced by returning soldiers; or to the Moynihan Report of 1965, when Senator Daniel Moynihan blamed African American women in the workforce for a crisis in black masculinity; or, as we have seen, to the economic recession in the 1980s, when then president Ronald Reagan blamed the recession on increasing numbers of women in the workplace, suggesting that they had displaced men.[5] In the first decades of the twenty-first century, it has been suggested that the economic environment that is emerging from global financial collapse is "better suited for women." Reporter Hanna Rosin, in her book *The End of Men*, argues, "The working class, which has long defined our notions of masculinity, is slowly turning into a matriarchy, with men increasingly absent from the home and women making all the decisions" (2012, 21).

The idea that women are "making all the decisions" and somehow oc-cupying positions of power is conceptualized here as happening at the expense of men, as if decision making were done only by men or only by women.[6] And for all Rosin's statistics about the good economic shape of American women, there is, of course, copious evidence that women continue to be discriminated against economically. The continuing gap between a man's and a woman's wages for the same job may sound like an old-fashioned complaint, but it is persistently, and depressingly, justified.[7]

If work, or lack of work, provides a context for the crisis of masculin-ity, so too do feminism and a perception that women are succeeding in the workplace like never before, because of their newfound confidence. The visibility of popular feminism over the past few decades has helped to deepen the well from which a crisis in masculinity can spring, one that finds expression in intimate relations for heterosexual men. The "ma-triarchy" that is apparently taking over the workplace is seen by many men as a threat to their very selves. Indeed, the idea that women are to blame for job loss, personal rejection, or other forms of "emasculation" was key to the 2016 political campaign of Donald Trump, who uses social media to express his misogyny and racism to his white, male, working-class constituency, precisely the demographic of men most saturated by both economic and masculinity crises. As Daniel HoSang and Joseph Lowndes write, Trump marshaled dystopic rhetorics of loss and emas-culation as his key campaign logic: "While Trump's campaign slogan was 'Make America Great Again' he foregrounded themes of a fully real-ized and even irreversible loss, defeat and abandonment" (HoSang and Lowndes, forthcoming). Here, "making America great again" is explicitly about recuperation—and primarily the recuperation of men whose very masculinity has been threatened.

This apparent injury to men's self-confidence has been a key issue for men's rights organizations. Like other forms of popular misogyny, men's rights organizations operate within the economy of visibility that supports popular feminism. These organizations appropriate the issues around which popular feminism is centered, such as confidence and em-powerment, and mirror them in a way that distorts and transforms the target of confidence and empowerment so that it is men (and particularly white men) who suffer, not women. This dynamic is precisely conditioned by an economy of visibility, which makes these popular feminist concerns available for appropriation for popular misogyny. As I argued in the introduction, in every economy there must be capital. In the economy of visibility within which men's rights activism is organized, one of the most dominant forms of capital is erotic capital. In 2011, sociologist Catherine Hakim (2011) published *Erotic Capital: The Power of Attraction in the Boardroom and the Bedroom* (unfortunately titled *Honey Money* in the United Kingdom, where it first appeared). The basic premise of the book, using Pierre Bourdieu's typology of different kinds of capital (financial, social, cultural, and political), is that we need to consider "erotic capital" just as important in how we construct our identities and improve our social standings. Hakim argues that, like the acquisition of knowledge that gives an individual more cultural capital, we should work assiduously on improving our sexual attractiveness in order to improve our social standing. Additionally, Hakim argues that women work harder at gaining erotic capital than men, thus allowing her to (ironically) position her theory as "empowering for women."

Hakim offers her "theory" of erotic capital as a needed extension of Bourdieu's typology, but her argument is not any different from those that hundreds of plastic surgeons, Instagram bloggers, and the entire beauty industry have insisted upon: women need to constantly improve upon their bodies and physical appearance in order to get ahead in life. While Hakim vaguely gestures to different sorts of beauty standards in different parts of the world, her argument is most applicable to the same constituents that the beauty industry targets: thin, white, Western, middle-class, heterosexual women.

It is easy to critique Hakim's theory of erotic capital—and many have done that (e.g., North 2010; Day 2011; Zevallos 2011)—for the way it privileges a particular kind of individual, thus excluding the majority of people who cannot acquire the kind of "erotic capital" she finds so valuable. Yet it is precisely this idea that one must "invest" in erotic capital as a strategy that is the context for men's rights organizations' focus on masculine confidence. The sexual agency of women that is celebrated within both post- and popular feminism is a residual element here; it is presumed by many men's rights organizations that men no longer have sexual agency because the increased sexual agency of women has apparently emasculated them, robbing them of their natural masculine confidence. This is constructed as a specific injury to men, caused by women. And, much the same as the twinned dynamic of injury and capacity functions for popular feminism, the capacity of men to overcome this injury is the focus of much of popular misogyny. An industry thus emerges around the *recuperation* of masculine sexual agency, an industry that utilizes erotic capital as currency, and that finds traction in an economy of visibility.

In this way, contemporary men's rights organizations do not *deny* women's sexual agency; while clearly sexual objectification of women is still a central logic within all realms of social and cultural life, this objectification clashes with an increasingly recognized sexual subjectification. This dynamic is part of the response and call of popular feminism and popular misogyny: the response by women to a history of objectification is to claim sexual agency, and this reclaiming then mobilizes a "call" on the part of popular misogyny. Indeed, as I discussed in chapter 1, Rosalind Gill argues that a key element of a "postfeminist sensibility" is the celebration of this sexual agency, in which we see a shift from "sex object to sexually desiring subject" (Gill 2007, 151). This results in the funhouse mirroring effect, in which the politics of popular feminism are distorted and shaped to serve the purpose of popular misogyny: an industry has emerged to regain control of the gaze, to reimagine and reframe women as objects, and to rebuild masculine sexual confidence.

This rebuilding of masculine sexual confidence *requires* a reframing of women as sexual objects, but objects with sexual agency. While this seems to be a contradiction, it is not so for masculine confidence campaigns. Men's rights organizations often assume that women have more sexual confidence and sexual power than men, and thus give instruction on how to understand confidence as capital that can be exchanged. Indeed, according to these organizations, it is precisely the breaking down of women's confidence that gives men sexual confidence.

There are scores of online organizations dedicated to rebuilding masculine confidence. One website organization, Men's Confidence Project, offers an audio series, *The Collection of Confidence*, for $67. This series covers a range of confidence issues in five modules: "Reinventing Yourself," "Refusing Rejection," "Daring to Decide," "Assert to Achieve," and "Collecting More Confidence." The leader of the Men's Confidence Project, a man who goes by the name Hypnotica, promises to share with consumers an "astonishing secret" for how to get virtually any woman one might desire into bed. Using a familiar tactic, Hypnotica promises that his secret is backed by "government-funded studies" and "scientific research,"

and that once a consumer hears the secret, he "will effortlessly sleep with beautiful women you once thought were out of your league."

I purchased the tapes, so that I now know what the "astonishing secret" is: "shutting off that annoying voice in your head" that says you are not good enough, not sexy enough, not attractive enough. The "astonishing secret" of the Men's Confidence Project is much like the self-help book and project *The Secret* (2006), which is based on the "law of attraction," claiming that one need only utilize positive thinking to create a life of increased happiness, health, and wealth. *The Collection of Confidence* is essentially applying *The Secret* to misogyny, and like other self-help products within neoliberalism, it is based in self-governance and self-care and is an intensely individual project.

Other organizations, such as the Art of Manliness, AskMen, Confident-Man, and Menprovement, also focus on how men can regain erotic capital. Each of these organizations, along with more mainstream men's media outlets such as *Men's Fitness* and *Men's Health*, offer "tips" and lists for men to increase their erotic capital and have success in attracting women into bed. While a few of these also focus on general self-esteem, the overwhelming majority of the confidence-building guides assume a heterosexual male consumer who is having trouble attracting women and having sex. Many of the "tips" are actually just basic physical hygiene; on the Art of Manliness website for example, the authors of "How to Increase Confidence" write that "manly men are confident men," and the first steps to this achievement are things like showering every day and brushing one's teeth and hair (McKay and McKay 2008). The *Men's Health* article "9 Easy, Effective Ways to Be More Confident" exclaims, "Simply put, bravado gets the girl. So if you want to be more attractive to women, show your swagger" (Grish 2015, para. 3). "Swagger" here apparently means things such as "walking confidently," looking her in the eyes (this was a key point made in several of the organizations tip lists), taking a compliment, and so on. Unlike the more aggressive *Collection of Confidence*, which is explicit in instructing consumers in how to construct women as sexual objects in order to have sex with them, many of these organizations offer basic grooming tips to men as a way to "build confidence."

I am not necessarily interested in *how* men are instructed to build confidence in these organizations, as these often seem to be relatively normative suggestions for being social in the world. I am, however, interested in the fact that there is a *confidence industry* for men that has developed in part due to the injuries ostensibly incurred because of popular feminism. Again, simultaneously mirroring and distorting the popular feminist themes of confidence and empowerment, men's rights organizations that focus on sexual confidence argue that heterosexual men need to acquire more erotic capital because feminists have wrenched this away from them.

This confidence industry takes specific shape in what Rachel O'Neill calls "seduction communities" and pickup artist "community-industries" (O'Neill 2015). While it is impossible to completely generalize about the primary perpetrators of popular misogyny (in part because it is such a multilayered, complex network), it is clear that the men with the most visibility in men's rights organizations—seduction and pickup artist communities—are white, heterosexual, working- and middle-class men. Seduction and pickup artist communities fit within a larger, broader context that ranges from valorization of the "alpha male" to sexual violence. Popular and digital culture—the economy of visibility—has provided a rich, and embracing, space for such communities to emerge and flourish. One of many examples of how mainstream misogyny has become, as we'll see, is that in 2007, the burgeoning industry of seduction communities and pickup artists became the topic of a reality television

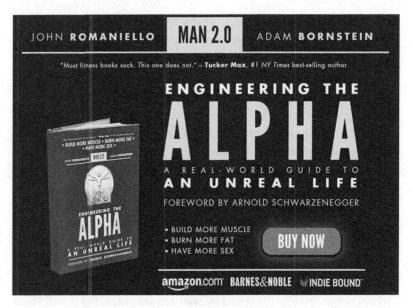

FIGURE 3.6. *Engineering the Alpha*, Male Confidence Movement, 2016.

show aired on VH1. While the cable reality show signaled the profitability of misogyny, it has been the Internet that has signaled its vastness.

The Manosphere in an Economy of Visibility

Digital media has been a crucial element in an economy of visibility in the coalescing of men's rights activism, as the Internet allows for a connection of scattered groups, a more coherent "public" sphere, and, again, what is referred to as the "manosphere," an (increasingly large) corner of the Internet that is by turns absurd and depressing, hilarious and terrifying. Here, hundreds of websites and social media platforms are dedicated to opining, training, and expressing the urgency of the "alpha male" in a land-scape apparently emasculated by feminism in particular and by women in general. Pickup artists, seduction communities, and topical threads on social media sites such as 4Chan and Reddit are dedicated not only to the accumulation of more erotic capital for men but also to recouping that capital that has been lost. However, the issues of the manosphere cover a wide range: from the more moderate, such as support for father's rights and custody rights, doubts over the prevalence of domestic violence, and reflexive support of the military, to the more extreme, such as normalizing rape and sexual violence, manipulating and controlling women into sex, and making death threats against a vast number of people (mostly women) who disagree with these views (Marwick and Lewis 2015).

Men's rights activism is not new to the contemporary moment, but it is precisely digital media sites like Reddit that allow for men's rights activists to flourish and widen their reach (Massanari [2015] 2017). For example, organizations such as Men'sActivism.org and the National Coalition for Men (NCFM) have been around since the 1970s, but it is in the twenty-first century that they have become more widely visible, both online and in public. The mission statements of these organizations focus on what they call "promale" activism. NCFM's mission statement reads, "Since 1977 NCFM has been dedicated to the removal of harmful gender based stereotypes especially as they impact boys, men, their families and the women who love them" ("About Us" n.d., National Coalition for Men). Mens Activism.org claims to have two purposes: "to provide pro-male activists with news and information that will aid them in working toward establishing equal rights for men and the improvement of men's lives" and "to encourage participation in activism projects, and to promote membership in men's rights organizations which coordinate activism efforts and serve as a supportive network for men" ("Our Philosophy" 2006, n.p.). Again, the activism projects of men's rights organizations range from expanding fathers' rights and custody issues to men as victims of domestic violence to limiting the presence of women in the military. While the ostensible purpose of most men's rights organizations is to provide a "supportive network for men," many of the organizations instead cohere around aggressive tactics and narratives that are antiwomen and antifeminism.

Thus, men's rights organizations officially take relatively "safe"—if still misogynistic—positions about custody, women in the military, and so on. But the culture that these organizations create, and the online spaces they inhabit, foster a platform for far more extreme views. For example, Paul Elam, of A Voice for Men, a prominent men's rights organization, has written that some women "walk through life with the equivalent of a I'M A STUPID, CONNIVING BITCH—PLEASE RAPE ME neon sign glowing above their empty little narcissistic heads" (Blake 2015, para. 7). While viciously misogynistic statements such as Elam's are perhaps on the extreme end of the manosphere spectrum, this network of organizations and digital spaces has, on the one hand, been normalized in contemporary culture so as to become practically imperceptible as misogyny, and, on the other, is seen as the province of a few, deranged individuals.

In other words, men's rights organizations should be understood not as distinct units or groups but rather as interconnected nodes in a network of misogynistic discourses and practices. For example, in September 2015, Anthony Williams circulated the Twitter hashtag #MasculinitySoFragile as a way to bring attention to the rampant killing of black men in the Unites States by police and to general racist violence against men (Thomas 2015). However, #MasculinitySoFragile was quickly taken up by popular feminism, and it then became a signal for gendered consumption. The hashtag then became a repository to poke fun at what users referred to as "toxic masculinity," a (heterosexual) masculinity that is so precarious it is threatened by anything containing just a whiff of femininity. Some men who reacted to the hashtag interpreted this as an attack on men in general (as opposed to a construction of masculinity), and commented about the campaign in a hostile and violent way. One in particular, Twitter user Mech of Justice (@mechofjusticewz) sneered, "I challenge any female tweeting unironically with #MasculinitySoFragile to last three rounds against me in a fight. We'll see who's fragile" (Banet-Weiser and Miltner 2015, 171). This defensive reaction to #MasculinitySoFragile is indicative of a more general popular misogyny, one that is networked across and within multiple media platforms. Again, popular misogyny is expressed on and within networks, implicating a technological, social, and economic infrastructure, and the manosphere is its beating heart (Banet-Weiser and Miltner 2015). The violent misogyny of Elam is but one node in a broader network, and the extremism of his comments work to support other nodes that are seen as milder by comparison. What is important to recognize, however, is that popular misogyny works as a broad networked structure, not as distinct expressions or outbursts. Popular misogyny is a *system* of shared interconnections and links; when a more extreme men's rights organization such as Return of Kings features headlines such as "27 Attractive Girls Who Became Ugly Freaks Because of Feminism" or "Why Abundance and Ruthlessness Are Needed to Get Hot Girls in 2017," this is interconnected to formalized political attempts to roll back reproductive rights for women, in turn interconnected with online misogyny and harassment. Within an economy of visibility, various modes of networked misogyny *authorize* and support one another, even if they give the appearance of being distinct. Popular misogyny, in all its forms, capitalizes on men's apparent injuries, caused by women and feminism, and offers routes to recoup men's natural capacities.

Networks often require a lingua franca to communicate and form a system (Castells 1996, 2013), and the concepts of masculine injury and capacity provide this common language for popular misogyny. Indeed, there is a whole new vocabulary that has developed to address masculine injury: words such as "negging," which means to subtly insult a woman to lower her self-esteem so that she will be more interested in having sex; "incel," an abbreviation for "involuntarily celibate," a term used by men who feel that women owe them sex but who cannot seduce women; Anti-Slut Defense (ASD), a label men give to women who claim to have been raped because they were incapacitated, say by alcohol; Social Justice Warriors (SJWS), a label for women who advocate for equal rights for women and minorities; Men Going Their Own Way (MGTOW), a label for men who refuse to have contact with women because of how they assume they will be treated, and more. This vocabulary helps to create community within the manosphere and consolidate its networked nature; a misogynistic lingua franca coheres varied groups around the sexual objectification of women and the mandate to achieve heterosexual confidence.

Again, one of the more extreme men's rights organizations is Return of Kings. Daryush "RooshV" Valizadeh founded the site. RooshV is an American who began his career as a microbiologist but then wrote a book called *Bang*, which he describes as a "textbook for picking up girls and getting laid." Leaving the field of microbiology behind, he created Return of Kings, which claims to be based on the values of "neomasculinity," defined by RooshV as "combining traditional beliefs, masculinity, and animal biology into one ideological system. It aims to aid men living in Westernized nations that lack qualities such as classical virtue, masculinity in males, femininity in females, and objectivity, especially concerning beauty ideals and human behavior" (Valizadeh 2015b, para. 1). Return of Kings is a blog format, where bloggers identify as "heterosexual, masculine" men (just to make matters entirely clear, there is an explicit statement on the home page: "Women and homosexuals are strongly discouraged from commenting here"). On a typical day the most-shared posts are something like "6 Ways Liberal Democracy Destroys the Goodness of Humanity" (Roscoe 2016), "6 Slut Tales Every Man Needs to Be Aware Of" (Sharpe 2016), and "Why Feminism Is a Terrorist Movement" (Savage 2016). This last blog post begins, "There exists a noxious ideology with fanatical followers who use tactics of intimidation, manipulation, and outright violence to attack and suppress both men and women to further their quest for power and control. We are, of course, referring to the cancer that is feminism" (Savage 2016, n.p.).

Like many men's rights organizations, Return of Kings specifically and explicitly targets feminism as the reason that the "masculine man" has apparently disappeared from the world. Return of Kings also sees this lack of confidence in heterosexual men as a specific injury caused by feminists and feminism: it "aims to usher the return of the masculine man in a world where masculinity is being increasingly punished and shamed in favor of creating an androgynous and politically correct society that allows women to assert superiority and control over men. Sadly, yesterday's masculinity is today's misogyny. The site intends to be a safe space on the web for those men who don't agree with the direction that Western culture is headed" ("About" n.d., Return of Kings). Yet for Return of Kings, the notion of safety clearly doesn't extend to women. In February 2015, RooshV published a blog post titled "How to Stop Rape" (Valizadeh 2015a). The main argument in the post was that rape should be legal "if done on private property." After a digital media maelstrom (including coverage on well-trafficked sites such as *BuzzFeed* and the *Daily Beast*) condemning him for this, RooshV then tweeted that it had been satire.

Then, a year later, in February 2016, RooshV canceled a Return of Kings International Meeting Day, a simultaneous worldwide meeting to be held in the United Kingdom, Ireland, Canada, and Australia, among other places. He cancelled the global meetup after numerous media reports warning about what was characterized by many feminists as a "rape gathering," stating that he could "no longer guarantee the safety or privacy of men who want to attend the meeting" (Valizadeh 2016, para. 1). The irony of his claim that men are unsafe, when the website has dozens of articles that range from fat shaming to justifying rape to objectifying women, is apparently lost on the founder. Yet this is precisely how the twinned discourses of injury and capacity work as a dynamic between popular feminism and popular misogyny, where the popular feminist claim of gendered injuries such as rape culture is taken up and distorted by popular misogyny, transforming the injury into one that affects men. While the number of readers of Return of Kings is unknown (there is no formal membership requirement, and readers can submit articles to the site as well), the group has thirteen thousand followers on Facebook, and has been officially named by the Southern Poverty Law Center as an extremist hate group. Not surprisingly, in the spring of 2016 the group officially endorsed Donald Trump for president of the United States.

Masculine Sexual Confidence

As offshoots of men's rights organizations, seduction and pickup artist communities are a more visceral attempt to strengthen a man's place—a literal attempt to sleep with the enemy, to go inside the belly of the beast, as it were, to boost one's confidence not via policy but in the most intimate arena of all—sex. These communities focus even more specifically and intensely on confidence—and lack thereof—for men. The rise of seduction communities is apparently a response to large numbers of heterosexual men who have for the most part achieved some financial and career success but have yet to overcome the "hurdle" of seducing a woman (Chu 2014a, 2014b; O'Neill 2015). There are hundreds of websites and organizations dedicated to the practice of picking up and seducing women, such as the American company Real Social Dynamics, which is advertised as a dating service and lifestyle coach and is one of the most active brands of the pickup artist community-industry. Real Social Dynamics offers classes and workshops on how to pick up and seduce women, charging around two hundred dollars for a course that consists of twenty-three instructional videos, or anywhere up to a few thousand dollars for a ticket to a live event. There are seminars and boot camps held all over the world that charge similarly exorbitant fees to participate; the pickup artists' bible, *The Game*, by Neil Strauss, has been widely covered in the media and was the impetus for the vh1 reality show, *The Pickup Artist.*

These seduction communities have been pilloried in the press, with the men who lead them and those who participate being cast as losers and pathetic. One particularly visible leader in seduction communities, Julien Blanc, who works for Real Social Dynamics, was the subject of a *Time* magazine article in 2014 that was headlined "Is This the Most Hated Man in the World?" (Gibson 2014). Blanc describes himself as an "international leader in dating advice," and, as reporter Megan Gibson notes, on his Twitter account has posted things like "Dear Girls, could you please save me the effort and roofie your own drink?" (Gibson 2014, para. 4). Because of his implied sexual violence toward women, Blanc became the focus of several online petitions, including one in Australia that resulted in the country revoking Blanc's visa before he was to hold a seminar in Melbourne. According to Gibson, Australia's immigration minister explained why they revoked his visa: "This guy wasn't putting forward political ideas, he was putting forward abuse that was derogatory to women and that's just something, those are values abhorred in this country" (Gibson 2014, para. 1). Since Australia took action, other nations, including the United Kingdom, have followed suit, so that Blanc holds the dubious honor of being the first person denied entry into a country due to sexism (Gibson 2014).

Blanc is only one individual in the pickup artist community who has been identified as dangerous because of his explicit threats of sexual violence to women. Elliot Rodger, the twenty-two-year-old who shot and killed six people in Santa Barbara, California, in 2013, was described in the press as a "frustrated pick-up artist" (Dewey 2014). In 2009, George Sodini shot and killed three women outside a gym in Pennsylvania, claiming that "30 million women" had rejected him in his life. A self-declared pickup artist, Roissy, wrote on his blog that if Sodini had only learned "game,"[8] women's lives would have been spared (because apparently then he would have been able to seduce women); RooshV made a similar statement about Rodger (Valizadeh 2014). In these communities, men achieve a sense of self-confidence through seducing and controlling women. Yet, despite the derision by the press, as O'Neill (2015, 2) argues, seduction communities represent "less a deviation or departure from current social conventions surrounding sex and relationships than an extension and acceleration of existing cultural norms." Indeed, the fact that seduction communities have so much traction in an economy of visibility, where websites, blogs, and other media productions circulate with ease, is part of how these communities reflect existing cultural norms about masculine injury and capacity and are not an anomaly.

In fact, this extension of cultural norms, and the validation of seduction communities within an economy of visibility, is clearly present in the vh1 series that aired for two seasons in 2007–8, *The Pickup Artist*. It is important to make a distinction between companies such as Real Social Dynamics, men's rights activism, and a reality television show on a commercial network; the motivations behind each of these are different, and they employ different tactics to achieve their goals, ranging from seminars to boot camps to social media to ridiculous spectacle. Real Social Dynamics is a for-profit company, for example, Return of Kings suggests sexual violence as a way to control women, and vh1 is more interested in getting better ratings than in encouraging rape. But it is also important to consider them together, because they are all nodes in the *network* of networked misogyny. As such, they validate and authorize each other.

The Pickup Artist featured a group of men who had difficulties talking to and dating women being mentored by a "master" pickup artist named Mystery, who eliminated the men, one by one each week, in a conventional reality television manner, until he "crowned" a new master pickup artist.[9] Mystery's perspective was simple: learn the requisite techniques of seduction and control, and you will be able to have sex with any woman you want. It is difficult not to see this as absurd: the premise of the show, like other competitive reality television shows, is to bring in a group of men, presumably randomly selected, who have a demonstrated issue with picking up and sleeping with women. The men arrive at a "mansion" (a staple in competitive reality television, from *The Bachelor* to *America's Next Top Model* to *Big Brother*) in a party bus with the license plate reading "Destination Manhood." The show then proceeds by gathering the men in front of the "master" pickup artist, Mystery, and his two fellow mentors, Matador and J-Dog (apparently one needs a call name to be a pickup artist; Bob or Mark or Ted simply won't do). Each week there is a different "skill" taught and then practiced at a club with hidden cameras. These skills include the previously mentioned "negging" but also "peacocking," which is wearing an unusual piece of clothing (for example, Mystery wears a variety of fur and otherwise ostentatious hats), explaining 101s, or Indicators of Interest (such as a woman playing with her hair or jewelry, apparently understood as interest), and tactics such as false time constraint (always acting like you have somewhere to be, something more important to do), separating one's target from the pack, identifying the "mother hen," and so on. Each week, the man who demonstrates the weakest pickup artist skills is eliminated and sent home, and the program concludes with the "crowning" of a new master pickup artist, who receives $50,000 and tours the globe with Mystery to train new pickup artists.

The norms of seduction communities, the rules of the "game," are primarily about manipulation and control over women. These norms are not seen as malicious or out of the ordinary. On the contrary, they are, as O'Neill puts it, "reconfiguring intimate and sexual subjectivities and producing distinctly antisocial forms of sociability" (2015, 17). This "antisocial form of sociability" is in part a response to the way that masculine injury and capacity circulate in an economy of visibility, an economy that is itself part of the proliferation of neoliberal rationalities and the way that these increasingly structure intimate relations. That is, neoliberal rationalities focus intensely on the self and individual satisfaction, and as such are fundamen-

FIGURE 3.7. *The Pickup Artist* reality television show cast, VH1, 2007.

tally antisocial. But because these same rationalities mandate that individuals should be entrepreneurs, an inherently social subjectivity, sociability is also needed. This combination produces a curiously antisocial sociability. Through the production of antisocial forms of sociability, within intimate and sexual relations a level of sexual manipulation and violence may well be not only tolerated but expected, particularly in a context of popular feminist confidence, where gender equality is assumed. This combination produces what Rosalind Gill (2008) calls "compulsory sexual agency." In other words, the pickup artist industry is not understood by the men who participate as teaching them to treat women like objects but rather as cultivating confidence in themselves. Of course, the route to that self-confidence *is* to treat women like objects, but, like other neoliberal practices, the focus is on the self, while the violence that often underpins that focus is obscured *as* violence, and is transfigured into self-confidence.

The pickup artist and seduction community emerged as a way to "teach" confidence, to instill mastery in men who had been *denied* this skill because of popular feminism and the confidence of women. In other words, the men who are depicted in the VH1 series are not randomly selected but are seen as those with damaged or stunted masculinities (understood within the assumption of heteronormative masculinity). These men never had confidence in the first place—they admitted they couldn't talk to women; they were forty-year-old virgins; they were socially awkward. So sexual confidence is depicted as something that is denied to them. Again, the mechanisms are similar to the "confidence movement" for girls and women—and both are engaging in a neoliberal project of the self as an enterprise. Yet, not only have women taken away confidence from men, but feminists in particular have *too much* confidence; overconfidence is a familiar stereotypical characteristic of feminism. For centuries, a common tactic to trivialize and dismiss feminist demands and struggles has been to focus not on the demands themselves but on the bodies of those women who are making the demands: they are unfeminine, ugly, hairy, unkempt, overweight. This stereotype is well used by men's rights activism and the manosphere in general, and has taken on new valence in a context of what Gill and Orgad (2015) call "confidence culture": feminists are, as Sara Ahmed (2016) points out, perceived as overconfident.

This theme is picked up in a seminar video on how to pick up women sold by Real Social Dynamics (RSDTyler n.d.). In this video, "Tyler," a master pickup artist, tells a group of men that they need to continue trying to pick up women, even if "nine out of ten reject you." "You create your own reality," he tells them, and if you don't try to seduce a woman after rejection, then "you're a scared little bitch." In the reality the men are told to create, confidence is everything: "You have to tell yourself, I'm fucking awesome," and eventually a woman "will fuck you." In this seminar, Tyler does not deny that women have sexual agency; rather, the training focuses on the men, in an attempt to cultivate sexual confidence and the "right attitude." The pickup artist community sees sexual relations as a game (hence the title of their go-to guide), and thus victory just requires the right strategy. Consequently, men are taught things like "negging," in which, as we've seen, a man insults a woman in order to lower her self-esteem, and, the logic goes, as her self-esteem lowers, she's more likely to be interested and willing. Sexual relationships here are always a gamble, a game in which the victory is not only gaining confidence in oneself but also stripping it from women.

Within popular misogyny, violence toward women and validation of rape culture are interconnected with more heteronormative practices. These interconnections form networked misogyny. On the one hand, the fact that leaders in the industry are making a profit by "training" men to seduce and control women is seen as outside cultural and social norms; on the other hand, these communities fit perfectly well within a cultural context of what RooshV calls neomasculinity. Here, we can see popular

FIGURE 3.8. Real Social Dynamics, "How to Get the Woman You Want," 2015.

misogyny as moving toward a more mainstream brand, and labeling it-self, as Real Social Dynamics does, "lifestyle coaching." This not only ob-fuscates the misogyny of this industry but folds that misogyny into neo-liberal structure. In so doing, popular misogyny is often not recognized *as* misogyny but merely as the recuperation of traditional masculinity. Even RooshV recognizes this when he says, "Sadly, yesterday's masculin-ity is today's misogyny" (Valizadeh n.d., n.p.). This captures the dynamic of masculine injury and capacity—the injury is that masculinity has been lost, and the role of popular misogyny is to find and restore it.

Through the focus on the individual, self-mastery, and entrepreneur-ship, neoliberalism and popular misogyny are just as interconnected as neoliberalism and popular feminism, despite a general mediated discourse that positions popular misogyny as an outlier, a break from norms of tra-ditional masculinity. The "skills" needed to be a pickup artist, the train-ing needed to master the game, are forms of that self-mastery that has long been valued and validated by neoliberalism's version of meritocracy. But while there has been some attention to networked misogyny, it is rou-tinely dismissed as an outlier, an anomaly, a technological "glitch." Writing about a similar process with racism, Lisa Nakamura discusses how racism is interpreted online: "Everyday online racism is a 'glitch' or malfunction of a network designed to broadcast a signal, a signal that is hijacked or polluted by the pirate racist" (2013, para. 2). In other words, Nakamura argues that while online racism is dismissed as a "glitch," digital cultures actually provide a context in which racism *is* the agent that makes racist memes spreadable. This works similarly within the context of seduction and pickup artist communities, where men are venerated and given prestige because of their sexual conquests, but when it is taken to its extreme—as in the pickup artist—he is cast as deviant, a glitch, rather than part of a misogyny that is far more pervasive than most of us like to admit.

Overconfidence in Confidence

In some ways, confidence is hard to theorize, because why would anyone want to *not* be confident? Yet confidence, as it is defined by popular feminism and popular misogyny, is a concept that circulates in an economy of visibility, where it is enough to stand in its own visibility, untethered to other pathways or avenues for social change. We need to think through what this "confidence culture" means for gender relations rather than simply accept it as an aspirational goal (Gill and Orgad 2015). In an insightful and incisive essay about confidence, Sara Ahmed traces some of the ways, both historically and presently, that girls and women are expected—and not expected—to be confident. Confidence, she argues, is often something women feel like they lose—confidence in a person, an ideology, a practice. Here, confidence again recalls the con game, where confidence is always precarious. Confidence comes easier for some women than for others; if one is already white and cis-gendered, for instance, she already *has* confidence; she exists in a culture that tells her that the body she was born into is the best way to be, she is capable, even if eventually, of leaning in. Confidence, as Ahmed states, is a "manner of existence . . . the word confidence rests on faith or trust. To be confident can thus mean to have trust in an expectation" (Ahmed 2016, para. 11). In this way, if expectations of women are below those of men, then confidence itself can be about women trusting these lower expectations of themselves (which is one reason why feminists are so often seen as "overconfident"). These lower expectations appear in career options for women, in the realm of the family and divisions of labor, in our intimate relations.

Indeed, Ahmed argues, "We need to throw our confidence in confidence into crisis. Maybe what confidence is doing depends upon what values we are upholding. . . . You lose confidence in the world that rewards you for compliance. But you also need to acquire confidence in order not to comply with that very world: you have to have confidence that you can survive the experience of challenging the system" (2016, paras. 40–43). Because women seem to expect less of themselves (indeed, are *expected* to expect less of themselves), and because in the United States success is judged primarily around one's paycheck and job title, many feminists have been concerned with a general lack of confidence held by women. In other words, confidence is a feminist issue, and an important one. But when it circulates within a popular feminist economy of visibility, and when it becomes visible when white, middle-class, and cis-gendered girls and women are seen to be deprived of it, it is transfigured as a kind of commodity that is available only for some. This confidence in confidence, as Ahmed points out, "could be another way that women are made responsible for what happens to them; as if our task in challenging gender relations is to modify ourselves" (2016, para. 13). The burden of confidence is thus placed on the individual woman or girl, rather than on the structure of inequality that mobilizes the lack of confidence that emerges at an early age in girls, and grows more pernicious, if more subtle, as girls become women.

This logic reinforces not only the idea that girls and women are vulnerable but also that empowerment is an individual achievement rather than something that should be worked for from the ground up. Rather than marshaling confidence as a way to challenge patriarchal structures, it becomes a popular feminist mandate for women to feel good about themselves, and a tool of popular misogyny to *shore up* those very patriarchal structures. Achieving confidence thus happens in a cyclical relationship. Confidence organizations are responding to and challenging an economy of visibility that values girls and women primarily for their bodies, but in doing so they are emphasizing and validating those same gendered, neoliberal characteristics. Through this cyclical logic, girls and women are unintentionally made *more* vulnerable, not less. When activism and empowerment organizations are primarily legible within an economy of visibility, when confidence itself becomes a commodity within a market, then the value of girls and women is also understood through these terms. This allows for an easier transformation of confidence by popular misogyny into a frame of masculine injury, caused by overconfident women and girls. Through the economy of visibility, popular feminism and popular misogyny have transfigured confidence into a commodity. Only certain forms of confidence become visible: those that validate particular kinds of gendered injuries and capacities.

FOUR. COMPETENCE

Girls Who Code and Boys Who Hate Them

There's a toxicity within gaming culture, and also in tech culture, that drives this misogynist hatred, this reactionary backlash against women who have anything to say, especially those who have critiques or who are feminists. There's this huge drive to silence us, and if they can't silence us, they try to discredit us in an effort to push us out. — ANITA SARKEESIAN, 2014

In 2014, after pressure from the Equal Employment Opportunity Commission, the media company Google finally released the demographic statistics of their current employees. The report confirmed what had long been suspected: 70 percent of Google employees are male, and 62 percent of the company's US employees are white (even in Google outlets in racially diverse cities such as New York and Atlanta) (Catalan 2014). When jobs at Google are further separated into categories, the gender disparity becomes even more pronounced: men hold 83 percent of technology positions, and 79 percent of leadership roles are held by men. The only category that has a semblance of gender balance are the nontechnology jobs at the company, including administrative and clerical positions.

The "woman problem" in the technology industries has become a key component of popular feminism; scores of nonprofit and corporate initiatives now teach girls to code, encourage girls to become more engaged in science, and address gender disparities in technology companies. Why does popular feminism pay so much attention to women in technology? In great part because the technology industries, are, in Laurie Penny's words, "the most important fields both of human development and social mobility right now, the places where power is being created and cemented right now" (Penny 2014, n.p.). Because the technology industries are increasingly the centers of power (financial, political, and cultural), and because the gender and racial disparities in employment in giant technology companies such as Google have moved into a media spotlight, it makes sense that popular feminism would focus efforts to include women in these industries. The attention to the technology industries is also indicative of the limitations of a market-focused popular feminism, in which encouraging girls and women toward technology aligns with broader neoliberal principles about expanding markets, and often works to implicitly and explicitly devalue other career paths whose economic rewards are less certain. The deeply embedded sexist structure of technology industries has thus become both more visible and more defended. For example, in August 2017, there was a media maelstrom over an internal "manifesto" written by a Google engineer, James Damore, who argued that the reason more men had leadership positions in the technology industries is biological. According to Damore, "female" characteristics such as empathy and emotion are not well-suited for the engineering profession; in his words, "women have a stronger interest in people rather than things" (Damore, quoted in Jones 2017, n.p.). The manifesto was leaked to the press, and became the subject of intense media attention, eventually leading Google to fire Damore (Jones 2017). The manifesto provided evidence for a feminist insistence that there is structural sexism in the technology industries, and raised the question yet again about inclusion within these industries. Yet, as I mentioned in the introduction, the "add women and stir" method also comes at a cost, as simply including women in technology industries doesn't necessarily address sexist structure.

And efforts to include more women in the tech industries incur a response. Because technology industries are a center of power, it is also not surprising that there is a significant response by popular misogyny to gender inclusivity; the territory of technology is one that is defended vehemently against potential interlopers. Indeed, Damore quickly became a hero for misogynists, who defended his faulty science as fact and decried his firing (Jones 2017).

What is a bit surprising, however, is the level of violence and vicious-
ness of the misogynistic response to efforts to include more women in
technology. While women who work in the technology fields have repeatedly reported sexual harassment,[1] those in the gaming industries routinely report death and rape threats. As I discuss later, there was even a
game created called "Beat Up Anita Sarkeesian," in which the only goal
was to violently beat Anita Sarkeesian, a feminist vlogger who critiqued
the representation of women in video games (Shaw 2015). The dynamic
between popular feminism and popular misogyny within the realm of technology is framed by hostility and violence that has particular purchase in
an economy of visibility. The tropes of injury and capacity that I have discussed throughout this book are in bold relief in the context of technology
industries: women have been injured through a long history of exclusion
from the science and technology fields, and popular feminism redirects that
injury into a capacity, realized through organizations that work to include
girls and women in technologically based spaces, such as engineering and
coding. In turn, men who occupy positions of power within the technology
industries are often those whose masculinity has been shaped by historical
injury: geeks, nerds, and the socially awkward (Ensmenger 2015). In other
words, the kinds of people who are drawn to technology fields are typically not the same kinds of people who are drawn to other forms of labor,
whether that is factory labor or the labor of financial capital. Indeed, tech
labor, as Gina Neff (2012), Fred Turner (2006), and others have described, is
emergent labor, and doesn't have the same settled social forms that factory
labor or financial labor have had in the past. Thus, as dominant power is
decentered from financial capital and recentered within technology industries, the injury that comes from social and cultural exclusion because one
is a geek or a nerd is reimagined as a source of capacity. In this chapter, I explore this intertwined dynamic of popular feminist and popular misogynist
tropes of capacity and injury within the context of technology industries,
particularly in the context of "toxic geek masculinity."

Toxic geek masculinity is a vicious manifestation of the broader realm
of popular misogyny that I have been exploring; indeed, we can think of
it as the technological branch of men's rights activism (Johnson 2016). I'm
arguing that toxic geek masculinity is not an isolated phenomenon but is
bolstered by a larger cultural context of popular misogyny. This context energizes toxic geek masculinity; the sheer popularity of popular misogyny
offers more platforms and faster distribution for this kind of toxicity. This

FIGURE 4.1. Beat Up Anita Sarkeesian video game, 2015.

networked misogyny, like other networks, connects and supports its different forms, from hateful tweets to pickup artist seminars in hotel rooms to revenge porn. Like other versions of men's rights activism, toxic geek masculinity "seek[s] to provide a masculinized counterpoint to feminism"; but more than simply a counterpoint, toxic geek masculinity is a call to arms against feminism, because feminism apparently poses a terrible threat to livelihood and identity (Massanari 2017). Feminism is seen as encroaching on territory not belonging to women (unless they adopt a clear masculinist subjectivity, and even then women are subjected to harassment and violence). Adding to the threat that feminism apparently embodies, geek masculinity has historically been an embattled identity, a subject position deeply insecure. It is an identity category that, until the global technology boom of the last two decades, has been belittled, emasculated, and mocked, especially in comparison to hypermasculinity, represented by the "alpha male" subject and "bro" or frat culture (Chu 2014; Dunbar-Hester 2016).

An economy of visibility provides platforms where particular forms of redress for these injuries become visible. For example, just like the organizations that we have seen devoted to confidence building, there are scores of organizations—ranging from nonprofit to corporate to state-funded—that are dedicated to girls and women in technology: Girls Who Code, Black Girls Code, Ladies Who Code, Women 2.0, Webgrrls, Women Who Tech, Women in Technology, Tech Girlz, The Science Club for Girls, and the list goes on. Furthermore, long-standing social service organizations such as the Boys and Girls Club and the Lower East Side Club for Girls in New York City now offer classes on science, math, and coding, as do innumerable after-school programs and summer camps and workshops. Huge technology companies, such as Verizon, have partnered with these smaller, girl-focused organizations, such as Girls Who Code; this particular partnership created the "Inspire Her Mind" campaign, as well as ads promoting the joys and empowerment of being a "maker," and classes that teach girls to produce apps. Verizon's website claims that the company is "inspiring young minds to get involved with STEM and build brighter futures" (Tilstra 2016). These organizations and initiatives, as we'll see, share the goal of integrating more girls and women into STEM fields, but not surprisingly, have varied relationships with and investments in feminist politics. Black Girls Code, for example, is explicitly dedicated to challenging not only sexism but also racism in technology fields; *Glamour* magazine's partnership with Girls Code, or Verizon's encouraging girls to pursue science and technology ("Not Just Pretty, but Pretty Brilliant"), however, maintain a commitment to dominant gender norms, and are presumably quite content with existing patriarchal structures, at least when it comes to heteronormative constructions of femininity. Not surprisingly, the latter form of popular feminism becomes more visible within an economy of visibility, as these expressions and practices connect to more palatable forms of feminism—inclusion, coding organizations, and so on—rather than addressing the intersectionality of structural racism and sexism.

Popular misogynistic tropes of injury and capacity also circulate within an economy of visibility, often as a direct response to popular feminism. The popular feminist focus on girls and women in technology has not been received well, to say the least, by the men who have dominated these fields. Indeed, the response from men, especially in gaming and game development, has been astounding: women who dare to enter these fields as professionals, not to mention women who critique gender disparities in technology, have been targeted with extreme vitriol and even violence. The backlash from tech communities against women and their participation within these communities involves not only general resentment from "geeks" but also the creation and perpetuation of what Adrienne Massanari (2017) has called "toxic technocultures." Within the world of toxic technocultures, a variety of tactics have become commonplace: rape and death threats, doxing (revealing one's personal information on social

FIGURE 4.2. #GirlsWhoCode, 2012.

media), public shaming, and myriad other efforts to block women from entering the tech community in any way. In this chapter, I examine, among other things, the culture of (mostly) white geek masculinity. Most of these communities (initially centered in Silicon Valley in the United States, but now clearly global) were formed by small coteries of young techies, and abound with the cultural patterns of young male bonding—think of the in-jokes and casual sexism and white privilege of "bro" culture but with a technological spin. These communities operate according to a logic that not only deliberately excludes women but also diminishes them. Thus, although there are a number of examples of remarkable women in technological innovation and in the electronics industry, the barriers women face to excel in the world of technology appear to be greater than in most other fields (in contrast, for instance, with medical research).

As with previous chapters, in this chapter I examine the deeply intertwined relationship between popular feminism and popular misogyny in the context of injury and capacity. However, within the specific context of the technology industries, this dynamic tension between popular feminism and popular misogyny frequently erupts into more specific violence; the call by popular misogyny to respond to popular feminist demands for inclusion in these industries is often interpreted as a call to arms. The injury that popular feminism claims occurs when girls and women are excluded from technology industries is interpreted not as an injury by popular misogyny but rather as an affront: it is a competition over labor, both labor in the technology fields and domestic labor. As I discuss later in this chapter, one prominent narrative of geek masculinity is that despite the fact that geeks are finally experiencing a moment when they are receiving both cultural and economic capital because of the rise in prominence of the technology industries, they have not acquired "erotic capital," and continue to be denied the attention of heterosexual women. Thus, when women encroach upon the cultural and economic territory of geek men in technology, it is seen as an injury that demands a reaction. In this narrative, women are *not* doing what they are supposed to do (partner with geek men), and then they are doing what they are *not* supposed to do (work in the technology industries).

The fact that technology fields are "the places where power is being created and cemented right now" also means that we need to account for the political economy of advanced capitalism that supports these fields (Penny 2014, n.p.). As I've been arguing throughout this book, the varied practices of neoliberalism both enable and constrict our identities, and are always simultaneously an opening and a foreclosure around social categories such as gender, race, and sexuality. The normalized logic of neoliberal practices—in trade, government, education, and employment—often touts its ability to create new markets, to expand older ones, and to provide opportunities for entrepreneurship, whether for Fortune 500 companies or for the small investor, the teenage vlogger, or the "stay-at-home mom." Through the relentless expansion of markets, rather than, say, aiming to correct the ways markets do *not* work, the logic of neoliberalism follows that logic perfected by liberalism over the last three centuries: through affirming language and the material privileging of the individual and entrepreneurship, neoliberal capitalism maintains structural asymmetries of power, asymmetries that manifest in everything from sexism to racism, from homophobia to poverty. We see this clearly in the popular feminist framing of girls and women in technology, where girls are encouraged to be makers and learn code so that they can compete as entrepreneurs in technology fields. Inclusion in this field is not the problem; it is the goal of this inclusion—to compete as an entrepreneur in ever-expanding markets, to be a better economic subject within neoliberalism—that is problematic. This route secures and maintains dominant systems of capital—precisely those systems that have excluded women for centuries. The response from popular misogyny is thus recuperative in some ways: it is dedicated to securing, and continuing, capitalism as the privileged site of patriarchy.

Twenty years before Google released their diversity report, the American Association of University Women (1991) released another report, *Short-changing Girls, Shortchanging America*, which detailed the wide disparity in US education in terms of gender. The report surveyed self-esteem, and in particular, the growing gap between the genders as girls and boys go through adolescence. Most damning, the report found a connection in the gendered asymmetry in self-esteem in terms of how math and science were being taught in schools. As I detailed in chapter 2, self-esteem has become a key issue for popular feminism; indeed, a lucrative market for self-esteem emerged after this report, primarily aimed at white middle-class girls who were seen as suffering from the injury of low self-esteem. The survey found a significant relationship between a person's self-esteem and how he or she perceived their math and science skills: "Of all the study's indicators, girls' perceptions of their ability in math and science had the strongest relationship to their self-esteem; as girls 'learn' that they are not as good at these subjects, their sense of self-worth and aspirations for themselves deteriorate" (American Association of University Women 1991, 10). Though Heather Huhman wrote in 2012 in Forbes magazine that the science, technology, engineering, and math (STEM) fields have "always had a woman problem," it is also the case that, as Janet Abbate (2012) and Marie Hicks (2017) have argued in their histories of women in computing, computer science in particular has *not* always had a "woman problem." Rather, women worked more widely in these fields when they were seen more as *service* work than a center of cultural and economic power. In the 1960s, when computing began to emerge as a valuable (culturally, politically, and economically) career path, the "woman problem" was created by institutionalized sexism and misogyny, in which women were systematically pushed out of computing fields to make room for men (Abbate 2012; Ensmenger 2012; Hicks 2017). As Nathan Ensmenger argues, "The use of low-wage, low-skilled female programming labor was integral to the design of early electronic computation systems. For the leaders of many of the pioneering computer projects, the assumption was that the process of 'coding' a computer was largely rote and mechanical—and therefore work that could best be assigned to women. Or, to borrow a relevant metaphor from computer programming itself, the presence of women in early computing was a feature, not a bug" (Ensmenger 2012, 44).[2]

This history, however, has been largely obscured; in the contemporary moment, the "women problem" in STEM fields and computing is seen to have a number of origins: as the AAUW report documents, girls are less likely to be encouraged to pursue math and science, especially since math and science are often thought of as a "male" endeavor, whether consciously or unconsciously, while humanities and arts are thought of as "female" fields. The problem centers in education: in the United States in 2013, only 18.5 percent of the students who took the Advanced Placement Computer Science test were girls, only 0.4 percent of girls entering college intended to major in computer science, and women made up only 14 percent of all computer science graduates (which was actually a decrease from twenty years earlier) (Tiku 2014). Much of the world abounds with essentialist, and surprisingly resilient, beliefs about the supposedly innate abilities of men to comprehend science and math quicker and more easily than women. No surprise, then, that the products of that culture—namely, our educational systems—further that gap between men and women. Also not surprisingly, popular culture, ranging from film to television to comics, largely features male characters as those who do technological things; in the last decade or so, alongside the explosion of the Internet, we have now embraced the stereotype of "geek masculinity." The popular veneration of key male figures in the field of technology, such as Steve Jobs, Bill Gates, and Mark Zuckerberg, enhances this stereotype—indeed, there have been mainstream films that detail the lives of Jobs and Zuckerberg.

This gendered asymmetry has prompted educators, policy makers, and state officials to take an interest in those fields with the most pronounced gaps. After the AAUW report, even the toy company Mattel was apparently motivated to modify its Teen Talk Barbie, who had lamented, among a wide range of proclamations and complaints, "Math class is tough!" (Mattel also created a STEM Barbie). The efforts inspired by popular feminism have been numerous, and varied, including corporate initiatives that focus on STEM fields; pop culture, often humorous, endeavors to reveal the sexism that has structured STEM fields and gaming since their beginning; and federal programs, nonprofit organizations, and others that encourage girls to learn code. To that end, the Obama administration was also active in promoting gender equity in science and technology, pairing the Office of Science and Technology Policy with the White House Council on Women and Girls to increase engagement of girls and women in STEM fields. In a 2013 speech, President Barack Obama said,

FIGURE 4.3. STEM Barbie, 2016.

"One of the things that I really strongly believe in is that we need to have more girls interested in math, science, and engineering. We've got half the population that is way underrepresented in those fields and that means that we've got a whole bunch of talent . . . not being encouraged the way they need to" (Fried 2013, n.p.).

Yet, as Mary Celeste Kearney (2006) has eloquently argued, despite the continued gender disparity in technology fields, girls have always been makers, often creating media as a way to express anger and general dissatisfaction over precisely the exclusion of girls and women in these fields. Technological skill and knowhow has only become more prevalent in the contemporary moment—a different moment from when Kearney initially wrote about girls as makers—in part because of the ubiquity of social media. Indeed, the economy of visibility that is the backdrop for popular feminism has been a key mechanism in encouraging girls and women to creatively use technology and make media: using Instagram, Twitter, Tumblr, and other social media sites has become normal among those girls who have access to smartphones and the Internet (which is clearly not all girls). This increased visibility and digital presence and activity has been the focus of feminist scholarship.[3] As I wrote in 2012, much of this work has challenged traditional communication research that links technological use (ranging from watching television to participating in chat rooms to taking selfies) to harmful social effects; in turn, we have become more willing to see the potential benefits, especially for girls, of exploring the Internet as a space in which creative identity making, among other things, might be possible (Banet-Weiser 2012). This increasingly normative presence of girls and women online has tapped into the popular feminist discourse of empowerment I discuss throughout this book; the notion that girls can be producers as well as consumers both draws upon and authorizes the neoliberal mandate to be an entrepreneur.

Thus, many girls and women have used technology itself to launch popular feminist critiques about their marginalization within technology, as well as to challenge the essentialist notion that women and girls lack what in 2005 then Harvard president Larry Summers called "intrinsic aptitude" (Jaschik 2005), a resilient ideology about gender essentialism that appeared yet again in 2017 in the Google manifesto discussed at the beginning of this chapter, which stated that "female qualities" such as emotion and cooperation are not suited for technological work. Not surprisingly, given the ubiquity of satire within social media, many popular feminist expressions use satire and humor to critique the masculinist framing of technology. For example, in May 2016, the nonprofit organization Girls Who Code created a three-part satirical YouTube series of girls explaining why they can't code: they have boobs, they menstruate, and they are too pretty. The videos, titled "Why Girls Can't Code," are a series of hilarious laments: one girl complains, "I can't code because my cleavage is too distracting"; another says, "I can't code because my long eyelashes get in the way and I can't see the screen"; one young woman says, "My boobs, like, really prevent me from coding"; a younger girl says, "I don't even have boobs yet and they still get in the way. It's crazy." Each young woman or girl delivers these lines in a straight-faced, deadpan manner, followed by the text "Girls Do Code." The final young woman says, "Coding is just *too* rational when I am *this* emotional," leading to the final text frame: "Every other theory is ridiculous" ("Why Can't Girls Code?" 2016). According to their website, Girls Who Code created the series because "teen girls are bombarded with messages that coding is not for them. In fact, several studies cite negative stereotypes and media portrayals as top reasons why girls are opting out of coding. We wanted to tackle these messages head on and reclaim them! These absurd theories have been used for decades to keep girls out of male-dominated industries. Enough is enough" ("Why Can't Girls Code?" 2016, n.p.). The use of humor was a strategic way to stand out among the media clutter of popular feminist challenges to the masculine dominance of technology; according to the founder and CEO of Girls Who Code, Reshma Saujani, "There are already a

FIGURE 4.4. "I've tried to get into coding, but my cleavage is just so distracting," Girls Who Code campaign, 2016.

ton of inspirational videos about why girls should code. We wanted to try something different and use humor and satire to question the stereotypes that tell our girls that coding is not for them. Our hope is these videos will spark a much-needed conversation about the messages we send our young women and what we can do to create a more inclusive, well-rounded image of a programmer" ("News" 2016, n.p.).

Saujani's strategy to "try something different" by using humor and satire is important for a number of reasons: the "popular" in popular feminism, as we have seen, often requires a kind of easy access to grave topics such as discrimination, harassment, racism, and sexual violence. However, while humor is often used effectively as scathing critique, the use of humor in popular feminism, especially when created on social media, frequently means a distillation of politics, in which words and images are used ironically to create an easy-to-digest critique. This doesn't mean that these forms of popular feminism are apolitical, but rather that too often the joke just stays a joke, living for a brief time in your feed before disappearing into the cloud. Again, this is indicative for how an economy of visibility functions; rather than a politics of visibility, where the visibility itself is a route to politics, visibility becomes enough in itself. This video is a particular kind of response to the injury of structural sexism in the technology industries, one that emphasizes the capacity of women through the debunking of gender stereotypes. The kind of discourse and practice that circulates most easily within an economy of visibility often has a particular tone, one of soft, humorous rebuke rather than rage or anger; it needs to be framed in a way that is palatable. As Girls Who Code CEO Saujani emphasizes, teaching girls to code means to encourage a "more inclusive, well-rounded image of a programmer" ("News" 2016, n.p.). In this way, the video's humor fits well within popular feminism and its desire to be "fun." When feminists do marshal anger, or occupy the position of what Sara Ahmed (2010) calls the "feminist killjoy," this often positions the feminist squarely back in the bitter, angry stereotype—or at the very least, as a finger-wagging "bad mom" feminist that doesn't understand the younger generation.

A humorous video, such as "Why Can't Girls Code?," can stimulate awareness in those watching that there is a problem, but it is not clear it will lead more girls to learn to code—or companies to hire women who do. It is also not clear that simply teaching girls to code will fundamentally disrupt the deeply embedded sexism that has shaped the technology industries. The biting satire of the Girls Who Code video makes an important point. But I also want to point out that the political efficacy of humor often depends on the platform on which it is delivered; while "hashtag" activism on Twitter, for example, has been important in stimulating public awareness, it also relies upon the logic of an economy of visibility, and so often becomes something retweeted or reposted rather than engaged politically. Of course, not all hashtag activism is the same, or has the same political valence. To be sure, there are some campaigns that have gone beyond a first step and have mobilized social change beyond the hashtag, such as #BlackLivesMatter, which initially brought widespread attention to police brutality against black men and women and has since spread beyond this issue to broader issues of racism and violence in the United States and elsewhere. After a videotape was leaked featuring then presidential candidate Donald Trump encouraging sexual assault, a hashtag campaign #NotOkay began, and scores of women detailed their own stories of sexual assault on social media. This was an important move, as it forced a public awareness of the widespread, normative problem of sexual assault, and motivated women to come forth and publicly detail their stories—a move that a year later became the #MeToo movement when several men in the entertainment industries were accused of sexual harassment in the workplace, and scores of women came forward to tell their stories. However, while hashtag campaigns may be the first step to such change, most remain in place, as a first step.

Another example of the use of the humorous hashtag to challenge the masculine dominance of science and technology emerged after Tim Hunt, a Nobel Prize–winning biochemist, publicly said that women in science labs were "distractions" for men. According to Hunt, when women are in the science lab, one of three things typically happens: the woman falls in love with the male scientist, the male scientist falls in love with the woman, or women cry (Quinn 2015). After this statement about the "trouble with girls," a number of female-identified scientists started the Twitter hashtag #timhunt, and responded in a humorous, satirical way, tweeting things like "Had *such* trouble doing good science today. What with the crying, and battling my way through hordes of suitors. So distracting" (Twomey 2015), or "Dear department: please note that I will be unable to chair the 10 am meeting this morning because I am too busy swooning and crying" (Devlin 2015). These responses to powerful men justifying sexism in technology and science fields as a natural state of affairs are important in the way they expose the fallacy of this logic after years of, well, *scientific* research and empirical data of girls and women performing equally to or better than men in STEM fields. As the Girls Who Code website points out, these theories are not only absurd, they have remarkable longevity. However, like the Girls Who Code video series, #timhunt has done little to change the structural inequities within STEM fields, in part because they use individuals—girls and women who are scientists—as "evidence" of inequity.

In turn, the #timhunt campaign also employs shaming an individual—Hunt—as a disciplinary tool, what Laura Thompson calls a "name and shame" technique (Thompson 2018). Publicly shaming or humiliating someone can possibly work to call attention to forms of gendered violence, but mostly it is used as a way to discipline and police female bodies. Shaming is a slippery slope, and humiliation is always a suspect politics. In the case of Hunt, the campaign singles him out for his comments, thus shaping gender discrimination in technology as the ill-advised mindset of the individual. In other words, even if the intentions of a campaign are to disrupt sexist structure, when these campaigns circulate in an economy of visibility, the focus of the message is on individual injury, which distracts from understanding the problem as a systemic one. To be clear, there were particular consequences with this hashtag campaign, which I discuss below. Yet the source of the problem this campaign identifies is *Hunt*, not patriarchy or structural sexism. Revealing the absurdity of sexist claims hasn't changed the numbers of women who are employed at Harvard's

FIGURE 4.5.
#HeyaTimHunt
campaign, 2015.

science departments, or those who have been awarded a Nobel Prize in chemistry. It is not that #timhunt isn't political or important—efforts to reveal gender discrimination are crucial. Yet, within the economy of visibility, again, these campaigns are absorbed after a few retweets and a new one comes along. And these circuits of visibility are particularly amenable to publicly shaming individuals as a politics or to call out culture. These manifestations of popular feminism follow the logic of what Jodi Dean (2005) has called "communicative capitalism," in which political messages are circulated, rather than engaged—indeed, it is precisely the *circulation* that becomes the politics rather than a route to politics. Nonetheless, the fact that a whole slew of girls and women used technology—creating videos for YouTube, or using Twitter hashtags to aggregate responses to Tim Hunt—to demonstrate the absurdity of sexism within technology is important in in its own right.

Another popular feminist response to women in technology is the documentary *GTFO: The Movie*, about gaming, the online misogynistic harassment campaign #GamerGate (which I discuss at length later in the chapter), and the exclusion of women and girls from the world of gaming generally. Written and directed by Shannon Sun-Higginson (2015), GTFO premiered at the South by Southwest (SXSW) film festival in 2015. Unlike the two previous examples, GTFO—slang for "Get the Fuck Out"—is quite serious in its tone and aesthetic; it details not only some of the specifics of #GamerGate but also broader forms of gender discrimination in technology fields. The fact that the film was made is as important to popular feminism as what the film chronicles; feminist media production is a key popular feminist practice, as is revealing misogynistic responses to popular feminism.

The documentary details the role of women in the $20 billion gaming industry, arguing that most mainstream male gamers see gaming as their own, implicitly gendered domain: girls and women are grudgingly admitted into this realm (because we can't ban people outright), but they are meant to stay only temporarily, and should eventually leave to do things that are more relevant to their gender identity. Actually engaging in creative activity, such as gaming full time or working as a game designer, is not seen as an option—or if it is, it means, according to one gamer featured in the film, just "willing to take shit forever." The film features several women who are part of the gaming industry, or gamers themselves—including Anita Sarkeesian and Brianna Wu—who became victims of well-orchestrated harassment campaigns (such as #GamerGate), and Jennifer Hepler, who worked on the creation of the game *Dragon Age* and who was targeted on Reddit and other media sites because she included gay romances in the game.

GTFO does not merely focus on particular individuals, however. The film covers a variety of issues that frame gaming and the gaming industry, including marketing and representation, as well as some of the ways that female-identified gamers have used activism to challenge marginalization and discrimination. The film cites a game scholar, Jennifer Hammer, who offers free coding classes for girls and women, and who mentions the statistic that while 96 percent of teen girls play games, only 10–12 percent of people involved in the game industry overall are women (Sun-Higginson 2015). Another game industry professional claims that the industry is a "self-perpetuating cycle." He continues by asking, "Who is buying games? Straight white men in their twenties. So they make games to appeal to that demographic" (Sun-Higginson 2015). Yet the statistic that 96 percent of teen girls play games would certainly seem to disrupt this "self-perpetuating cycle." The argument that a target audience is young men is one that is often marshaled in the entertainment industry, from film to television to video games. This is an easy, consumer-as-sovereign defense of both the continual creation and perpetuation of underrepresentation of girls and women characters, but as the film repeatedly demonstrates, is illogical given the fact that so many girls and women are interested in gaming, at least before they are hounded out of it or get absorbed by the message that they are supposed to do other things. According to *GTFO*, any major innovation within the gaming industry remains constrained by a tried-and-true formula of violent and sexist representation. As one game developer said, "You get innovation within these genres that have already been established as interesting to men—not all men, but this very specific type of young man" (Sun-Higginson 2015). The conventional wisdom of the industry is, again, familiar: "If a whole company relies on that world [the world of straight young men] to stay afloat, it's too big a risk" to include games with a different logic and a different kind of character or plot. Despite copious evidence to the contrary, the stereotype is that gamers are men—and game developers perpetuate this stereotype by catering to it.[4]

The film thus emphasizes a dangerous fallacy: that the gaming industry sees itself as "depoliticized." A common refrain from game developers is "We're just making a game, we're not sending a message." Any game that diverges from the standard fodder of games—sports, violence, war—is seen as "political," which is why, as I elaborate on later, Zoe Quinn's *Depression Quest* was seen as an affront to the entire industry, and why adding gay romances to *Dragon Age* was considered such a threat. Of course, the fact that creating games that glorify war, violence against women, racism, and homophobia is considered somehow *not* political—"just making a game"—is a function of long-standing norms where whiteness and masculinity become invisible as vested identity categories, and are instead "just the way things are" (H. Gray 2013).

The documentary ends with a section titled "Boys Club," and argues that the sense of entitlement and cover of anonymity that provides the logic for the gaming world creates a space where men feel like they can attack women. And, like other feminist (or more broadly, even just women-identified) interventions into popular misogynistic logics and structures, the idea that the gaming world could be transformed into a more inclusive space is terrifying to some men. Feminism threatens the status quo of gaming; but in the contemporary moment of popular misogyny, this threat is countered with heightened intensity and violence.

The "boy's club" metaphor indicates a particular kind of clubhouse, one that is not simply an enclave for men but rather encompasses the entire field of gaming as one of ownership. As the film points out, misogynistic responses to women and girls in the gaming world is, like GamerGate, about desperately holding on to this ownership: as one woman in the film says, the common refrain by men in gaming is "I own this. If you're going to participate, you better shut up. Or you can get the fuck out."

GTFO, as a media production, can be situated along a continuum of popular feminism. Indeed, the recent efforts by women to develop games that challenge the industry standard in their narrative, logic, and characters are bolstered by the broader context of popular feminism. GTFO is much more overtly critical of the marginalization of women in gaming than, say, the Girls Who Code video series, which certainly points to the problem but doesn't directly challenge misogyny and patriarchy. While the Girls Who Code series is certainly funny, and points out the ridiculousness of "theories" as to why girls shouldn't be in STEM fields, the GTFO documentary calls out the deeply embedded misogynistic infrastructure of gaming. The documentary makes it clear *why* it is that there is such vitriolic harassment online; it makes an argument that men feel threatened by potential change in an industry in which they are entitled and they feel that they own. Changing the industry to be more inclusive of women as intelligent— let alone as emotionally and psychologically complex individuals—rather than merely bimbos or prostitutes, makes no sense to the group of men who violently harass women online (and indeed, might force a questioning of the violent harassment itself). A change in the logic, narrative, and characters within gaming so that women are represented as humans rather than objects would be a change for a reason that is devalued by mainstream gamers. In an industry in which, when one gamer beats another gamer, the common phrase is "I just raped you," it is clear that women, and women's bodies, are dehumanized and devalued (Sun-Higginson 2015).

A final example of media production that challenges the marginalization of women in STEM fields is the corporate campaign of the technology company Verizon. Since 2014, Verizon has paired with Girls Who Code and MAKERS, both nonprofit organizations invested in "closing the gender gap in STEM fields." Verizon sponsors a summer coding camp for girls and created an ad called "Inspire Her Mind." While these efforts, like other examples of popular feminism, may stoke public awareness of gender marginalization in STEM fields, the company frames its involvement as a matter of international competition and neoliberal entrepreneurship. Verizon's website reported, "Not enough girls are encouraged to pursue their love of science, technology, engineering and math (STEM). The greatest opportunities in the future will be high-tech jobs in STEM fields, but we're lagging behind the rest of the world, currently ranked 36th in math and 28th in science" ("Girls in STEM" 2016). Here, Verizon points to global competition as the reason girls should be encouraged to go into STEM fields. In a way similar to the "Girl Effect" campaign discussed in chapter 2, Verizon is focusing on girls becoming better economic subjects within a context of global competition, not on how, and in what ways, patriarchy and misogyny encourage a structural and ideological exclusion of girls and women from STEM fields.

The "Inspire Her Mind" ad is shot as if it were a home movie of the life of Sammy, a young white girl. The voiceovers are clearly the girl's mother and father, and each shot depicts a different stage in the girl's young life. It begins with soft focus shots of Sammy as a baby girl, with the mother saying, "Who's my pretty girl?" The next shot depicts Sammy, now about four years old, walking in a creek, picking up sticks. The mother says, "Sammy, sweetie, don't get your dress dirty." Cut to the next shot, where Sammy is about seven, at the beach playing with a starfish. The father says, "Sam, honey, you don't want to mess with that. Let's put him down." The next cut depicts Sammy as an eleven- or twelve-year-old, painting Styrofoam balls as planets, and hanging them from her bedroom ceiling as a solar system. The mother says, in a sterner voice, "Samantha. This project has gotten out of control." The next shot features a young teenager using a drill while her brother holds a science project for her. The shot begins on Samantha's painted, glittery nails, and then the father says, "Whoa! Be careful with that! Why don't you hand that to your brother." The final shot of Samantha depicts her as a high school student, walking down a hallway. She stops in front of a flyer that announces an upcoming science fair; she pauses, and then uses the reflective glass covering the flyer as a mirror as she puts on her lipstick. Text appears on the screen: "66% of 4th grade girls say they like science and math. But only 18% of all college engineering majors are female." A new voiceover begins, and says, "Our words can have a huge impact. Isn't it time we told her she's pretty brilliant too? Encourage her love of science and technology, and inspire her to change the world" ("Inspire Her Mind" 2014).

While ostensibly the Verizon campaign encourages girls to enter STEM fields, it is also, of course, an ad for a profit-driven technology company.

Situated along the popular feminism continuum I've discussed throughout this book, corporations such as Verizon are more in line with popular feminist social responsibility efforts than the independent film GTFO. "Inspire Her Mind" is like many other neoliberal feminist media artifacts in its engagement of the individual rather than a patriarchal structure. The ad, while seemingly challenging gendered constraints on femininity, nonetheless reaffirms these constraints through the play on "pretty." The statement—"isn't it time we told her that she's pretty brilliant *too*"— implies that being pretty is still just as important as using her mind. Most significantly, there is an abstraction that is key to the logic of the ad: the message that "we" should "inspire her to change the world" is not a *critique* of that world necessarily, and squarely positions individuals as agents of change, rather than positioning a context of exclusion, discrimination, and outright hostility. Her parents, not patriarchy, are to blame for her choosing lipstick over science.

In these four examples of popular feminist media productions—an online "series" created by a nonprofit organization, a corporate ad, an independent documentary, and a Twitter hashtag campaign—each makes its own intervention into the issue of girls and technology, and each relies on an economy of visibility for its circulation. Their range of political valence demonstrates the reach of popular feminism—as well as the ambivalence that is created by this broad spectrum. Each narrative occupies a different place on the continuum of popular feminism. Each production positions different actors as the key drivers of their respective narrative— accomplished female scientists, generalized "every girls" in "Inspire Her Mind" and "Why Girls Can't Code," and victims of #GamerGate and other gaming-based harassment. While all four productions are about gender discrimination within STEM fields and the gaming industries, Verizon's ad is the only one that does not directly juxtapose girls and boys in an oppositional relationship (except for the one oblique reference to "hand that to your brother"). This, of course, is logical given the late capitalist context of advertising: using "Sammy" as a generalized every girl (though she's clearly not "every girl," as she is white and middle class), and focusing on the "positive" message of inspiration and changing the world, and resisting a sharp feminist, or even political, critique of the gendered nature of STEM fields even while pointing out gendered inequities, the ad works diligently to not alienate the consumers of Verizon. While the "Why Girls Can't Code" is a series created by the nonprofit organization Girls Who

Code, the organization hired an ad firm, New York–based McCann, for guidance on how to demonstrate the ridiculousness of the idea that girls can't code simply because they are girls. The series is funny to be sure, and the deadpan discussion of female biology as the reason the girls don't understand technology is certainly clever. Susan Young, group creative director at McCann, commented, "There's been a lot of work done about the gender gap in STEM, but it's been more emotional and kind of encouraging girls, that if you like science you should get involved.... This campaign is a little bit more about provoking a response and reaffirming what girls already know and that is that this is really ridiculous that people think that just because you're a girl you can't do something" (cited in Monllos 2016, n.p.).

The two other media productions, however, did "provoke a response," but not necessarily one that created inclusion from the gaming and technology industries. The #timhunt campaign is politically engaged in a way that is different from either Verizon or Girls Who Code, though its focus on one individual's sexist comments clearly directs its critique toward Tim Hunt—rather than patriarchy, or even structural sexism. It is important to call out influential members of the scientific community on their sexism, but this move also contains the critique of sexism to one misguided person rather than to a misguided cultural, political, and economic context. And shaming individuals rather than focusing critique on institutions or structural formations is a political move that is often targeted to women, so it is worth considering the efficacy of these politics. Indeed, the response by Hunt himself was to resign from his position at the University of London, a move that arguably consolidates even further the individualism of the whole conflict. While it is remarkable that a handful of women tweeting out responses could cause a prominent scientist to resign, it is not clear that this move inspired the scientific community to call for a more systemic investigation into sexism in the sciences. Yet the hashtag campaign did stimulate a "backlash to the backlash," which, according to the *Washington Post*, has "some saying the problem isn't with Hunt but with those who took offense and ultimately drove him out of his position. It reflects more broadly increasing tension over shaming and blaming on social media and the willingness of people to say what's on their minds" (Bever 2015, n.p.). The article continues by citing individuals who commented on Facebook about the issue. One commenter, Gabriel Bartash, wrote on Facebook, "I think it's tragic that political correctness has become so toxic that it destroys the careers of brilliant individuals" (Bever 2015, n.p.). Again, the "broadly increasing tension over shaming and blaming on social media" is not just *any* tension; as I've argued throughout this book, the tactics of shame that characterize social media are overwhelmingly directed at women, not men. Within the tropes of injury and capacity framed within an economy of visibility, the injury here is to men, from "politically correct" women. This deflects from the possibility that it is women in science who have been injured by Hunt's comments; it is not "political correctness" that has become toxic, it is a particular version of masculinity that is toxic. This deflection is rather easily made when the logic of shaming is the political mechanism.

Toxic masculinity was a key ingredient in the reception of GTFO. The documentary is clearly the most pointedly political of the four media productions discussed here, and explicitly names misogyny as the driving force behind sexism in the gaming industry. While the three other media productions do call attention to gender exclusion in STEM fields, the documentary sees the issue as deeply structural to the gaming industry. While GTFO focuses only on the gaming industry, it implies a connection of the misogyny of #GamerGate to a wider popular feminist context, explicitly stating that the toxicity of the gaming environment is about misogyny, not a bland "political correctness." And, sure enough, after the film's release, some men responded with misogynistic vitriol. For example, on the film's IMDB page, there are a number of comments that rank the film between one and five stars. While there are some that rank it highly, the majority of the commenters gave it a ranking of one star.[5] More than that, the comments about the film are revealing in the ways in which they reiterate a by now familiar version of toxic geek masculinity. Using the lack of "veracity" of the film as a launching point for statements about whether women belong in the gaming world, the comments are disturbingly familiar in the way they characterize women as bitter, angry, stupid, and engaged in strategic warfare against men. As "Joseph Godfrey" comments on the site,

> They [women in gaming] speak on harassment commonly found in multi-player games believing the fact that they are women induces said harassment. It's an ineptitude by pervasive idiotic self-proclaims that ignore the customary "trolling" found in multi-player games. The unorganized absurd lengths that trolls will go to becomes ridiculous

in its devotion. The agenda of a troll typically is unleashing one or more cynical or sarcastic remarks on an innocent by-stander in order to frustrate them into outrage. Yet these women persistently entertain & bait these trolls; they document the absurdity and then claim it's the same as violence in the real world. ("GTFO" 2015)

Again, this is a familiar tactic: blaming systemic misogyny on a few anomalous trolls is an effective argument not merely within the #Gamer-Gate controversy but also within the pickup artist industry, men's rights organizations, and other forms of popular misogyny discussed in this book. Indeed, as Whitney Phillips (2015) has pointed out, the dynamic of trolling is that anyone who responds to "troll bait" then *deserves* to be trolled. When it then happens, it is their own fault. The tactic of positioning men as the victims of feminism, the ones who suffer injuries, is also well rehearsed; as "Joseph Godfrey" continues, "That very negativity is both where the film begins to lose some of its authenticity and possibly appeals to the misandry of absolutist feminism. The documentary spends most of its energy accusing the gaming industry of 'sexism' based solely on female characters being attractive." Another commenter, "Pepe Frijoles,"[6] makes an even bolder claim:

This is a dishonest propaganda piece in similar vein to one's you'd see from the church of Scientology or even similar to how the Nazi party did with Jews after World War 1. The sole intent of this movie was to demonize. And it does a relatively good job at that. It paints the attackers (Gamers) as not humans with rational thoughts and feelings. But as nothing but hate mongers, in order to assassinate that identity and to shame any viewer who is a gamer to feel bad. . . . Online gaming is not your hugbox, stop pretending online gaming is preschool. ("GTFO" 2015)

This commenter, like so many others within the toxic geek masculinity, sees any feminist critique of misogyny as an "attack," an "assassination," targeted at men who cherish their identities as gamers. These kinds of expressions are a call to arms for other misogynists, a call to protect the apparently rightful position of men in the gaming industry. Again, this is an example of how injury and capacity function within an economy of visibility: popular misogyny is used to recuperate men's capacity as the "true" subjects of the gaming world.

During the National Basketball Association Championships that aired on US television in 2016, General Electric (GE) debuted a new ad. The ad features a middle-aged white couple talking to their twenty-something son about his new job at GE. The father is depicted as excited that his son will be in the field of manufacturing, and brings out a heavy iron hammer his own "pappy" used to use. The son, looking nervous, says, "Yes, GE makes powerful machines, but I'll be writing the code that will allow those machines to share information with each other." His father interrupts, and says, "You can't lift it up, can you? Go ahead, lift the hammer!" The son awkwardly looks on, while the nervous mother ends the commercial by reassuring her son, "It's okay, though, you're going to change the world." In these thirty savvy seconds, GE capitalizes on a generational conflict within industries, and nods to technology's rise; the ad's tagline is "It's an industrial company. It's a digital company." But more subtly, the ad captures a conflict with the way we see masculinity: a familiar, and enduring, conflict about whether manliness is about brawn or brains, but updated here for the age of code.

The ad reflects the cultural infrastructure within the contemporary realm of science and technology, one that both legitimates and perpetuates popular misogyny: toxic geek masculinity.[7] The term "geek" in popular parlance typically refers to someone who likes computers and/ or science; but as important, it also refers to some kind of broader social awkwardness, as well as, perhaps, a love of arcane trivia or science fiction. As Christina Dunbar-Hester (2015) points out, a dictionary definition of "geek" depicts geeks as unsociable and obsessive, especially when it comes to computers and technology. Indeed, geek masculinity has emerged from a more depreciative connotation in recent years, in large part because there has been a larger cultural acceptance and appreciation of those "geeks" who have been instrumental in changing the technological landscape (and thus the political and economic landscapes as well) in the United States (and beyond). Yet, there remains a struggle for subject-position in a culture that continues to value hypermasculinity above all other masculinities. As Kristina Bell, Christopher Kampe, and Nicholas Taylor (2015, n.p.) point out, the stereotype of geeks as "weak, easily bullied, and socially awkward males who lack social skills, athletic abilities, and physical attractiveness" remains intact but is also challenged in the contemporary historical moment when technology is a center of power, because those same socially awkward males "are perceived as possessing mastery over digital technologies" (Bell, Kampe, and Taylor 2015, n.p., citing Kendall 1999 and 2011).

The prominence of Silicon Valley, and the emphasis on technological creativity, has propelled the socially awkward, white, heterosexual techie to new heights of cultural visibility. Bill Gates, Steve Jobs, and Mark Zuckerberg, all self-admittedly socially awkward white men, are the most famous of geek men, occupying very visible spaces in cultural and economic life, and embodying a new, albeit precarious, version of masculinity. But geek masculinity is certainly not new to the twenty-first century. Indeed, the 1990s was a key decade for this variation of masculinity, in which Kevin Smith movies such as *Clerks* (1994) and *Chasing Amy* (1997) highlighted the socially awkward man desperately trying to get the girl, and television series such as *My So-Called Life* (1994–95) and *Freaks and Geeks* (1999–2000) offered a popular platform for geek subjectivity. Thus, this brand of geek has also become fodder for popular culture, and the twenty-first century has seen a bevy of top-rated television shows that feature male geeks as lead characters (and characters who are attractive to women), such as *The Big Bang Theory, Community, Silicon Valley, Dr. Who*, and *The IT Crowd*, among others. Blogs and websites are dedicated to the difficulties of living in the West as a geek; with names such as Dr. Nerdlove and The Good Men Project, these sites offer dating advice, parenting advice, and general reassurance about living as a geek in a culture that values a more alpha hypermasculinity. As an added reassurance to actual geeks, the geek characters in media culture are often paired up with conventionally beautiful women, which offers a popular kind of "evidence" that geeks are not only the new center of power in terms of their occupation but that they can also get the (right) girl.

So when does geek masculinity become toxic masculinity? Toxic masculinity is at the heart of the culture of popular misogyny I discuss throughout this book, but it is certainly not a new phenomenon. Toxic masculinity involves a sense of entitlement in all realms of culture, economy, and social life: careers, activities, habits, routines, and rituals. I've explored a variety of manifestations of toxic masculinity in this book, from public shaming of women's sexual practices and bodies to revenge porn and the pickup artist community to rape culture. And, as I've detailed throughout this book, the varied expressions and practices that compose what I call popular misogyny do not emanate from any one, generalized constitu-ency, and, in fact, do not emerge solely from men. However, within an economy of visibility, toxic masculinity circulates more widely than ever before, and often finds validation within a discourse of injury of men by women (and feminists in particular).

The toxicity of toxic geek masculinity is connected to the historical moment in which it emerges; in the contemporary moment of the early 2000s, it is a toxicity that is both aided and distributed by social media. Toxic geek masculinity requires both structural and ideological scaffolding for validation (Turner 2009). In the contemporary moment, when technol-ogy is widely understood as a center of power, geek masculinity finds new validation and support—for once, geeks and nerds are seen as powerful, rather than weak, versions of masculinity. Thus, when women, through popular feminism, challenge this newfound validation and masculine sub-ject position by insisting on inclusion and recognition, the injury to geek masculinity is seen as severe, a return to a historical moment when geeks and nerds were victims of other versions of toxic masculinity in the form of the aggressive alpha male who humiliated them (Penny 2014).

However, unlike the earlier, more benevolent versions of geek mascu-linity that we saw in popular media, contemporary toxic geek masculinity is a culture that encourages violence against women, and creates a context within science and technology communities that is not only unwelcoming but dangerous. The injury to male geeks is framed as a call to arms, in which women are targeted as the instigators of the injuries. Indeed, women are framed within toxic geek masculinity as the central problematic issue in their lives: the narrative here is that not only are women encroach-ing on economic territories that are apparently rightly owned by men, but women have also rejected geeks throughout their lives. Toxic geek masculinity is partly a response to a perception (created and sustained through popular cultural representations, high school cliques, and frat culture on college campuses) that women are not interested in geeks because they are socially awkward and insecure. As Adrienne Massanari (2017, 332) argues, geek masculinity "both repudiates and reifies elements of hegemonic masculinity . . . geek masculinity often embraces facets of hypermasculinity by valorizing intellect over social or emotional intel-ligence. At the same time, geek masculinity rejects other hypermasculine traits, as 'the geek' may show little interest in physical sports and may also demonstrate awkwardness regarding sexual/romantic relationships."

Yet, unlike "bro" culture, which by its very name is defined as exclusively male, geek masculinity is a culture that is, ironically, founded on disrupting traditional norms of masculinity and power, especially in the ways these coalesce in conventional positions of mobility and economic success. Indeed, in 1972, Stewart Brand published an article in *Rolling Stone* magazine in which he vaunted the "computer bum," men who were dedicated to computing as a way to challenge dominant relations of power and masculinity (Turner 2006; Ensmenger 2015). As Nathan Ensmenger points out, when computer bums (always men in these histories) were seen to be violating conventional norms, "it was as the heroic outsider or iconoclast" (Ensmenger 2015, n.p.). As I discussed earlier, computing was initially a labor force occupied by women; it was only after powerful computers were created, and in turn, computers were deemed to be powerful, and salaries for programmers increased, that this field became one dominated by men (Abbate 2012; Ensmenger 2015). The masculine culture of technology, then, is not a recent phenomenon; as Susan Douglas (1989) has argued about ham radio enthusiasts in the early 1900s, technological mastery is at the heart of an American construction of masculinity. But it is often a masculinity seemingly at odds with other hegemonic constructions of masculinity, characterized by self-confidence, attractiveness to heterosexual women, and adherence to an alpha-male persona. Traditional realms such as finance and corporate culture have long been the mainstay of masculine dominance. In contrast, the realm of technology is framed through discourses of creativity, innovation, and the counterculture, and takes pride in disrupting traditional capitalism (Turner 2006; Castells 2017). The technology industries emphasize creativity and innovation as a new kind of economy, challenging traditional and conventional economies, such as finance, which work overtly to secure systems of capitalist production and consumption. This history of challenging traditional boundaries and parameters, especially the parameters of traditional masculinity, seems to be at odds with the aggressive policing of boundaries by geeks when it comes to women. If, as Manuel Castells and I have argued (Banet-Weiser and Castells 2017, 18), "the transformation of creativity in the digital culture ushers in new processes of wealth creation and destruction, as well as new forms of expressing and feeling the human experience," then why the violent reaction to feminism and women in general by geek masculinity?

When feminists in the media have pointed out the misogyny and racism of the reaction by geek men to women in technology, it is often met with a sense of disconnect, because geek men often feel that the world has been hostile to *them*, and are "likely to view themselves as perpetual outsiders and thus are unable or unwilling to recognize their own immense privilege" (Massanari 2017, 4). This assemblage of features—technical prowess, social awkwardness, and cognitive dissonance about privilege—yields a contradictory subjectivity. According to this frame, geek men have been injured by the world and, more importantly, by women. The aggressive and violent regulation and exclusion of women is a way to regain masculine capacity. Indeed, this theme of regaining masculinity forms a central logic in most forms of popular misogyny, not just geek masculinity; here I find Martha Nussbaum's (2010) rethinking of the Nietzschean idea of "ressentiment" particularly useful. Nussbaum frames online misogyny within the framework of ressentiment, where those who feel themselves to be inadequate—specifically in relation to another group—seek out ways to validate themselves. The logic of popular misogyny is that of a zero-sum game: men lose and become invisible when women win and become more visible. Popular misogyny takes a particular shape in a crisis in hegemonic masculinity, a crisis brought on by global economic collapse (as men lose their jobs and future security), by more visible efforts to diversify workplaces and cultural spaces (exemplified by a few visible successful women in technology fields), and by increasing popular feminist activism. Within this crisis, some men (particularly white working- and middle-class men, as well as men who work in technology industries) see themselves as losing cultural and political ground, relinquishing patriarchal authority (Rosin 2012; Negra and Tasker 2014). Popular misogyny is a set of discourses and practices that aim to reset the gender balance back to its "natural" patriarchal relation. As Nussbaum points out, "The weak need to affirm themselves, relieving the psychic distress that comes with subordination, by creating a virtual world, an expressive world, in which they hold sway" (Nussbaum 2010, 80). This need presents itself as a "revaluation of values," a revaluation that can occur only if women are objectified, shamed, and positioned as the means to a masculinist end.

Through this notion that the "weak need to affirm themselves," geek masculinity, again unlike "frat boy" or "bro" masculinity, is characterized by a kind of *overt* fragility—and in particular, white fragility. The privilege of whiteness is rarely acknowledged by geeks. The misogynistic reactions to popular feminism come, primarily, from often young, cis-gendered, white, heterosexual males. Again, this demographic is the group that simultaneously feels most "injured" by any form of feminism, popular or not, and that feels most entitled to react, an entitlement born of race and class privilege. As I discussed in the introduction, this seemingly contradictory move—embracing an alternative economy and way of being while simultaneously maintaining structural impediments to that very way of being, such as racism and sexism—has a history in other identity movements, especially when we look at racial identity. This injury is most often felt as a kind of threat—a threat to a kind of masculine confidence, or a threat to what is seen as an "earned" sexual expectation, or a threat to a job in a realm that has historically catered to men (and continues to): technology. Indeed, I argue throughout this book that all forms of hypermasculinity are deeply, and ambivalently, intertwined with fragility; there are a number of contextual factors that have contributed to a contemporary form of white masculine fragility—many of which are outside the realm of technology, such as economic recession, shifting gender roles in both workplaces and households, and precarious labor positions. However, it is helpful to understand the broader picture of white masculine fragility as a way to understand its embeddedness within toxic geek masculinity.

Not all masculinities are inevitably toxic and/or violent. But toxic geek masculinity finds a home within a broader context of popular misogyny, and as such, is illuminated within an economy of visibility. Much as the spectacular visibility of popular feminism works to secure it as a primary way of understanding all feminisms, the visibility of toxic geek masculinity functions in a similar way, so that it often becomes the lens through which all geek masculinity is interpreted. As Bell, Kampe, and Taylor (2015) argue, much of the scholarship on toxic masculinity within technology focuses on the misogyny and racism of specific mainstream gaming communities, rather than other communities within the tech world that reject toxic masculinity. There are multiple, and intersectional, masculine subject positions within technology. Part of what I am arguing throughout this book is that in any given cultural and economic landscape, certain subject positions become especially visible—this does not, however, obscure the existence of others. On the contrary, I am suggesting that this lack of visibility is *actually part* of the problem.

It is precisely the fragility, the precariousness, of toxic masculinity that is at issue here; it is the *instability* of masculinity that requires a constant maintenance. It is the ambivalence of masculinity, the ways in which it is a constantly negotiated terrain, that is of interest to me. This negotiation of masculinity transforms into an often literal call to arms, in which popular misogyny often turns to violence as the only way to express itself. The ways in which masculinity is secured through misogynistic and racist expressions and acts demonstrates the ambivalence of masculinity, not its certainty: "It is the product/ongoing production of contingent, historically situated relations of power" (Bell, Kampe, and Taylor 2015, n.p.). Geek masculinity is ambivalent because it is, again, a constant struggle between the embodiment of race, gender, and economic privilege and, at the same time, a kind of alienation from hypermasculine norms (Bell, Kampe, and Taylor 2015). Gender is always a *crisis*, always something that finds itself in a defensive posture. Contemporary masculinities, characterized by fragility, need to be sutured consistently.

Geek masculinity, we might say, is in the throes of an unprecedented validation within popular culture and the media. Yet there has also been a great deal of media attention to the continued hardships involved in being a geek—hardships that predominantly involve social awkwardness around women. There have been dozens of self-reflective articles and blog posts just in the last few years that have detailed, often from a personal perspective, the personal difficulties of being a male geek, especially in light of accusations—from feminists and others—of the tech world's rampant misogyny. For example, in 2014, MIT professor Scott Aaronson (2014) wrote a comment on his blog about how he, as an awkward shy guy, doesn't feel "privileged," the accusation that many women in tech communities were lobbing against men and the increasing misogynistic violence. According to Aaronson, he has himself felt awkward, especially during his attempts to attract women, even though he says explicitly that he has read feminist theory (Aaronson 2014). One interpretation of his explicit acknowledgement of feminism is that feminism itself is to blame for his lack of success with women; since feminism fights for resources for women who are victims of harassment and sexual assault, those who benefited from feminism were then *more* privileged than men. In Aaronson's words, he felt victimized by the fact that there are apparently no resources for shy, awkward men such as himself. Not surprisingly, there were a variety of heated responses by women and feminists to Aaronson's comments, and the exchange soon became widely circulated. While it doesn't make sense to deny Aaronson's feelings of being "bullied" for being shy and awkward (especially in a culture that is still dominated by alpha hypermasculinity), seeing this affective dynamic as the "fault" of feminism is to obfuscate the varied ways in which the reproduction of masculine privilege occurs within the guise of victimhood. As feminist Laurie Penny has stated about Aaronson, "Feminism, however, is not to blame for making life hell for 'shy, nerdy men.' Patriarchy is to blame for that" (Penny 2014, n.p.).

The Aaronson example is instructive: it reveals that, at least for some men—especially those who are not conventionally hypermasculine—patriarchy is also hostile. And thus geek culture, along with feminism, might be a place to challenge these kinds of social and cultural barriers. But patriarchy is not the target of most of the vitriol coming from masculine geek culture, because it is not seen as the problem. Instead, it is usually the encroachment of women in a traditional male domain that is the issue. Making women, and feminism, the problem works to preserve patriarchy, not challenge it. Above all else, feminism is the threat to geeks fully realizing their masculinity. This is remarkably consistent with the logics and rationales of other practices of neomasculinity that I have detailed in this book. I say "remarkable" because the economic and cultural context for, say, the pickup artist industry, or revenge porn, is seemingly quite different from geek masculinity.

The injury to geek masculinity, apparently caused solely by the presence of women within technology fields, took a particularly horrific turn in what came to be called GamerGate, a calculated series of attacks by male gamers on female gamers and game developers, under the guise of "ethics of games journalism."

Hidden Injuries: GamerGate

In August 2014, a relatively small group of mainstream male gamers and social media users began to use the #GamerGate hashtag; their purported purpose was ostensibly legitimate—to register their objection to questionable journalistic ethics. That purpose, however, was a ruse for a chilling misogyny.[8] As Derek Johnson writes, "These self-identified gamers branded as 'social justice warriors' those feminist, queer, and antiracist critics and developers who wanted to expand the all-white straight boys club of gaming" (Johnson 2016, 2). These gamers were primarily concerned with a few increasingly prominent women in the gaming world, whom they labeled "social justice warriors": Anita Sarkeesian, Brianna Wu, and Zoe Quinn. Sarkeesian is a feminist media critic who hosts a web series on YouTube, Feminist Frequency, intended to create a space where feminist theory is accessible to everyone, not merely those trained in feminist theory, such as academics. The series takes a feminist approach to a variety of popular cultural forms, but it wasn't until Sarkeesian took on the gaming industry that she received national attention. Sarkeesian used the crowdsource funding of Kickstarter to launch a series of episodes devoted to gaming's gender representations, "Women v. Tropes in Video Games." This installment of Feminist Frequency critiqued the long-standing sexist representations of women in video games, who surface most frequently as bimbos or prostitutes or hyperfeminine subservient beings, and who are often violently killed during the course of a game. Within hours, the comments section of Feminist Frequency was filled with threats of rape and other violence, and Sarkeesian's Wikipedia page was hacked. After the episode was funded, Sarkeesian came under attack for her "questionable ethics" in reporting what has been a long-known feature of many video games. Unlike other reporters whose ethics are questioned, however, Sarkeesian was threatened online with rape and death; images of video game characters raping her were sent to her; she was doxed (her personal information, such as her phone number and address, was revealed online); and one gamer created a game, "Beat Up Anita Sarkeesian," that had the simple premise of making Sarkeesian's face as bloody as possible. Sarkeesian became globally visible when she was scheduled to give a lecture at Utah State University and a terrorism threat was reported; apparently, a man called the university and said he would shoot her and the whole auditorium if she spoke. When Sarkeesian asked the university if they would temporarily lift their concealed-carry law, the university refused and Sarkeesian canceled the talk (Robertson 2014).

Also in 2014, Zoe Quinn, a game developer, released her game *Depression Quest*, a game about emotions and affect, intended to be an alternative to the violent nature of many video games. After the game received positive reviews from some in the gaming world, an ex-boyfriend of Quinn's wrote a lengthy blog post that insisted that Quinn had sex with a game reviewer in order to receive the positive reviews (despite the fact that this particular reviewer did not, in fact, review Quinn's game). The blog post went on to accuse Quinn of cheating on the ex-boyfriend with five different men. After the blog was posted, Quinn was subject to violent harassment, including rape and death threats. As David Whitford (2015, n.p.) points out, "Quinn argues that this is what happens when an overlooked but nevertheless proud male subculture feels threatened by the main-

FIGURE 4.6. Anita Sarkeesian, Feminist Frequency, "Women v. Tropes in Video Games," 2013.

stream. Women represent 'an invasion into a territory they've become quite comfortable in.'"

Brianna Wu is also a game developer with her own game development company, and she produces a podcast. On one of her podcasts, Wu discussed the increasing online harassment of women in the gaming world. According to legal scholar Danielle Citron, 70 percent of online attacks are on women and involve some kind of sexual comment or threat (Citron 2014). Wu took aim at these harassers: "You cannot have 30 years of portraying women as bimbos, sex objects, second bananas, cleavage-y eye candy. Eventually it normalizes this treatment of women. And I think something is really sick and broken in our culture" (Wu, quoted in Whitford 2015, n.p.). Wu has also been outspoken about the sense of alienation that many gamers apparently feel, especially when it comes to attracting heterosexual women. When Wu exposed this "defensive misogyny," she was then subject to its violent expression. In one series of especially vicious tweets, @spacekatgai went on a rampage, beginning with a (by comparison) moderate "You just made a shitty game nobody liked. That's it. Nobody will care when you die." The tweets escalated in violence: "If you have any kids, they're going to die too. I don't give a fuck. They'll grow up to be feminists anyway"; "Your mutilated corpse will be on the front page of Jezebel tomorrow and there isn't jack shit you can do about"; and "I've got a K-bar and I'm coming to your house so I can shove it up your ugly feminist cunt."

The violence in these tweets is directed at Wu not only because she's a woman but also and especially because she's a *feminist.*

As Arthur Chu, a gamer who has been critical of #GamerGate, has argued, the popular identity of gamers (by those outside the gamer world) has been demonized, characterized as a group of alienated losers (the oft-heard stereotype of the man in his pajamas playing games in his mother's basement). Because gamers have been mocked and alienated within popular media culture, the world of gaming is seen as a refuge, a respite from this humiliating emasculation. Unfortunately, the space of refuge for geeks takes shape by demonizing and objectifying women, especially those women who criticize the politics of this refuge. That is, women who dare to critique the world of gaming—which at least some male gamers hold dear as the only space in which they hold a semblance of power—are invading territory in need of protection. As Chu argues, many male gamers "readily invoke the high-school language of 'bullying' to characterize the opposition they face from the gaming 'establishment' and the mainstream media. The relentless attacks on the women they target as 'attention whores' bear all the earmarks of defensive misogyny, the nasty attitude of the nerdy, awkward guy who's convinced 'popular girls' are all secretly taunting him" (Chu 2014a).

Adrienne Shaw offers a crucial insight into gaming culture, arguing that "we must contextualize the sexism, racism, homophobia, and other biases of game culture within broader systems of oppression. Violence in games, game culture, and the gaming industry are not unique to gaming" (Shaw 2014). While the tweets sent to Brianna Wu threatening to rape and kill her and the "Beat Up Anita Sarkeesian" game are horrific in their bold misogyny, they are also part of a larger continuum of more mainstream misogynistic expressions and practices. As Shaw points out, "Treating gaming as an isolated realm makes this misogyny a spectacle at the same time it normalizes the oppressive behavior within mainstream gamer cultures" (Shaw 2014). Like Lisa Nakamura's (2013) concept of the technological "glitch" that I discuss in chapter 2, the move to characterize misogyny as isolated events, whether in the form of anomalous trolls, mentally ill individuals, or as mere social media spectacle, is a key strategy in the contemporary moment. And this strategy, as Shaw argues, normalizes all forms of oppressive behavior.

Yet, as Shaw points out, there does seem to be something about gaming that strikes a particular kind of powerful—and violent—chord. The sexism in mainstream video games, evident in their relentlessly cleavaged design, as well as in their production and promotion, is long documented; in 2001, when the game *Tomb Raider* was created, the hypersexual character of Lara Croft was debated—and defended—over multiple media platforms (Shaw 2014). The critique of Lara Croft was not met with death and rape threats, however. What is new in the current moment? While I agree with Shaw that "many of the attacks [in GamerGate] did not merely deny a woman's right to be present in a male-dominated virtual space but flat out rejected *anyone's* right to critique games as cultural texts," I also feel that an emphasis on rejecting anyone's rights to critique games *masks* the misogyny inherent in these attacks (Shaw 2014). #GamerGate can be considered alongside other "toxic technocultures" populated by users who employ online forums to spew hatred about and encourage violence against women. This networked misogyny also includes the open-source platform Reddit, which is a particularly inviting site for toxic technocultures, because anyone can create their own community of interest, called a "subreddit," that is moderated by a subreddit user.[9] Reddit is, as Massanari ([2015] 2017) has pointed out, a rich context for geek culture, precisely because of the sheer multitude of subreddits, many of which focus on technology, science, popular culture, and gaming. Massanari also argues that Reddit serves "as a nexus for various toxic technocultures to thrive," in part because the assumed subject of many subreddits is a cisgendered white male (Massanari [2015] 2017, 333). Indeed, Reddit, like other manifestations of popular misogyny I discuss in this book, is part of the "manosphere," that increasingly relevant term referring to the portion of the web that supports and encourages misogyny—a portion that seems to be growing every day. As the Southern Poverty Law Center's *Intelligence Report* "Misogyny: The Sites" states, "The so-called 'manosphere' is peopled with hundreds of websites, blogs and forums dedicated to savaging feminists in particular and women, very typically American women, in general. Although some of the sites make an attempt at civility and try to back their arguments with facts, they are almost all thick with misogynistic attacks that can be astounding for the guttural hatred they express" (SPLC 2012). Among other sites, SPLC has identified the subreddit Mens Rights as a hate site.

Using the technological idyll of freedom and choice, Reddit operates under a mandate of "free speech," which means that, except in particularly egregious cases, it does not moderate content. Interviewed by the BBC in 2012, the former CEO of Reddit, Yishan Wong, stated, "We stand for free speech. This means we are not going to ban distasteful subreddits. We will not ban legal content even if we find it odious or if we personally condemn it" ("Reddit Will Not Ban" 2012, n.p.). The site also protects the identity of all users, and does not require an email address for a user to post something. While these policies have been lauded as encouraging truly democratic communication and the open sharing of information, it has also allowed for hundreds of misogynist and racist subreddits to flourish, with only the most odious being banned from the site (and then only after media attention and protests by other Reddit users). After an exposé in the mainstream media in 2011, Reddit closed down the subreddit "jailbait," a site that depicted teenage girls in provocative poses. Reddit has also hosted "creepshots," in which sexualized images of women were posted without the women's knowledge, as well as "beatingwomen," which featured graphic depictions of violence against women. As I discuss in chapter 2, "The Fappening" (slang for masturbating) was a subreddit that hosted nude photos of celebrities that were hacked from their personal computers, and was eventually closed down, but not before hundreds of photos were distributed without consent.

In 2013, amid increasing media scrutiny, Reddit hired Ellen Pao as interim CEO. Pao was already known in the technology community for bringing a lawsuit of sexism against her former employer, venture capitalist firm Kleiner Perkins Caufield Byers, when she was passed over for a major promotion. After being hired, she immediately created new antiharassment policies and rewrote the Reddit user rules to prevent the harassment of other users. Using these new policies, she banned five subreddits, all known for their violent personal harassment and glorification of racist murders and rape: "fatpeoplehate," "hamplanethatred," "transfag," "neofag," and "shitniggerssay" (Lopez 2015). The backlash was swift. Reddit users not only created hundreds of racist, misogynistic threads about Pao but also began to advocate for her dismissal, including a Change.org petition calling for her termination that garnered over 200,000 signatures (Lopez 2015). In 2015, Pao resigned. As Susanna Schrobsdorff said in *Time* magazine about Pao's resignation, "Pao became the face of change. The controversial, 'difficult' female face of unwelcome, unholy change" (Schrobsdorff 2015, n.p.).

While Pao managed to shut down five of the more controversial subreddits, thousands more exist, and new ones emerge every day. Pao should be commended for highlighting some of the most egregious subreddits, but when they are seen, and challenged, as discrete message threads rather than as an intricate part of a structure that nurtures misogyny within the guise of free speech, there is nothing to stop other subreddits that crop up in their stead.[10] The misogyny of these subreddits is not limited to merely abstract expressions of hate; threats, harassment, doxing, stalking, and other violence, both cyber and offline, occur on a regular basis. For example, a prominent subreddit, "The Red Pill," proclaims its link to a "red pill" moment, a metaphor from the dystopic film *The Matrix*, in which the hero swallows a red pill and awakens to the way the world "really" is, rather than the enslaved, docile obliviousness he had previously inhabited. In 2016, "The Red Pill" subreddit had 141,966 members, who were primarily white, early thirties, male, and conservative (Lopez 2015). Some of the different threads on this subreddit are titled "Donald Trump's statement is really more about women being whores than him being a sexual predator," "Selecting a wife: you can lower your odds of divorce around 10% through proper vetting," and "Can MGTOW [Men Going Their Own Way] ever be a valid choice, or is it just giving up?" The last thread led with this summary, which also summarizes many of the subreddit threads about women: "Women want to be led. Leading is an inherently masculine treat that makes you more attractive (and not only in the eyes of women). The opposite—being undecided and doubtful—is a sign of weakness. It's always better to ooze decisiveness and leadership as in most cases girls will follow. Just that can get you much further and quicker than trying to work out compromise or—yuck—asking her for everything" ("Women Want to Be Led" 2016, n.p.). Indeed, many of these subreddits and other manifestations of toxic masculinity end up sounding almost exactly the same—women have stolen power from men, women just want to be dominated, men need to have more confidence.

To be clear, there is nothing inherent in geek culture that determines toxicity or misogyny. Those men who have offered explanations for geek culture have noted that they felt generally alienated from a hypermasculine, corporate-dominated culture and economy, and thus found solace, and authority, in the world of computers, algorithms, and games (Chu 2014; Rensin 2014; Bell, Kampe, and Taylor 2015). Yet what we are seeing is a move from a general sense of alienation and marginalization—an affective state that nearly all of us, except for the very few privileged by gender, race, and class, feel either sporadically or constantly—to a violent

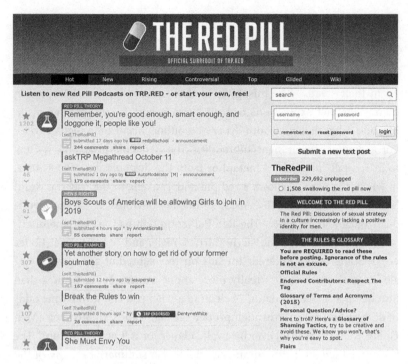

FIGURE 4.7. "The Red Pill" subreddit, 2015.

attack on those who are seeking change or justice. This move from general alienation to misogynistic violence is encouraged by an economy of visibility, as well as the tropes of injury and capacity. In an article detailing his own past as a "troll," Emmett Rensin (2014) insightfully parses the reasons that "trolling" has shifted from admittedly annoying, but merely adolescent, pranking to violence, hatred, and vitriol. In the early 2000s, as a teenager, Rensin and his troll friends would prank Microsoft executives or celebrities, who were targeted not only because of their positions of power but also because they responded in a defensive way—precisely the goal for trolls. But they weren't targeted because they were critiquing sexism or racism in games and technology.

This shift in trolling from annoying to violent is in part because of the economy of visibility that supports digital culture. In wondering what changed, or what motivated this shift in target, tone, and intensity of harassment, Rensin speculates that in the early 2000s there weren't as many visible spaces to create and produce media; the self-reflexivity of bloggers, who increasingly write about their own vulnerabilities as well as larger social and cultural injustices, has created a landscape that exposes dominant power relations in a less constrained way, and in turn, has made it easier for trolls to identify these individuals as targets. Again, this is the crux of the dynamic between popular feminism and popular misogyny, in which an economy of visibility allows for more popular feminist expressions to be circulated, which in turn has allowed for the increasing visibility of popular misogyny as a response to popular feminism. Certainly this landscape is a crucial element in the reactionary response of toxic technocultures, though it is not the only element. That is, the barriers of entry for ordinary people writing and expressing and making media has certainly relaxed in the past ten years, and thus the space of visibility has grown. But patriarchy has, in many ways, disturbingly remained the same. Acknowledging the confluence of factors involved in trolling, Rensin points out:

> To subscribe to the theory that trolling targets anything trolls see as a sacred cow without any underlying political agenda of their own is to believe that trolls are now taking aim at the least among us is just a reaction to how much the mainstream has begun to accept those voices. Feminism is in—therefore, it ought to be mocked. Yet this explanation seems inadequate. It strikes me as too easy to see trolling as some force of nature not explicable by political motive. Moreover, such an explanation would seem to place the blame on activists for their harassment—"If you want to be left alone, stop being so successful and popular." (Rensin 2014, n.p.)

The visibility of popular feminism, then, allows for, indeed demands, a response from popular misogyny. As Whitney Phillips (2015) has pointed out regarding trolls, this instinct to blame the victim is a familiar conservative move, one that uses the guise of individual "freedom" and "free choice" as a justification for discrimination and targeted violence. Focusing on individuals is a key mechanism within the economy of visibility, where the visibility of individuals becomes the focus, rather than the structure of racism and sexism. We can see this logic at work in dismissive "if you want" statements: "If you want to work at Google, then go work at Google," "If you want to be left alone, stop being so popular," and in 2016, when Kim Kardashian was tied up and her jewelry stolen, "If you want to not be robbed, stop posting Instagram pictures of your jewelry." Blaming victims for their harassment, or claiming that they bring the violence on themselves, not only abdicates responsibility from those being aggressive or hostile but also relies on a vague notion of endless choice, the implicit assumption that we are all able to do exactly what we "want." Claiming that women and people of color should simply accept the consequences of doing "what you want" deflects blame from the perpetrators of violence, obscures the way racist and sexist structures are sustained not only by individuals but also by policy, law, and material life. As Rensin (2014, n.p.) states, "Trolling as an impulse has always been largely the domain of white men—and especially of those acutely aware of a world where the theoretical foundation of their inherited power is crumbling. They—we—are all anxious. The difference is in how we cope." This anxiety, the state of injury that many white men find themselves to be in, a state not simply made more complicated by women and anyone of color, but explicitly seen as *caused* by them, forms the core logic of popular misogyny. Women and people of color, who have decidedly not inherited power, are more and more often struggling for space and place in a world that continues to be dominated by white men. As I've argued in this chapter, some of that struggle takes place in the world of technology, where technological competence has long been thought to be a naturally masculine—and in the United States anyway, an implicitly white—domain.

Networks of Popular Feminism and Misogyny

None of the examples discussed here is a discrete, isolated example of popular feminism or popular misogyny. Each is a node in a wider network of popular feminist and popular misogynistic discourses. The links that connect these nodes are multiple: they are media sites such as YouTube, which allows users to upload documentaries such as *GTFO*; they are the blogosphere, where spaces for critical, self-reflective (and critically self-reflective) expression are available and accessible in wider ways for both viewers and authors. Some of the links that intersect networks of popular feminism and popular misogyny involve media production itself, such as coding or creating a video game. Some involve education, and how children are taught differently based on their genders. Within popular feminism, though the wider goal—inclusion of women and girls in STEM fields and gaming industries—might be shared, each node also has an individual emphasis: *GTFO* recognizes and directly critiques structural misogyny; Girls Who Code argues for a more "inclusive, well-rounded" realm of technology; #timhunt challenges specific sexist stereotypes in the world of science; and Verizon encourages girls to pursue science and technology so that they can become better economic players in a global capitalist competition.

Within popular misogyny, #GamerGate is a reflection of a deeply insecure, fragile toxic geek masculine community that attacks women as a way of reassuring themselves that they are masculine enough. Open-source platforms such as Reddit are shaped by ideologies of free speech and belief in open access and freedom of choice and expression; these "freedoms" then function as a way to justify hosting scores of misogynistic hate sites. Toxic technocultures are deeply ambivalent, a context that attempts to maintain a dominant, though always precarious, masculinity.

I point out these differences not to make sharp hierarchical distinctions between forms of political expression. Both popular feminism and popular misogyny are networked continuums, with a variety of nodes that are triggered depending on historical context, power relations, and neoliberal markets. So, toxic geek masculinity is validated by a broader context of white masculine fragility, one that extends historically to the civil rights era. #GamerGate occurs at a particular historical moment because of an increasing visibility of female gamers and game developers, and a gradually decreasing set of barriers to entry for women using their technological skills. Reddit relies upon a much broader ethos of creativity that has become a center of power in capitalism, extending well beyond Silicon Valley to Silicon Alley to London to Hong Kong. While the specificities of the examples discussed here are important, I'm just as interested in how they are all part of a constantly moving terrain of popular feminism and popular misogyny. Because this terrain moves, and is often fraught, it is difficult to pin down, to determine its exact goals and motivations. The Verizon campaign feels like a crass version of what Andi Zeisler has called "marketplace feminism," commodifying a feminist ideal of inclusion and harnessing it to build Verizon's brand and enhance the company's bottom line; but it is also the case that commodifying feminism does not always neutralize it (Zeisler 2016). Indeed, even a banal ad campaign can spread a version of feminism, and make it more available and accessible.

But it is precisely this availability—the fact that the globe's biggest companies now pander to feminist ideas, however distorted or market-driven they may be—that encourages and validates popular misogyny. The popularization is a kind of war cry—no longer confined to scholarly feminist enclaves or radical activism, popular feminism has opened up a debate among feminists and nonfeminists alike. But it has also generated uproar among misogynists, a call to arms fueled by fear and panic. There is something crucial at stake in popularizing feminism. The struggle, the response and call between and within popular feminism and popular misogyny that I have examined in this book, is a struggle over power, meaning, and identity.

CONCLUSION. RAGE

Rage. The most conventional definition of "rage" is powerful, extreme, sometimes violent anger. But "rage" is also used as a verb: one can rage *against* something one hates; or it can refer to something out of control, like a raging fire. And "rage" can also mean something very popular, the latest trend: it's *all the rage.*

As I reflect on the years I spent researching and writing this book, I realize that one of the central logics of the relationship between popular feminism and popular misogyny is rage, in all its manifestations. These different meanings of "rage," as violent anger, as a hateful or out-of-control action, or as something very popular, trace the dimensions of the mirroring of popular feminism and popular misogyny. The very *popularity* of popular feminism, as something that is all the rage in the contemporary moment, provokes the violent rage of misogyny. That is, the visibility of popular feminism, the way it occupies a spotlight in multiple media platforms, brings into bold relief gender asymmetries in culture, politics, and economics. This focus, in turn, incurs a misogynistic reaction, marshaling the tropes of injury and capacity emanating from feminism and transforming these into specific injuries felt by men. Indeed, the *transformation* between these senses of rage—from "all the rage" to angry rage—maps onto the funhouse mirror distortion that I have traced throughout this book.

While popular misogyny is not overtly celebrated in the mainstream in the way popular feminism has been for the past several years, misogynistic expressions seem to more easily translate into actual *structural* changes. As I've traced in this book, at a time when there is a dramatic increase in organizations (both corporate and nonprofit) dedicated to empowerment and equality for girls and women, there is a similar increase in men's rights organizations and "meninism," a series of discourses and practices about the apparent difficulties of being a man in the twenty-first century, amid all this feminism. At a time when girls' self-esteem and sexual agency are the focus of new corporate industries, federal funding, and educational programs, there is also what seems to be an explosion of rape and sexual assault cases on college campuses and elsewhere, as well as the cultural and media trope of "the pickup artist," a set of guides on how to seduce women who would not otherwise be interested. At a time when women and girls are told to "lean in" and demand more for themselves in the workplace, there is a dramatic uptick in the number of reproductive rights that have been formally retracted. At a time when there is a robust consumer market *for* girls and women, emphasizing confidence and self-love, there is a growing market *in* girls, as we see in the harrowing increase in sexual and human trafficking around the globe. And at a time when girls are encouraged to become a central part of the world of technology, from coding to STEM fields, there are online misogynistic movements such as #Gamer-Gate, where men threaten women with death and rape for their participation in the technological sphere. Feminist logics of confidence, competence, self-esteem, and sexual agency are rerouted by popular misogyny, which then uses these logics to center men as discriminated against and in need of recuperation and reparation. If successful, this rerouting works to *shore up*, rather than challenge, structural sexism and racism.

Both popular feminism and popular misogyny revolve around vulnerability and resistance—and often, resistance *to* vulnerability. Popular feminism recognizes the vulnerability of women (and thus is distinguished from the "girl power" of postfeminism), but it then turns to already established structures of paternalistic power to challenge that vulnerability, thus wanting women to be more "confident" in the economic and political spheres, with calls for female CEOs and for more girls and women to learn to code. As Judith Butler, Zeynep Gambetti, and Leticia Sabsay (2016, 3) ask, "How, then, is the political demand to address these issues to be directed towards those institutions that should be responding to those conditions, at the same time that we seek to resist the models of power represented by those institutions? Are we stuck in the situation in which there are two opposing alternatives, paternalism and victimization? And in accepting those alternatives, do we not reinstate a gendered opposition?" This is a key point: this is why the refusal of popular feminism to challenge or even seriously critique patriarchy can potentially only reproduce those conditions that create and support gender asymmetry in the first place.

Vulnerability is the central logic to the tropes of injury and capacity I trace in this book, those tropes that amplify and mobilize both popular feminism and popular misogyny in an economy of visibility. As Butler, Gambetti, and Sabsay point out, claims of vulnerability can shore up power for those without it, but vulnerability can also "be claimed by those who seek to rationalize the subjugation of minorities," such as when "feminism is figured as a castrating 'threat' to ostensibly vulnerable men" (2016, 9; see also Gilson 2014). Injury, or vulnerability to injury, is recast in the relationship between popular feminism and popular misogyny as fragility, thus defanging it as a condition of possibility for politics, social change, and racial justice.

But while the politics of popular feminism may be attenuated through a discourse of vulnerability, the stakes of misogynistic rage and vulnerability are high. Misogyny has been weaponized in the political institutions of the US state, as well as in other state institutions around the world. I therefore turn now to where I started this book, with the campaign and subsequent election of Donald Trump as the president of the United States. The election of this unapologetically racist, misogynist candidate at a time when feminism is supposedly more popular than ever only makes sense when understood in the framework of the funhouse mirror of popular feminism and popular misogyny.

"I'm With Her": Hillary Clinton and Popular Feminism

Despite the high visibility of popular feminism's aspirational messages of self-confidence, high self-esteem, and empowerment, the US presidential race in 2016 often rendered these messages meaningless. When Trump consistently remarked upon women's appearances during his campaign and after his election, comparing them with animals ("dogs" and "pigs"), fat shaming, and generally criticizing all women who did not follow a conventional, highly idealized definition of feminine beauty, it was difficult to reconcile with the popular feminist exhortation for women and girls to accept themselves as "beautiful the way they are." This struggle manifested in the campaign of US presidential candidate Hillary Clinton, which broadly adopted a popular feminist mantle as a way to appeal to voters.

As I've argued throughout this book, the messages and practices of popular feminism are those that circulate within an economy of visibility, and we were certainly witness to this circulation with the campaign of Clinton. As the first woman from a mainstream party to have a chance at becoming US president, Clinton's *femaleness* stood in for *feminism*. Fifteen years ago, in 2003, the satirical news site the *Onion* featured an article titled "Women Now Empowered by Everything a Woman Does," mocking the overuse of the word "empowerment" and implying that this overuse vacates the concept of any real meaning because if women are empowered by *everything*, they are empowered by *nothing*. In some ways, Hillary Clinton's feminism operated under the same logic.

Clinton's political history of continuing the dismantling of welfare that Bill Clinton initiated when president, her ties to Wall Street, and her varied relationships with corporate culture were hardly feminist achievements. She did not adequately fight against economic inequalities in the United States, a context in which women and children, and especially women and children of color, suffer disproportionately. In 1994 she lobbied for the Violent Crime Control and Law Enforcement Act, which encouraged stricter sentences on crime and mass incarceration, also disproportionately affecting people of color to a tragic extent (Featherstone 2016; Savali 2017).

Yet despite (or perhaps because of) this, Clinton was a very good representative for popular feminism—she clearly knew how to lean in, and she was a stellar example of an entrepreneurial woman. There were many examples of popular feminist framing in the Clinton presidential campaign, from her slogan "I'm With Her" to the reappropriation of Trump's campaign trail insults, such as "the woman card" and "nasty woman," as empowering messages. The Facebook group Pantsuit Nation was created by Clinton supporters, and by Election Day had more than 2.5 million members. Clinton thus fit well within popular feminism's relationship with corporate capitalism, a relationship that circulates with relative ease within an economy of visibility.

Clinton's actual politics did not stray far from those of some of the more conservative politicians. But her gender did. As Peter Beinart pointed out in the pages of the *Atlantic* just prior to the election, Clinton's gender was relevant because "the Americans who dislike her most are those who most fear emasculation. According to the Public Religion Research Institute, Americans who 'completely agree' that society is becoming 'too soft and feminine' were more than four times as likely to have a 'very unfavorable' view of Clinton as those who 'completely disagree.' And the presidential-primary candidate whose supporters were most likely to believe that America is becoming feminized—more likely by double digits than supporters of Ted Cruz—was Donald Trump" (Beinart 2016, para. 2). Clinton's political experience, her foreign policy background, her position as secretary of state in the Obama administration—none of that mattered to those who thought that a female president would necessarily mean a feminized nation.

The attacks on Clinton by politicians on the left and on the right and by pundits, the mainstream media, and individuals on social media were vicious and full of misogynistic rage. Clinton was routinely labeled a bitch or a witch; her appearance was ridiculed in the media; at Trump rallies political buttons were sold that read: "KFC Hillary Special: Two fat thighs, two small breasts, one left wing"; and Trump agitated his followers to "Lock her up!" at rallies across the United States. Many of us watched the televised debates in horror as Trump called Clinton a "nasty woman" and menacingly hovered over her. However one felt about Clinton as a possible president, it was absolutely clear that the vitriolic rage directed against her during the campaign (and indeed, like most female politicians, throughout most of her career) was a rage of misogyny, a hatred of her because she was a woman who dared to let herself be positioned as a feminist. This misogyny had the uncomfortable effect of turning Clinton into a feminist icon just for being the target of it, as Liza Featherstone (2016) and others in the book *False Choices: The Faux Feminism of Hillary Rodham Clinton* argue. Voters and the media could then interpret electing a woman as president—whatever her politics were—as the ultimate feminist act.

We Are Losing So Much

There have been literally thousands of articles, think pieces, rants, interviews, and other forms of communication about the election of Donald Trump as the president of the United States. Needless to say, Trump's shortcomings as leader of arguably the most powerful country in the world are both legion and obvious: he has no political experience; he lies routinely about just about everything; he is racist; and he has no respect for the free press. Yet perhaps his most distinctive trait is his aggressive misogyny. In an opinion piece in the *Guardian*, columnist Jonathan Freedman listed some of Trump's many offenses:

> His serial outrages are well known. He has called women dogs and pigs; he humiliated the winner of his Miss Universe beauty pageant for gaining weight, forcing her to exercise in front of the cameras; he rates women's bodies out of 10; he dismissed Republican rival Carly Fiorina on the grounds that no one would vote for "that face"; he suggested TV anchor Megyn Kelly was hostile because "she had blood coming out of her wherever." Even when seeking to rebut the charges of sexual assault, he couldn't help himself. His defence amounted to: "Have you seen what these women look like? I don't think so." This is such a swift degeneration from the public mores that America and the wider world had arrived at—and which had seemed steady and settled—that it can be hard to take in. (2016, paras. 3–4)

Hard to take in, indeed. That violent misogyny is continually expressed by the president of the United States is enough of a travesty; the fact that Trump uses the social media site Twitter for this expression so that the reach of his misogyny is even broader makes it worse. Trump's misogynistic ways of not only characterizing but also treating women as a means to an end (the end being the restoration of patriarchy) circulate in the economy of visibility, but often without acknowledgment that these expressions and practices are misogyny. The relentless coverage of his words and actions by virtually all media channels enables the routine dismissal of Trump's misogyny by his supporters and even by more moderate Republicans as "locker room talk" or as "boys being boys." Just as damaging, Trump's tweets and behaviors are often covered with the façade of journalistic objectivity; his words and actions are thus not challenged but rather validated through their visibility.

Trump's misogyny has been met with outrage by many in the Democratic Party, by feminists, and by women in general. It has been interpreted by many of Trump's supporters as a crucial kind of authenticity, a glorious refusal to play the game of politics, finally a moment when a person in power says what the rest of us are apparently thinking. Misogyny here is folded into state structure *because* of its apparent authenticity, its "realness" in a context of "fake news," "alternative facts," and post-truth society. Indeed, it was clear that in the months leading up to the election—especially after the release of the *Access Hollywood* video in which Trump excused sexual assault by saying that men in power "can do anything" to women, even "grab 'em by the pussy"—that misogyny didn't hurt his campaign. It *bolstered* it, because it was seen not as misogyny but as telling it like it is.

In many ways, this makes perfect sense. After at least a decade of an increasingly visible—and increasingly normative—popular misogynistic culture, the United States elected a man for president who is openly and unrepentantly racist and misogynistic.

Trump is not only faithful to the logics of popular misogyny but perpetuates and fortifies them. Misogynists like Trump see everything within the frame of a zero-sum game: for them, politics, like other practices of popular misogyny, is just about winning. In familiar heteronormative hypermasculine logic, to win means to affirm male superiority over women, at women's expense. Just as popular misogynists do, Trump presents himself (and his supporters see him) as being on a recuperative mission, a pursuit to restore patriarchy, to repair injuries caused by women, to return capacity to men.

Trump has weaponized white rage specifically by emphasizing voters' hopelessness and fear—a fear of being emasculated by a woman leader. Trump's success is contingent on this rage, this popular misogyny, a success that validates a reactionary response, a structural violence. As Daniel HoSang and Joseph Lowndes write,

> The unabashed language of white supremacy and misogyny, rage and even violence at Trump rallies was like nothing seen in decades. It was a rage also undergirded with references to permanent loss and mourning. While Trump's campaign slogan was "Make America Great Again" he foregrounded themes of a fully realized and even irreversible loss, defeat and abandonment. Throughout his campaign, Trump told crowds: "We don't win any more." "We don't make anything." "We are losing so much." Unlike the leaders of past populist revolts, Trump seemed less a champion of working people than a figure who confirmed their debased status, reveling in such terms as "disgust," "weakness," "losing," and "pathetic." (HoSang and Lowndes, forthcoming)

This defensive posture from the Trump campaign mirrors the defensiveness of popular misogyny. But this defensiveness is not simply a posture; it manifests in the actual use of "violence and intimidation as ordinary practices of politics" (HoSang and Lowndes forthcoming). The "popular" of popular misogyny both validates and trivializes its violence; in a historical moment and political economic context in which white men feel vulnerable and threatened, popular misogyny becomes both reaffirmed as a norm and simultaneously newly weaponized as a call to arms. This is, in other words, not just about online harassment, or revenge porn, or the other forms of misogyny I detail in this book. It *is* about those forms of popular misogyny, and how they work to normalize this misogyny so that it becomes the backdrop, the justification, for eruptions of violence. As Carol Anderson eloquently writes, white rage "is not about visible violence, but rather it works its way through the courts, the legislatures, and a range of government bureaucracies. It wreaks havoc subtly, almost imperceptibly. Too imperceptibly, certainly, for a nation consistently drawn to the spectacular, to what it can *see*" (2016, 3). The economy of visibility I have discussed throughout this book works to render the spectacular visible, but it is just as important to attend to what is eclipsed by that spectacle, what is authorized to continue as a norm. And when rage becomes the norm, it is also inevitable that there will be moments when it will erupt into violence, as we witnessed in August 2017, in Charlottesville, Virginia, where hundreds of neo-Nazis, white supremacists, and misogynists openly gathered to "Unite the Right." It was clear that they came to commit violence; armed with bats, clubs, mace, and other weapons, they attacked the counterprotestors, and one man, in an act of terrorism, drove a car into a group of people, killing a woman. The rage of white supremacy and misogyny manifests in violence as an ordinary act; the normalization of racism and misogyny combine to form what Roxane Gay has called the "hate that doesn't hide" (2017, n.p.).

Nevertheless, She Persisted

The Clinton/Trump presidential campaign was, in many ways, a perfect symbol of the funhouse mirror of popular feminism and popular misogyny that I've traced in this book. As I've argued, misogyny has been more efficiently folded into the institutions of the state over the past decade, while popular feminism has importantly stoked public awareness but has for the most part remained in the realm of visibility rather than structure.

Feminism may be popular, but it is not always powerful. In fact, it is poetically fitting that Hillary Clinton actually won the *popular* vote in the United States, while Trump won the electoral vote—and the power of the presidency.

Postelection, one of the most visible examples of contemporary popular feminism was the Women's March of 2017. The march was a popular feminist reaction to the election of Trump as president, although it expanded from that specific issue in the United States to a global demonstration about women's rights, economic disparities, rape culture, and other gendered forms of violence. The Women's March originated in Washington, DC, from a Facebook post, and quickly expanded its reach through "sister" marches all over the world. Indeed, with its social media origins and wide circulation on all media platforms, the march was an important illustration of the *potential* of the circulation of popular feminism within an economy of visibility to have a broader reach, to push back against the limitations of visibility.

Hundreds of thousands of demonstrators participated in the march, a positive sign for the organizers' hope of "a sustained campaign of protest in a polarized America, unifying demonstrators around issues like reproductive rights, immigration and civil rights" (Hartocollis and Alcindor 2017, n.p.). The march was visible in many forms, with news media publishing images of huge crowds in Washington, DC, New York, Chicago, and Los Angeles, images of protest signs making the social media rounds, and, perhaps most widely shared, the image of the "pink pussy hat" circulated in all forms of media. (The "pink pussy hat" was a knitted pink cap with cat ears designed to challenge Trump's "grab 'em by the pussy" remark.) Thousands of photos depicting seas of pink pussy hats were circulated, giving clear visual evidence of a gendered collectivity. The hundreds of "sister marches" should not be underestimated; this was clearly a profound statement about gender inequality around the globe.

I participated in the march in Los Angeles, and was truly bolstered by the feelings of solidarity, not just with fellow demonstrators around me but also with the constant texting of images from my friends and family. The sheer numbers of people demonstrating were important politically, and I hope that the march really was the start of a "sustained campaign of protest in a polarized America." Again, the march was an example of the potential of popular feminism to bring attention to issues about gender discrimination to a wide swath of the population. But I also think that the march was an example of precisely the limitations of visibility, the way it works as an end in itself.

For one thing, the march was an example of a primarily popular white feminism, with many of its stated goals intended to empower white middle-class women, especially in the capitalist workplace. Indeed, many called out the march for its lack of intersectionality, and its refusal to recognize that vectors of power work differently if one is a woman of color. As Kirsten West Savali noted, "Cocooned in the white privilege that many of them deny, this type of white feminist expects black feminists with legitimate concerns to push those concerns aside for the so-called greater good—a good, to paraphrase both Harriet Tubman and Viola Davis, that exists over a line where there are 'green fields and lovely flowers and beautiful white women with their arms stretched out to us . . . but we can't seem to get there no-how. We can't seem to get over that line'" (2017, 37).

We can see this expectation for women of color to put aside race for the "greater good" of gender in the Women's March. When Brooklyn blogger and activist ShiShi Rose wrote to white women about the march that "now is the time for you to be listening more, talking less," some white women reportedly canceled their trips to the march (Rose, quoted in Valentine 2017, n.p.). As one woman quoted in the *New York Times* said: "This is a women's march. . . . We're supposed to be allies in equal pay, marriage, adoption. Why is it now about, 'White women don't understand black women'?" (Stockman 2017, n.p.). Of course, it isn't "now" that white women don't understand black women; this is the historical legacy of much of feminism, in which gender has been prioritized as the central identity category, and race has been marginalized. Mainstream feminist movements in the United States since the suffragettes have lacked an intersectional approach, often ignoring the ways in which racism discriminates against women of color. The demands of middle-class white women have long been prioritized over those of women of color in mainstream feminist movements. This is the line women of color "can't get over."

Another way that the Women's March demonstrated the limits of visibility was through its focus on individual women rather than on a more collective feminist politics. This was brilliantly demonstrated in a photo from the march in Washington, DC, that went viral, featuring Angela Peoples, an African American woman and director of the LGBT equality organization GetEqual, standing in front of three white women wearing pink pussy hats, all on their cell phones, texting and taking selfies. Peoples

FIGURE CONC.1.
Angela Peoples,
Women's March,
2017. Photo by
Keven Banatte.

stands in front of them, nonchalantly sucking on a lollipop, wearing a cap that says "Stop Killing Black People" and holding a sign that reads "Don't Forget: White Women Voted for Trump." While clearly this photo captures just one moment of the Women's March, it is also emblematic of popular feminism itself: a politics that both includes and affects mainly white women; a politics that focuses on individualism over the collective, symbolized in the taking of a selfie at the march; and a reminder that the messages of popular feminism for girls and women to be self-confident and have body positivity have little to do with the continued racial violence that affects black people in the United States.

Despite the spectacular visibility of millions of marchers in January 2017, a number of events soon occurred at the level of policy and legislation that have worked to bolster, not challenge, gender discrimination in the United States. Popular feminism, as I have argued throughout this book, poses a threat to those who are insecure, who feel injured by women and feminists, who see the "gender wars" only within a binary frame, a zero-sum game. This injury is explicitly about gender—it is about the threat of imagined emasculation. While the march worked to bring to the fore the gendered injuries of women, since that time we have witnessed the silencing, interrupting, and trivializing of these very injuries, as well as of the women who have articulated them. In perhaps one of the most blatant examples,

Massachusetts senator Elizabeth Warren was interrupted while reading a letter from civil rights activist Coretta Scott King written in 1986 during a US Senate debate over the appointment of Jefferson Sessions, Trump's nominee for attorney general of the United States.

The office of attorney general is the highest law enforcement post in the United States and heads the Department of Justice. As such, the attorney general is charged with enforcing federal law and antidiscrimination statutes. Many of these laws are crucially important to women, such as the Violence Against Women Act and the Freedom of Access to Clinic Entrances Act, as well as others that were created to protect women at school, at work, when voting, and so on. Sessions was a particularly poor candidate for attorney general because of his political history of attempting to retract rights for women. He voted against the reauthorization of the Violence Against Women Act; he has repeatedly voted to limit women's access to reproductive care; and he has a long history of hostility toward civil rights (Matsui 2016). When the *Access Hollywood* video featuring Trump's validation of sexual assault emerged, Sessions said it would be a "stretch" to consider grabbing a woman by her genitals sexual assault (Paquette 2016).

Warren, in an act challenging Trump's nomination of Sessions for attorney general, read the letter by King, and was interrupted and silenced by Senate majority leader Mitch McConnell in the middle of the reading. Citing a little-applied rule prohibiting speech portraying a sitting senator (which Sessions was at the time) in an "unbecoming" light, McConnell stated of Warren, "She was warned. She was given an explanation. Nevertheless, she persisted" (Wang 2017, n.p.). The incident, captured on video, instantly went viral, and McConnell's words became a rallying cry for popular feminism, appearing on signs at marches, T-shirts, and hundreds of memes and videos on social media platforms. Hashtags such as #letlizspeak and #shepersisted flourished on Twitter. "Nevertheless, she persisted" became another highly visible (and commodified) moment for popular feminism, and many reacted with appropriate outrage at the silencing of Warren. But ultimately, Warren (along with Coretta Scott King) was silenced in the halls of power, and Sessions was confirmed.

Aside from Sessions's confirmation, a number of other antiwoman measures passed in the wake of the Women's March of January 2017. Trump pushed to defund Planned Parenthood, and he nominated a Supreme Court justice who he promised would overturn *Roe v. Wade* (the ruling that made abortion legal in the United States). Over a thousand antiabortion measures have been introduced at the state level. Trump and the GOP congress have also repeatedly tried to repeal the Affordable Care Act, the health care plan Obama put in place while he was president. The repeal of this act would certainly make things much worse for all women, but especially poor women and women of color.

At the time of writing, the Women's March had occurred a mere six months earlier, hardly enough time to understand its lasting impact. But still, I think it is worth noting that in January 2017 we had a highly visible worldwide expression of the power of women, and it hasn't deterred politicians around the world from carrying out their misogynistic agenda. I opened this book with the sentiment that this is, in many ways, a remarkable moment to be a feminist. Feminism has become popular; it is embraced by more women—and men—than ever before, its expressions to be found not only at a radical bookstore or an activist gathering but now on T-shirts at a Target store and on Instagram, Facebook, Twitter, and other mainstream social media sites. The #MeToo movement, which emerged in force in 2017 after a flood of stories from women who had been sexually harassed in the workplace were finally heard, puts into bold relief widespread and normative misogyny and sexism. Feminism is visible like never before—although particular versions of feminism are more visible than others. These popular feminisms circulate with ever-greater ease within an economy of visibility.

As a scholar, I have found it hard to make coherent sense of the circulation of mediated popular feminisms and the subsequent reactions to these iterations. Trying to rein in this beast has been difficult, not simply because of information glut but also because there are many overlaps and convergences between popular feminism and feminist movements, and there are also clear ways in which feminisms differ in their circulation, response, and political practice. While popular awareness of feminist issues such as equality, rights, and agency is necessary for political practice, in an economy of visibility, popular awareness can become the goal rather than the route to activism. That is, while there are similarities, there are also differences between a feminist political practice that insists upon a structural critique of patriarchy and gender discrimination, and what Roxane Gay calls "the popular media feminist flavor of the week" (2014, x). I've tried to address the cultural, political, and economic conditions that amplify popular feminism, and the ways that they are different from the conditions that support other modes of feminist political practice, such as collective challenges to threats like the rollback of reproductive rights, the forced sterilization of women of color, or laws that fail to protect women from domestic and sexual abuse.

This moment is also, as I've detailed throughout this book, a remarkable one for the heightened presence of popular misogyny. Between 2012 and 2017, while I was researching and writing this book, popular misogyny became more and more normalized within social media and everyday life, often expressed in violent and vicious ways. No longer at the fringe, it seems that every day there is new violence directed at women, especially women of color, though it is rarely acknowledged *as* misogyny. These acts of violence are often justified by their perpetrators because they feel "injured" by women in general and by feminism in particular. As conservative reporter Matt Lewis has argued, "Rejection by women, it seems, has radicalized some men and made them bitter. The conservative instinct would be to work harder and succeed. Instead, these men have chosen to embrace their victim status" (2017, para. 10). Indeed, embracing victim status has fueled popular misogyny in a very specific way; deep gendered insecurity, the fear of being humiliated by women—or portrayed by them in an "unbecoming" light—is the impetus for a heightened misogyny, one easily circulated and exchanged in the media outlets that are created for its expression: subreddits, men's rights activist blogs, and seduction communities.

My argument in this book has been about this *relationship* between popular feminism and popular misogyny, and the fact that we need to give our attention to this relationship because it has structural consequences. Within an economy of visibility, popular feminist expressions and practices are important for public knowledge, but when their visibility *becomes* their politics, and this visibility hails us, asks us to pay attention to its spectacular expression, it also distracts us from the structural costs of popular misogyny's response, the aftermaths of this relationship, the violent effects of its rage.

To be "all the rage" is to have a feminism that is mainly concerned with individual women, not a collective politics. It is the feminism of neoliberalism, in a context in which gender equality is assumed to be possible, with only a few obstacles standing in its way, easily resolved through corporate and commercial intervention. It is a feminism that says "I'm with her," not "We're with each other." It is a feminism that is bounded by an antisocial neoliberalism, which not only tolerates but also expects individual women to be the targets of individual men's sexual manipulation and violence. It is in this neoliberal context that we are witnessing the transformation of popular feminism, feminism that is "all the rage," into the hateful rage of misogyny. What we need is a different sort of transformation, one that transfigures the rage of popularity into a powerful rage, an intersectional, collective rage, directed at a racist and sexist structure. We need a lasting feminist rage.

NOTES

Preface

1. This is adapted from a post I initially wrote on November 9, 2016, on the Culture Digitally blog at http://culturedigitally.org/2016/11/at-culture -digitally-were-thinking-about-our-scholarship-in-the-harsh-light-of-this-week /#banetweiser.

Introduction

1. The "risks" of feminism can be understood as part of a larger "risk society," as theorized by Anthony Giddens and Ulrich Beck. For both theorists, risk society is a manifestation of modernity; as Beck puts it, risk society is "a systematic way of dealing with hazards and insecurities induced and introduced by modernisation itself" (Beck 1992, 21). Feminism, in this context, is also a result of modernity, and presents itself to broader society as a set of "hazards and insecurities" that garner a reactive response.

2. See Trump's comments on the released video tape, where he said that powerful men can "grab 'em [women] by the pussy." These comments were dismissed by Trump as "locker room" talk ("Transcript" 2016).

3. Of course, as Duffy argues, these genres, and the women who labor within them, rely "on historically constructed notions of femininity—particularly discourses of community, affect, and commodity-based self-expression" (Duffy 2017, 9).

4. When visibility is an end in itself, it can also be transformed by the opposition, as when people of color signal something as racism, they are in turn called racists for seeing it. For more, see Ahmed 2012.

5. Indeed, Malala Yousafzai, the young woman who defied the Taliban in Pakistan by insisting the girls should be educated and was then shot for her activism, is a clear example of the "girl effect." In 2014, Yousafzai became the youngest person to receive the Nobel Peace Prize, and has continued her activism.

6. While Harris was theorizing a postfeminist, rather than a popular feminist, moment, the dynamic between the Can-Do and the At-Risk girls is similar in the current moment.

7. We see this conflation of the empowered girl and the At-Risk girl in the successful film franchise *Taken*, in which a privileged American girl is kidnapped by terrorists as part of a sex trafficking scheme.

8. Indeed, the "lone wolf" motif plays out in other acts of violence, such as terrorism. As many have pointed out, when white men commit acts of domestic terrorism in the United States, the media almost always frames these men as mentally ill, acting alone. When a Muslim man commits violence, it is almost always assumed to be a terrorist act (usually connected to radical Islam).

1. The Funhouse Mirror

1. In addition, I believe that the "power" in "girl power" is more complicated than the Nike posters and the valorization of the US women's soccer team would lead us to believe. The particularities of that power are just as important as the particularities of the girl herself, and still need rigorous theorization (Walkerdine, Lucey, and Melody 2001; Harris 2003; Gill 2007; McRobbie 2009; Projansky 2014).

2. Their campaign was also good counterpublicity for the sweatshop scandals of this same period: In 1995, when the "If You Let Me Play" campaign hit the airwaves, there was a stream of media and activist critiques detailing Nike's horrendous labor practices (especially outside the United States, in impoverished parts of the world), which would end up permanently damaging the company's reputation—especially in terms of gender, since most of the workers in the sweatshops were women. The "If You Let Me Play" campaign not only distracted consumers away from Nike's labor issues, it also established Nike as a company committed to gender equality. So while this video, and the general campaign, resonated with women, it also helped to obfuscate other issues involving the company, such as the women who make Nike products who can't afford to "play" even if someone lets them.

3. One of the key texts of second-wave feminism in the United States was Susan Brownmiller's *Against Our Will: Men, Women, and Rape* (1975), which called attention to the vast prevalence of rape in American culture. Almost twenty years later, in 1993, graduate student Katie Roiphe published her book *The Morning After: Sex, Fear, and Feminism on Campus*, where she argued, among other things, that feminism and its apparent culture of fear has made young

women afraid to be independent agents who take responsibility for themselves. Her argument took particular shape around sexual agency, and found a target in the growing discussion of date rape on college campuses. Date rape became an issue widely covered in the media, with Roiphe and others being offered screen time to frame date rape as a feminist strategy or plot, a campaign that worked to cast women as victims and not in control of their actions, including the decision to have sex. Roiphe's opinions found traction in postfeminist culture, which insists on women as active sexual agents and thus that date rape for the most part does not exist at all, and is instead just a bad decision on a woman's part, often fueled by alcohol. As Angela McRobbie has pointed out about feminine subjectivity in a postfeminist age, the definition of "sexual agency" in this context crucially involves an active "hostility to assumed feminist positions from the past, in order to endorse a new regime of sexual meanings based on female consent, equality, participation and pleasure" (2009, 18).

4. For example, Emma Sulkowicz, an undergraduate from Columbia University, staged a months-long activist campaign by carrying the mattress on which she was raped to class, as a way to protest the university's lack of response to her accusations.

5. See Noble 2017 for a discussion of the way algorithms such as Google's reproduce racist and sexist structures.

2. Shame

1. For more on practices of looking, see Berger 1972; Sturken and Cartwright 2003.

2. The concept "Love Your Body . . . or Else" was suggested to me by Brenda Weber.

3. The videos are predominately created and posted by "tween" or teenage white girls, all feature a girl speaking into a webcam, displaying photos taken of herself, asking "Am I Pretty or Ugly?," "Am I Ugly?," "Am I Pretty or Not?," and other variations of the same theme, and requesting audience feedback in the form of comments. The videos are generally amateur productions—the webcams do not typically have high resolution, the videos consist primarily of montages of still photos, and there is little to no sound editing. The dialogue is intimate and conversational.

4. ABC News, for example, also explains the videos as indicative of a self-esteem problem, albeit one that is a "normal" part of adolescence. The news program cites Dr. Joshua Klapow, PhD, a clinical psychologist at the University of Alabama–Birmingham, who says, "This is just an extreme version of something that's very normal. . . . Another piece that's normal is impulsivity. Give them a medium that is so easily accessible and so potent, you get the problem we're seeing" (Smith 2012, n.p.). The report continues by referencing Dr. Alan Kazdin,

PhD, a professor of psychology and child psychiatry at Yale, who agrees, saying, "There's a part of it that's unfortunate, but there's a part of it that's natural. Technology has made it so that it's not new in principle but new in practice" (2012, n.p.).

5. I discuss this at length in chapter 4, where I examine GamerGate.

6. "Fappening" is a reference to men masturbating; it is a portmanteau of "fapping" (masturbating) and "happening."

3. Confidence

1. Amoruso's business, Nasty Gal, was successful only for a short time; after she was sued by former employees for firing them for going on maternity leave, she filed for bankruptcy and the company was sold in 2016 (Schaefer 2017).

2. I examined the websites and other media productions of 118 organizations from a variety of sources, including SPARK Movement, Confidence Coalition, Amazing Women Rock, Idealist.org, World Association for NGOS (WANGO), and the girls' education links through the World Bank. The organizations I analyzed are primarily North American, and are those that have a web presence (many organizations in Africa do not have a web presence). For the large NGO databases, the word "girl" was used as a search term, so if there are girl-centered organizations that do not use the term "girl," they were less likely to be included. I am grateful to Tisha Dejmanee for this research.

3. The SPARK organization began as a response to a report by the American Psychological Association's Task Force on the Sexualization of Girls in 2007. Founded by well-known feminists Lyn Mikel Brown and Deborah Tolman and activist-artist Dana Edell, SPARK decided to take on the widespread sexualization of girls, focusing on the ways that the American Psychological Association defined the problem: "A person's value comes only from his or her sexual appeal or behavior, to the exclusion of other characteristics; a person is held to a standard that equates physical attractiveness (narrowly defined) with being sexy; a person is sexually objectified—that is, made into a thing for others' sexual use, rather than seen as a person with the capacity for independent action and decision making; and/or sexuality is inappropriately imposed upon a person" (Zurbriggen et al. 2007, 1). Part of this report called for grassroots mobilizing around the assumed dangers, and recommended ways to avoid this persistent cultural problem. SPARK took up this issue and offered a variety of ways to combat sexualization: "Alternative media such as 'zines' (Web-based magazines), 'blogs' (Web logs) and feminist magazines, books and websites encourage girls to become activists who speak out and develop their own alternatives. Girl empowerment groups also support girls in a variety of ways and provide important counterexamples to sexualization" (Zurbriggen et al. 2007, 4).

4. Girls of color in the United States occupy a different position as "at risk," as they are often seen as always already at risk, especially given the social, political, and cultural histories of institutionalized racism in the United States. However, it is beyond the scope of this chapter to discuss this aspect here.

5. For more on the scapegoating of women during the Reagan years, see Jeffords 1983 and Leonard 2009.

6. See the introduction to this volume for a more extensive discussion of this kind of zero-sum game.

7. In 2015, women earned 83 percent as much as men, and the gap becomes larger when specifically examining women of color. See Patten 2016.

8. "Game" refers to the pickup artist's premier guide book, Neil Strauss's *The Game*, in which he offers a tutorial on how to master a skill set ("game") to pick up women. It is worth pointing out that in recent years, Strauss has repudiated the arguments he made in *The Game* in a new book, *The Truth*, in which he lauds his new role as monogamous husband and loving father.

9. VH1's *The Pickup Artist* is premised on the idea that socially awkward men who lack self-confidence can be "trained" by a master to have more self-confidence and overcome their personal obstacles. However, it seems ironic that the structure of the show is based on a familiar reality television format in which contestants are eliminated one by one because they are not "good enough." This hardly seems to be a good technique for encouraging self-confidence.

4. Competence

Epigraph quote from Collins 2014.

1. For example, there have been recent revelations of widespread sexual harassment at Uber and Twitter.

2. The recent film *Hidden Figures* details this history in 1950s NASA, also pointing out that along with racism, sexism constructed women and women of color as primarily "service" workers and not integral minds that shaped the industry.

3. For example, Stern 2004; Mazzarella 2005; Kearney 2006; Dobson 2008.

4. See also Shaw 2015 for a compelling analysis of gender in this industry.

5. Giving films and documentaries a low ranking has become a familiar tactic for popular misogynists when a film is released that challenges their views. For example, even before the reboot of *Ghostbusters*, featuring an all-female cast, was released, the film had a very low rating on Rotten Tomatoes and other film ranking sites, the result of individuals who used rankings as a way to hurt potential box office profits.

6. Pepe the Frog is the global symbol of the alt-right; clearly this person is drawing on that symbolism.

7. Communication historian Fred Turner (2009) has analyzed the annual art and music festival Burning Man, known for its popularity among technology

companies and communities (especially Google). Turner calls Burning Man a "cultural infrastructure"—a social world that helps to both legitimize and further the particular kind of work that Google aims to do and the work, and also the values, of tech companies. Tech companies such as Google celebrate their "commons-based peer production"—seen in everything from their open-space floor plans to their emphasis on collaborative creation—but that corporate vision needs a "particular structural and ideological scaffolding" (Turner 2009).

8. Much has been written already about GamerGate, and thus I will only rehearse some key moments and issues here. For a detailed timeline of GamerGate, see "Timeline of Gamergate," RationalWiki, http://rationalwiki.org/wiki/Timeline_of_Gamergate.

9. Reddit is a privately held corporation, a subsidiary of Condé Nast.

10. Indeed, a friend likened this to the arcade game "Whack-a-Mole," in which players whack moles with a mallet as they pop up, only to have others pop up in rapid succession. They are always one step ahead.

REFERENCES

Aaronson, S. 2014. Comment #171: Walter Lewin. *Shtetl Optimized*, December 14. http://www.scottaaronson.com/blog/?p=2091#comment-326664.

Abbate, J. 2012. *Recoding Gender: Women's Changing Participation in Computing*. Cambridge, MA: MIT Press.

"About." n.d. Confidence Coalition. Accessed August 2016. http://confidencecoalition .org/about.

"About." n.d. Return of Kings. Accessed February 18, 2018. http://www .returnofkings.com/about.

"About Us." n.d. National Coalition for Men. Accessed February 18, 2018. http:// ncfm.org/ncfm-home/.

Adkins, L. 2001. "Cultural Feminization: 'Money, Sex and Power' for Women." *Signs: Journal of Women in Culture and Society* 26 (3): 669–95.

Ahmed, S. 2010. *The Promise of Happiness*. Durham, NC: Duke University Press.

Ahmed, S. 2012. *On Being Included: Racism and Diversity in Institutional Life*. Durham, NC: Duke University Press.

Ahmed, S. 2014. "Selfcare as Warfare." *Feminist Killjoys*, August 25. https://feminist killjoys.com/2014/08/25/selfcare-as-warfare/.

Ahmed, S. 2016. "Losing Confidence." *Feminist Killjoys*, March 1. https:// feministkilljoys.com/2016/03/01/losing-confidence/.

American Association of University Women. 1991. *Shortchanging Girls, Shortchanging America*. Washington, DC: American Association of University Women. http://www.aauw.org/files/2013/02/shortchanging-girls -shortchanging-america-executive-summary.pdf.

"Am I Pretty or Ugly?" 2010. YouTube video, 2:47. Posted by "sgal901," December 17. https://www.youtube.com/watch?v=8D9mqqkgH-0.

"Am I Pretty or Ugly?" 2012. YouTube video, 4:31. Posted by "SmileLoveBeauty8," January 15. http://www.youtube.com/watch?v=WoyZPn6hKY4.

Amoruso, S. 2015. *#Girlboss*. Portfolio.

Anderson, C. 2016. *White Rage: The Unspoken Truth of Our Racial Divide*. London: Bloomsbury Publishing.

Andrejevic, M. 2002. "The Work of Being Watched: Interactive Media and the Exploitation of Self-Disclosure." *Critical Studies in Media Communication* 19 (2): 230–48.

Arviddson, A. 2006. *Brands: Meaning and Value in Media Culture*. New York: Routledge.

Banet-Weiser, S. 2007. *Kids Rule! Nickelodeon and Consumer Citizenship*. Durham, NC: Duke University Press.

Banet-Weiser, S. 2012. *Authentic™: The Politics of Ambivalence in a Brand Culture*. New York: New York University Press.

Banet-Weiser, S. 2014. "Am I Pretty or Ugly? Girls and the Market for Self-Esteem." *Girlhood Studies* 7 (1): 83–101.

Banet-Weiser, S. 2015. "'Confidence You Can Carry!': Girls in Crisis and the Market for Girls' Empowerment Organizations." *Continuum: Journal of Media & Cultural Studies* 29 (2): 182–93.

Banet-Weiser, S., and M. Castells. 2017. "Economy Is Culture." In *Another Economy Is Possible: Culture and Economy in a Time of Crisis*, by M. Castells. Cambridge: Polity.

Banet-Weiser, S., and K. M. Miltner. 2015. "#MasculinitySoFragile: Culture, Structure, and Networked Misogyny." *Feminist Media Studies* 16 (1): 171–74.

Barker, M. 2004. *Girls on Track: A Parent's Guide to Inspiring Our Daughters to Achieve a Lifetime of Self-Esteem and Respect*. New York: Ballantine Books.

Baym, N. K. 2015. "Connect with Your Audience! The Relational Labor of Connection." *Communication Review* 18 (1): 14–22.

Beck, Ulrich. 1992. *Risk Society: Towards a New Modernity*. London: Sage.

Beinart, P. 2016. "Fear of a Female President." *Atlantic*, October. https://www.theatlantic.com/magazine/archive/2016/10/fear-of-a-female-president/497564/.

Bell, K., C. Kampe, and N. Taylor. 2015. "Of Headshots and Hugs: Challenging Hypermasculinity through 'The Walking Dead' Play." *Ada: A Journal of Gender, New Media, and Technology* (7). http://adanewmedia.org/2015/04/issue7-bellkampetaylor/.

Berger, J. 1972. *Ways of Seeing*. London: BBC.

Berlant, L. 2008. *The Female Complaint: The Unfinished Business of Sentimentality in American Culture*. Durham, NC: Duke University Press.

Berman, J. 2015. "Why That 'Like a Girl' Super Bowl Ad Was So Groundbreaking." *Huffington Post*, February 2. http://www.huffingtonpost.com/2015/02/02/always-super-bowl-ad_n_6598328.html.

Beusman, C. 2014. "What Does It Mean for Feminism If Feminism Becomes Trendy?" *Jezebel*, February 24. http://jezebel.com/what-does-it-mean-for -feminism-if-feminism-becomes-tren-1501305340.

Bever, L. 2015. "Sexism and the Nobel Prize Scientist: A Backlash to the Backlash." *Washington Post*, June 12. https://www.washingtonpost.com/news/morning -mix/wp/2015/06/12/nobel-scientist-tim-hunt-ignites-social-media-firestorm/.

Blake, M. 2015. "Mad Men: Inside the Men's Rights Movement—and the Army of Misogynists and Trolls It Spawned." *Mother Jones*, January/February. http://www.motherjones.com/ politics/2015/01/ warren-farrell-mens-rights-movement-feminism-misogyny-trolls.

boyd, d. 2010. "Social Network Sites as Networked Publics: Affordances, Dynamics, and Implications." In *A Networked Self: Identity, Community, and Culture on Social Network Sites*, edited by Z. Papacharissi, 39–58. New York: Routledge.

Bratich, J. 2011. "Affective Convergence in Reality Television: A Case Study in Divergence." In *Flow TV: Television in the Age of Media Convergence*, edited by M. Kackman, M. Binfield, M. T. Payne, A. Perlman, and B. Sebok, 55–74. New York: Routledge.

Brock, A. 2012. "From the Blackhand Side: Twitter as a Cultural Conversation." *Journal of Broadcasting & Electronic Media* 56 (4): 529–49. doi:10.1080/088381 51.2012.732147.

Brough, M. M. 2012. "'Fair Vanity': The Visual Culture of Humanitarianism in the Age of Commodity Activism." In *Commodity Activism: Cultural Resistance in Neoliberal Times*, edited by R. Mukherjee and S. Banet-Weiser, 174–94. New York: New York University Press.

Brownmiller, S. [1975] 2013. *Against Our Will: Men, Women, and Rape*. New York: Open Road Media.

Butler, J., Z. Gambetti, and L. Sabsay, eds. 2016. *Vulnerability in Resistance*. Durham, NC: Duke University Press.

Butler, J., and J. W. Scott, eds. 1992. *Feminists Theorize the Political*. New York: Routledge.

Castells, M. 1996. *The Rise of the Network Society*. Vol. 1 of *The Information Age: Economy, Society, and Culture*. Hoboken, NJ: Wiley-Blackwell.

Castells, M. 2007. "Communication, Power and Counter-Power in the Network Society." *International Journal of Communication* (1): 238–66.

Castells, M. 2009. *Communication Power*. Oxford: Oxford University Press.

Castells, M. 2012. *Networks of Outrage and Hope: Social Movements in the Internet Age*. Cambridge: Polity.

Castells, M. 2017. *Another Economy Is Possible: Culture and Economy in a Time of Crisis*. Cambridge: Polity.

Catalan, J. 2014. "Google Admits Lack of Diversity in Newly Released Report." *Diversity Inc.*, July 29. http://www.diversityinc.com/news/google-admits-lack -diversity-newly-released-report/.

Chambers, L. 2016. "'Don't Be That Guy' Campaign Tackles Sexual Assault." *Campus Lately*, August 10. http://campuslately.com/dont-be-that-guy -campaign/.

Chatman, D. 2017. "Black Twitter and the Politics of Viewing *Scandal*." In *Fandom: Identities and Communities in a Mediated World*, 2nd ed., edited by J. Gray, C. Sandvoss, and C. L. Harrington, 299–314. New York: New York University Press.

Chemaly, S. 2016. "If You Don't Take Women's Harassment Seriously, You Don't Want to Understand the Problem." *Huffington Post*, January 27. http://www .huffingtonpost.com/soraya-chemaly/if-you-dont-take-womens-harassment -seriously-you-dont-want-to-understand-the-problem_b_9082952.html.

Chernin, K. 1994. *The Obsession: Reflections on the Tyranny of Slenderness.* New York: Harper Perennial.

Chouliaraki, L. 2013. *The Ironic Spectator: Solidarity in the Age of Post-humanitarianism.* Hoboken, NJ: John Wiley & Sons.

Chu, A. 2014a. "Your Princess Is in Another Castle: Misogyny, Entitlement, and Nerds." *Daily Beast*, May 27. http://www.thedailybeast.com/articles/2014/05 /27/your-princess-is-in-another-castle-misogyny-entitlement-and-nerds.html.

Chu, A. 2014b. "I'm Not 'That Creepy Guy from the Internet': How Gamergate Gave the Geek Community a Bad Name." *Salon*, October 30. http://www .salon.com/2014/10/30/that_creepy_guy_from_the_internet_how_gamergate _shattered_faith_in_the_geek_community/.

Citron, D. K. 2014. *Hate Crimes in Cyberspace.* Cambridge, MA: Harvard University Press.

Collins, S. T. 2014. "Anita Sarkeesian on GamerGate: 'We Have a Problem and We're Going to Fix This'" [interview]. *Rolling Stone*, October 17. https://www .rollingstone.com/culture/features/anita-sarkeesian-gamergate-interview -20141017.

Confessore, N. 2016. "For Whites Sensing Decline, Donald Trump Unleashes Words of Resistance." *New York Times*, July 13, 2016. https://www.nytimes.com /2016/07/14/us/politics/donald-trump-white-identity.html?_r=0.

Cooky, C., and M. G. McDonald. 2005. "If You Let Me Play: Young Girls' Insider-Other Narratives of Sport." *Sociology of Sport Journal* 22 (2): 158–77.

CoverGirl. 2014. "#GirlsCan: Women's Empowerment" [Television commercial]. Accessed February 18, 2018. https://www.youtube.com/watch?v =KmmGClZb8Mg.

Cruikshank, B. 1999. *The Will to Empower: Democratic Citizens and Other Subjects.* Ithaca, NY: Cornell University Press.

Currie, D. 1999. *Girl Talk: Adolescent Magazines and Their Readers.* Toronto: University of Toronto Press.

Curtis, J. L., and L. Cornell. 2007. *I'm Gonna Like Me: Letting Off a Little Self-Esteem.* Los Angeles: Joanna Cotler Books.

Cyber Civil Rights Initiative. n.d. "38 States + DC Have Revenge Porn Laws." Accessed February 18, 2018. https://www.cybercivilrights.org/revenge-porn -laws.

Day, E. 2011. "Honey Money: The Power of Erotic Capital by Catherine Hakim— Review." *Guardian*, May 27. https://www.theguardian.com/books/2011/aug/28 /honey-money-catherine-hakim-review.

Dean, J. 2005. "Communicative Capitalism: Circulation and the Foreclosure of Politics." *Cultural Politics* 1 (1): 51–74.

Devlin, K. [drkatedevlin]. 2015. "Dear department: please note l will be unable to chair the 10am meeting this morning because I am too busy swooning and crying. #timhunt." Tweet, June 10. https://twitter.com/drkatedevlin/status /608554885785788416.

Dewey, C. 2014. "Inside the 'Manosphere' That Inspired Santa Barbara Shooter Elliot Rodger." *Washington Post*, May 27. https://www.washingtonpost.com /news/the-intersect/wp/2014/05/27/inside-the-manosphere-that-inspired -santa-barbara-shooter-elliot-rodger/?utm_term=.c877b225e065.

Dickson, E. J. 2014. "The History of Revenge Porn That Led to Hunter Moore's Arrest." *Daily Dot*, January 23. http://www.dailydot.com/crime/hunter-moore -arrested-indicted-california/.

DiSesa, N. 2008. *Seducing the Boys Club: Uncensored Tactics from a Woman at the Top*. New York: Random House Digital.

Dobson, A. S. 2008. "Femininities as Commodities: Cam Girl Culture." In *Next Wave Cultures: Feminism, Subcultures*, edited by A. Harris, 123–48. New York: Routledge.

Dockterman, E. 2016. "Barbie's Got a New Body." *Time*, January 27. http://time .com/barbie-new-body-cover-story.

Dosekun, S. 2015. "For Western Girls Only? Post-feminism as Transnational Culture." *Feminist Media Studies* 15 (6): 960–75.

Douglas, S. J. 1989. *Inventing American Broadcasting, 1899–1922*. Baltimore, MD: Johns Hopkins University Press.

Duca, L. 2016. "Donald Trump Is Gaslighting America." *Teen Vogue*, December 10. http://www.teenvogue.com/story/donald-trump-is-gaslighting-america.

Duffy, B. E. 2015. "The Gendered Politics of Digital Brand Labor." *Antenna*, March 18. http://blog.commarts.wisc.edu/2015/03/18/the-gendered-politics-of -digital-brand-labor/.

Duffy, B. E. 2017. *(Not) Getting Paid to Do What You Love: Gender, Social Media, and Aspirational Work*. New Haven, CT: Yale University Press.

Dunbar-Hester, C. 2016. "Geek." In *Digital Keywords: A Vocabulary of Informa- tion Society and Culture*, edited by B. Peters, 149–57. Princeton, NJ: Princeton University Press.

Durham, M. G. 2008. *The Lolita Effect: The Media Sexualization of Young Girls and What We Can Do about It*. New York: Overlook Press.

Dwyer, J. 2012. "A Real Girl, 14, Takes a Stand against the Flawless Faces in Magazines." *New York Times*, May 3. http://www.nytimes.com/2012/05/04/nyregion/seventeen-magazine-faulted-by-girl-14-for-doctoring-photos.html.

Edell, D., L. M. Brown, and D. Tolman. 2013. "Embodying Sexualisation: When Theory Meets Practice in Intergenerational Feminist Activism." *Feminist Theory* 14 (3): 275–84.

Edwards, S. R., K. A. Bradshaw, and V. B. Hinsz. 2014. "Denying Rape but Endorsing Forceful Intercourse: Exploring Differences among Responders." *Violence and Gender* 1 (4): 188–93.

Egan, R. D. 2013. *Becoming Sexual: A Critical Appraisal of the Sexualization of Girls*. Cambridge: Polity.

Elias, A., R. Gill, and C. Scharff. 2017. *Aesthetic Labour: Beauty Politics in Neoliberalism*. Basingstoke, UK: Palgrave Macmillan.

Ensmenger, N. L. 2012. *The Computer Boys Take Over: Computers, Programmers, and the Politics of Technical Expertise*. Cambridge, MA: MIT Press.

Ensmenger, N. L. 2015. "Beards, Sandals, and Other Signs of Rugged Individualism: Masculine Culture within the Computing Professions." *Osiris* 30 (1): 38–65.

Faludi, S. 1991. *Backlash: The Undeclared War against American Women*. New York: Crown Publishing Group.

Favaro, L. 2017. "Transnational Technologies of Gender and Mediated Intimacy." PhD diss., City University of London.

Featherstone, L., ed. 2016. *False Choices: The Faux Feminism of Hillary Rodham Clinton*. New York: Verso Books.

Feldman, J. 2016. "*Teen Vogue* Writer Battles Tucker Carlson: 'You're Actually Being a Partisan Hack.'" *Mediaite*, December 23. http://www.mediaite.com/online/teen-vogue-writer-battles-tucker-carlson-youre-actually-being-a-partisan-hack/.

Filipovic, J. 2014. "Emma Watson Named Celebrity Feminist of the Year." *Cosmopolitan*, December 19. http://www.cosmopolitan.com/entertainment/news/a34421/ms-foundation-feminist-celebrity-2014/.

Folkenflik, D. 2016. "Trump Essay Signals Shift in Approach for Teen Vogue." *All Things Considered*, December 23. http://www.npr.org/2016/12/23/506759094/trump-essay-signals-shift-in-approach-for-teen-vogue.

Foucault, M. [1977] 1995. *Discipline and Punish: The Birth of the Prison*. New York: Vintage.

Frank, N. 2017. "Visibility Is at the Heart of LGBTQ Politics. But Is It Always the Best Strategy?" *Slate*, June 26. http://www.slate.com/blogs/outward/2017/06/27/is_visibility_politics_the_best_strategy_for_advancing_lgbtq_movement_goals.html.

Freedman, J. 2016. "Donald Trump Is a Vile Misogynist—but He's Not the Only One." *Guardian*, October 21. https://www.theguardian.com/commentisfree

/2016/oct/21/donald-trump-rolled-back-gains-american-women-torrent
-misogyny.

Fried, B. 2013. "Students Speak: The Power of STEM." *The White House Blog*,
March 28. https://obamawhitehouse.archives.gov/blog/2013/03/28/students
-speak-power-stem.

Friedman, M. 2015. "Powerful Message of the #LikeAGirl Campaign." *Huffington
Post*, February 3. http://www.huffingtonpost.com/michael-friedman-phd/the
-powerful-message-of-the-likeagirl-campaign_b_6603714.html.

Gambetti, Z. 2013. "The Politics of Visibility: Hot Spots." *Cultural Anthropology*,
October 31. https://culanth.org/fieldsights/401-the-politics-of-visibility.

Garcia, S. E. 2017. "The Woman Who Created #MeToo Long Before Hashtags."
New York Times, October 20. https://www.nytimes.com/2017/10/20/us/me
-too-movement-tarana-burke.html.

Garza, A. n.d. "A Herstory of the #BlackLivesMatter Movement." *Black Lives
Matter*. Accessed August 2016. http://blacklivesmatter.com/herstory/.

Gay, R. 2014. *Bad Feminist*. New York: Harper Perennial.

Gay, R. 2017. "Hate That Doesn't Hide." *New York Times*, August 18.

Gibson, M. 2014. "Is This the Most Hated Man in the World?" *Time*, November 12. http://time.com/3578387/julien-blanc-feminism-real-social
-dynamics/.

Gibson-Graham, J. K. 2006. *A Postcapitalist Politics*. Minneapolis: University of
Minnesota Press.

Giddens, A. 1991 *Modernity and Self-Identity: Self and Society in the Late Modern
Age*. Cambridge: Cambridge University Press.

Gilbert, S. 2016. "Teen Vogue's Political Coverage Isn't Surprising." *Atlantic*, December 12. https://www.theatlantic.com/entertainment/archive/2016/12/teen
-vogue-politics/510374/.

Gill, R. 2007. "Postfeminist Media Culture: Elements of a Sensibility." *European
Journal of Cultural Studies* 10 (2): 147–66.

Gill, R. 2008. "Empowerment/Sexism: Figuring Female Sexual Agency in Contemporary Advertising." *Feminism & Psychology* 18 (1): 35–60.

Gill, R. 2011. "Sexism Reloaded, or, It's Time to Get Angry Again!" *Feminist
Media Studies* 11 (1): 61–71.

Gill, R. 2016a. "Postfeminism and the New Cultural Life of Feminism." *Diffractions*:
Graduate Journal for the Study of Culture (6). http://www.diffractions.net/.

Gill, R. 2016b. "'Post-postfeminism?': New Feminist Visibilities in Postfeminist
Times." *Feminist Media Studies* 16 (4): 610–30.

Gill, R., and A. S. Elias. 2014. "'Awaken Your Incredible': Love Your Body Discourses and Postfeminist Contradictions." *International Journal of Media and
Cultural Politics* 10 (2): 179–88.

Gill, R., and S. Orgad. 2015. "The Confidence Cult(ure)." *Australian Feminist
Studies* 30 (86): 324–44.

Gill, R., and A. Pratt. 2008. "In the Social Factory? Immaterial Labour, Precariousness and Cultural Work." *Theory, Culture & Society* 25 (7–8): 1–30.

Gilman, M. E. 2012. "The Class Differential in Privacy Law." *Brooklyn Law Review* 77 (4). https://brooklynworks.brooklaw.edu/blr/vol77/iss4/2.

Gilson, E. 2014. *The Ethics of Vulnerability: A Feminist Analysis of Social Life and Practice.* New York: Routledge.

"Girls in STEM." 2016. Verizon. Internet Archive, July 18. https://web.archive.org/web/20160718160442/http://www.verizon.com/about/responsibility/girls-in-stem.

Glennon, W. 1999. *200 Ways to Raise a Girl's Self-Esteem: An Indispensable Guide for Parents, Teachers, and Other Concerned Caregivers.* New York: Conari.

Goldstein, M. 2015. "Law Firm Founds Project to Fight 'Revenge Porn.'" *New York Times*, January 29. http://dealbook.nytimes.com/2015/01/29/law-firm-founds-project-to-fight-revenge-porn/.

Gray, E. 2012. "'Am I Ugly?' Videos: Young Teens Ask YouTube Users Whether They're Pretty or Not." *Huffington Post*, February 21. http://www.huffingtonpost.com/2012/02/21/am-i-ugly-or-pretty-videos-YouTube-teens_n_1292113.html.

Gray, H. 2013. "Subject(ed) to Recognition." *American Quarterly* 65 (4): 771–98.

Gregg, M. 2013. *Work's Intimacy.* Hoboken, NJ: John Wiley & Sons.

Grewal, I. 2005. *Transnational America: Feminisms, Diasporas, Neoliberalisms.* Durham, NC: Duke University Press.

Griner, D. 2014. "Ad of the Day: P&G Surges at Olympic Finish Line with Covergirls' 'Girls Can' Campaign." *AdWeek*, February 24. http://www.adweek.com/brand-marketing/ad-day-pg-surges-olympic-finish-line-covergirls-girlscan-campaign-155912/.

Grish, K. 2015. "Easy, Effective Ways to Be More Confident." *Men's Health*, March 19. http://www.menshealth.com/sex-women/self-confidence-sexual-turn.

Gross, L. 2012. *Up from Invisibility: Lesbians, Gay Men, and the Media in America.* New York: Columbia University Press.

"GTFO: Get the F*ck Out" [Reviews]. 2015. IMDB, June 10. http://www.imdb.com/title/tt3891970/reviews.

Gunn, C. 2015. "Hashtagging for the Margins: Women of Color Engaged in Feminist Consciousness-Raising on Twitter." In *Women of Color and Social Media Multitasking: Blogs, Timelines, Feeds, and Community*, edited by K. E. Tassie and S. M. B. Givens, 21–34. Lanham, MD: Lexington Books.

Hains, R. C. 2012. *Growing Up with Girl Power: Girlhood on Screen and in Everyday Life.* Bern, Switzerland: Peter Lang.

Hakim, C. 2011. *Erotic Capital: The Power of Attraction in the Boardroom and the Bedroom.* New York: Basic Books.

Hall, S. 1998. "Notes on Deconstructing 'the Popular.'" In *Cultural Theory and Popular Culture: A Reader*, edited by John Storey, 442. London: Routledge.

Harris, A. 2003. *Future Girl: Young Women in the Twenty-First Century.* New York: Routledge.

Harris, A., ed. 2004. *All about the Girl: Culture, Power, and Identity*. New York: Routledge.

Hartocollis, A., and Y. Alcindor. 2017. "Women's March Highlights as Huge Crowds Protest Trump: 'We're Not Going Away.'" *New York Times*, January 21. https://www.nytimes.com/2017/01/21/us/womens-march.html.

Hartsock, N. C. 1983. "The Feminist Standpoint: Developing the Ground for a Specifically Feminist Historical Materialism." In *Discovering Reality*, 283–310. Amsterdam: Springer Netherlands.

Hasinoff, A. A. 2015. *Sexting Panic: Rethinking Criminalization, Privacy, and Consent*. Champaign: University of Illinois Press.

Hearn, A. 2008. "Meat, Mask, Burden: Probing the Contours of the Branded 'Self.'" *Journal of Consumer Culture* 8 (2): 197–217.

Hearn, A. 2010. "Structuring Feeling: Web 2.0, Online Ranking and Rating, and the Digital 'Reputation' Economy." *Ephemera* 10 (3/4): 421–38.

Hearn, A. 2017. "Verified: Self-Presentation, Identity Management, and Selfhood in the Age of Big Data." *Popular Communication* 10 (2): 62–77.

Hegde, R. S. 2011. *Circuits of Visibility: Gender and Transnational Media Cultures*. New York: New York University Press.

Hicks, M. 2017. *Programmed Inequality: How Britain Discarded Women Technologists and Lost Its Edge in Computing*. Cambridge, MA: MIT Press.

Hochschild, A. R. 1983. *The Managed Heart: Commercialization of Human Feeling*. Berkeley: University of California Press.

Hochschild, A. R. 2012. *The Outsourced Self: Intimate Life in Market Times*. New York: Metropolitan Books.

Hong, G. K. 2006. *The Ruptures of American Capital: Women of Color, Feminism, and the Culture of Immigrant Labor*. Minneapolis: University of Minnesota Press.

HoSang, D., and J. Lowndes. Forthcoming. "Theorizing Race in the Age of Inequality." In *Post-Race Racial Projects*, edited by R. Mukherjee, S. Banet-Weiser, and H. Gray. Durham, NC: Duke University Press.

Hu, E. 2012. "'Seventeen' Magazine Takes No-Photoshop Pledge after 8th-Grader's Campaign." *Two Way*, July 5. http://www.npr.org/sections/thetwo -way/2012/07/05/156342683/seventeen-magazine-takes-no-photoshop-pledge -after-8th-graders-campaign.

Huhman, H. 2012. "STEM Fields and the Gender Gap: Where Are the Women?" *Forbes Magazine*, June 20. https://www.forbes.com/sites/work-in-progress /2012/06/20/stem-fields-and-the-gender-gap-where-are-the-women.

Illouz, E. 2008. *Saving the Modern Soul: Therapy, Emotions, and the Culture of Self-Help*. Berkeley: University of California Press.

"Inspire Her Mind." 2014. [Television commercial]. Verizon/Makers. https://www .youtube.com/watch?v=DQXZ_g2d5ao.

Jaschik, S. 2005. "What Larry Summers Said." *Inside Higher Ed*, February 18. https://www.insidehighered.com/news/2005/02/18/summers2_18.

Jeffords, S. 1983. *Hard Bodies: Hollywood Masculinity in the Reagan Era*. New Brunswick, NJ: Rutgers University Press.

Johnson, D. 2016. Unpublished paper in author's possession.

Jones, O. 2017. "Google's Sexist Memo Has Provided the Alt-Right with a New Martyr." *Guardian*, August 8. https://www.theguardian.com/commentisfree /2017/aug/08/google-sexist-memo-alt-right-martyr-james-damore.

Kanai, A. 2016. "Managing the Self-Social Tension: Digital Feminine Self-Production in an Intimate Public." PhD diss., Monash University, Melbourne, Australia.

Kantor, J., and M. Twohey. 2017. "Harvey Weinstein Paid Off Sexual Harassment Accusers for Decades." *New York Times*, October 5. https://www.nytimes.com /2017/10/05/us/harvey-weinstein-harassment-allegations.html.

Kashner, S. 2014. "Both Huntress and Prey." *Vanity Fair*, November. http://www .vanityfair.com/hollywood/2014/10/jennifer-lawrence-photo-hacking-privacy.

Kay, K., and C. Shipman. 2014a. *The Confidence Code: The Science and Art of Self-Assurance—What Women Should Know*. New York: HarperBusiness.

Kay, K., and C. Shipman. 2014b. "The Confidence Gap." *Atlantic*, May, 1–18.

Kearney, M. C. 2006. *Girls Make Media*. New York: Routledge.

Kendall, L. 1999. "'The Nerd Within': Mass Media and the Negotiation of Identity among Computer-Using Men." *Journal of Men's Studies* 7 (3): 353–69.

Kendall, L. 2011. "'White and Nerdy': Computers, Race, and the Nerd Stereotype." *Journal of Popular Culture* 44 (3): 505–24.

Kim, E. 2016. "The Politics of Visibility." *Disrupting the Digital Humanities*, January 6. http://www.disruptingdh.com/politics-of-visibility/.

King, S. 2006. *Pink Ribbons, Inc: Breast Cancer and the Politics of Philanthropy*. Minneapolis: University Minnesota Press.

Koffman, O., and R. Gill. 2013. "'The Revolution Will Be Led by a 12-Year-Old Girl': Girl Power and Global Biopolitics." *feminist review* 105 (1): 83–102.

Kolko, B., L. Nakamura, and G. Rodman, eds. 2013. *Race in Cyberspace*. New York: Routledge.

Lears, T. J. J. 1983. "From Salvation to Self-Realization: Advertising and the Therapeutic Roots of the Consumer Culture, 1880–1930." In *The Culture of Consumption: Critical Essays in American History, 1880–1980*, edited by R. W. Fox and T. J. J. Lears, 1–38. New York: Pantheon Books.

Leonard, S. 2009. *Fatal Attraction*. Hoboken, NJ: Wiley-Blackwell.

Lewinsky, M. 2015. "The Price of Shame" [video]. *TED*, March 2015. https://www .ted.com/talks/monica_lewinsky_the_price_of_shame.

Lewinsky, M. 2017. "Monica Lewinsky: Roger Ailes's Dream Was My Nightmare." *New York Times*, May 22. https://www.nytimes.com/2017/05/22/opinion /monica-lewinsky-roger-ailess-dream-was-my-nightmare.html.

Lewis, M. 2017. "The Red-Pill Right Swaps Chivalry for Misogyny." *Daily Beast*, April 26. http://www.thedailybeast.com/the-red-pill-right-swaps-chivalry-for -misogyny.

Lopez, A. 2015. "Ellen Pao's Resignation from Reddit." *Counterpunch*, July 15. http://
www.counterpunch.org/2015/07/15/ellen-paos-resignation-from-reddit/.

Lyons, M. N. 2016. "Alt-Right: More Misogynistic Than Many Neonazis." *three-
wayfight*, December 3. http://threewayfight.blogspot.com/2016/12/alt-right
-more-misogynistic-than-many.html.

Marcotte, A. 2014. "'The Fappening' and Revenge Porn Culture: Jennifer Lawrence and the Creepshot Epidemic." *Daily Beast*, September 3. http://www
.thedailybeast.com/articles/2014/09/03/the-fappening-and-revenge-porn
-culture-jennifer-lawrence-and-the-creepshot-epidemic.html.

Marwick, A. E. 2013. *Status Update: Celebrity, Publicity, and Branding in the
Social Media Age*. New Haven, CT: Yale University Press.

Marwick, A. E. 2017. "Scandal or Sex Crime? Gendered Privacy and the Celebrity
Nude Photo Leaks." *Ethics, Information, Technology* 19 (3): 177–91.

Marwick, A., and R. Lewis. 2015. "Media Manipulation and Disinformation Online." Report. *Data & Society*. https://datasociety.net/pubs/oh/DataAndSociety
_MediaManipulationAndDisinformationOnline.pdf.

Massanari, A. [2015] 2017. "#Gamergate and the Fappening: How Reddit's Algo-
rithm, Governance, and Culture Support Toxic Technocultures." *New Media &
Society* 19 (3): 329–46. First published online October 9, 2015.

Matsui, A. 2016. "Senator Jeff Sessions' Problematic Record on Women's Rights."
National Women's Law Center, December 20. https://nwlc.org/blog/sen-jeff
-sessions-problematic-record-on-womens-rights/.

Mazzarella, S. R., ed. 2005. *Girl Wide Web: Girls, the Internet, and the Negotiation of Identity*. Bern, Switzerland: Peter Lang.

McGee, M. 2005. *Self Help, Inc.: Makeover Culture in American Life*. Oxford:
Oxford University Press.

McKay, B., and K. McKay. 2008. "Increase Your Manly Confidence Overnight."
The Art of Manliness, January 10. http://www.artofmanliness.com/2008/01/10
/increase-your-manly-confidence-overnight/.

McKenzie, M. 2013. "On Defending Beyoncé: Black Feminists, White Feminists, and
the Line in the Sand." *Black Girl Dangerous*, December 16. https://www.bgdblog
.org/2013/12/defending-beyonce-black-feminists-white-feminists-line-sand/.

McKenzie, M. 2014. *Black Girl Dangerous: On Race, Queerness, Class and Gender*. Oakland, CA: BGD Press, Inc.

McNeal, J. U. 1992. *Kids as Customers: A Handbook of Marketing to Children*.
Lanham, MD: Lexington Books.

McRobbie, A. 2004. "Post-feminism and Popular Culture." *Feminist Media Studies* 4 (3): 255–64.

McRobbie, A. 2007. "Postfeminism and Popular Culture: Bridget Jones and the
New Gender Regime." In *Interrogating Postfeminism: Gender and the Politics
of Popular Culture*, edited by Y. Tasker and D. Negra, 27–39. Durham, NC:
Duke University Press.

McRobbie, A. 2009. *The Aftermath of Feminism: Gender, Culture, and Social Change*. London: Sage.

McRobbie, A. 2016. *Be Creative: Making a Living in the New Culture Industries*. Hoboken, NJ: John Wiley & Sons.

Mendible, M., ed. 2016. *American Shame: Stigma and the Body Politic*. Bloomington: Indiana University Press.

Mills, N. 2017. "Television and the Politics of Humiliation." *Dissent Magazine*. Accessed October 2017. https://www.dissentmagazine.org/article/television -and-the-politics-of-humiliation.

"Mission and Vision." n.d. *AfricAid*. Accessed August 2015. http://africaid.com /what-we-do/mission-and-vision.

Monllos, K. 2016. "Girls Explain How Boobs, Menstruation and More Keep Them from Coding in Satirical Campaign." *AdWeek*, May 17. http://www .adweek.com/digital/girls-explain-how-boobs-menstruation-and-more-keep -them-coding-satirical-campaign-171503/.

Mukherjee, R., and S. Banet-Weiser, eds. 2012. *Commodity Activism: Cultural Resistance in Neoliberal Times*. New York: New York University Press.

Mulvey, L. [1975] 1989. "Visual Pleasure and Narrative Cinema." In *Visual and Other Pleasures*, 14–26. Basingstoke, UK: Palgrave Macmillan.

Nakamura, L. 2013. "Glitch Racism: Networks as Actors within Vernacular Internet Theory." *Culture Digitally*, December 10. http://culturedigitally .org/2013/12/glitch-racism-networks-as-actors-within-vernacular-internet -theory/.

Neff, G. 2012. *Venture Labor: Work and the Burden of Risk in Innovative Industries*. Cambridge, MA: MIT Press.

Negra, D., and Y. Tasker. 2007. "Introduction: Feminist Politics and Postfeminist Culture." In *Interrogating Postfeminism: Gender and the Politics of Popular Culture*, edited by D. Negra and Y. Tasker, 1–26. Durham, NC: Duke University Press.

Negra, D., and Y. Tasker, eds. 2014. *Gendering the Recession: Media and Culture in an Age of Austerity*. Durham, NC: Duke University Press.

"News." 2016. *Girls Who Code*, May 31. https://girlswhocode.com/girls-code -releases-satirical-videos-stereotypes-computer-science/.

Nike. 1992. "If You Let Me Play" [Print advertisement]. *Vogue*, June.

Nike. 1995. "If You Let Me Play" [Television commercial]. Portland, Oregon. Accessed February 18, 2018. https://www.youtube.com/watch?v=AQ_XSHpIbZE.

Noble, S. U. 2017. *Algorithms of Oppression: Data Discrimination in the Digital Age*. New York: New York University Press.

Noble, S. U. 2018. *Algorithms of Oppression: Race, Gender, and Power in the Digital Age*. New York: New York University Press.

North, A. 2010. "3 Reasons Why 'Erotic Capital' Is Bullshit." *Jezebel*, March 26. http://jezebel.com/5502084/3-reasons-why-erotic-capital-is-bullshit.

North, A. 2016. "The Teen's Guide to the Trump Presidency." *New York Times,* December 19. https://www.nytimes.com/2016/12/19/opinion/the-teens-guide -to-the-trump-presidency.html.

Nussbaum, M. C. 2010. "Objectification and Internet Misogyny." In *The Offensive Internet: Speech, Privacy, and Reputation,* 68–73. Cambridge, MA: Harvard University Press.

O'Neill, R. 2015. "The Work of Seduction: Intimacy and Subjectivity in the Lon- don 'Seduction Community.'" *Sociological Research Online* 20 (4): 1–14.

Orenstein, P. 1995. *School Girls: Young Women, Self-Esteem, and the Confidence Gap.* New York: Anchor Books.

Ouellette, L., and J. Hay. 2008. *Better Living through Reality TV: Television and Post-welfare Citizenship.* Malden, MA: Blackwell.

"Our Philosophy." 2006. *Men's Activism.* Accessed November 2015. http://news .mensactivism.org/?q=node/5632.

Paquette, D. 2016. "It's Not Clear If Jeff Sessions Thinks Grabbing a Woman by the Crotch Is Sexual Assault." *Washington Post,* November 18. https://www .washingtonpost.com/news/wonk/wp/2016/11/18/its-not-clear-if-trump-attorney -general-sessions-thinks-grabbing-a-woman-by-the-crotch-is-sexual-assault.

Parkinson, H. J. 2016. "Who Will Take On Donald Trump? Teen Vogue." *Guard- ian,* December 12. https://www.theguardian.com/commentisfree/2016/dec/12 /who-take-on-donald-trump-teen-vogue.

Patten, E. 2016. "Racial, Gender Wage Gaps Persist in U.S. Despite Some Pro- gress." *Pew Research Center,* July 1. http://www.pewresearch.org/fact-tank /2016/07/01/racial-gender-wage-gaps-persist-in-u-s-despite-some-progress/.

Penny, L. 2014. "On Nerd Entitlement." *New Statesman,* December 29. http://www .newstatesman.com/laurie-penny/on-nerd-entitlement-rebel-alliance-empire.

Phillips, W. 2015. *This Is Why We Can't Have Nice Things: Mapping the Relation- ship between Online Trolling and Mainstream Culture.* Cambridge, MA: MIT Press.

Portwood-Stacer, L. 2013. "Media Refusal and Conspicuous Non-consumption: The Performative and Political Dimensions of Facebook Abstention." *New Media & Society* 15 (7): 1041–57.

Projansky, S. 2014. *Spectacular Girls: Media Fascination and Celebrity Culture.* New York: New York University Press.

Quenqua, D. 2014. "Tell Me What You See, Even If It Hurts Me." *New York Times,* August 1. https://www.nytimes.com/2014/08/03/fashion/am-i-pretty-videos -posed-to-the-internet-raise-questions.html.

Quinn, B. 2015. "Nobel Laureate Tim Hunt Resigns after 'Trouble with Girls' Comments." *Guardian,* June 11. https://www.theguardian.com/education/2015 /jun/11/nobel-laureate-sir-tim-hunt-resigns-trouble-with-girls-comments.

"Reddit Will Not Ban 'Distasteful' Content, Chief Executive Says." 2012. *BBC,* October 17. http://www.bbc.com/news/technology-19975375.

Remnick, D. 2012. "We Are Alive." *New Yorker*, July 30. https://www.newyorker
.com/magazine/2012/07/30/we-are-alive.

Rensin, E. 2014. "Confessions of a Former Internet Troll." *Vox*, December 16.
http://www.vox.com/2014/9/29/6840773/confessions-of-a-former-internet-tro.

Restauri, D. 2012. "Am I Ugly? Fat? Pretty? Tween and Teen Girls Ask YouTube
Strangers for Answers." *Forbes*. Accessed March 20, 2013. http://www.forbes
.com/sites/deniserestauri/2012/02/22/am-i-ugly-fat-pretty-tween-and-teen
-girls-ask-YouTube-strangers-for-answers/.

Robertson, A. 2014. "'Massacre' Threat Forces Anita Sarkeesian to Cancel University Talk." *Verge*, October 4. http://www.theverge.com/2014/10/14/6978809
/utah-state-university-receives-shooting-threat-for-anita-sarkeesian-visit.

Rochman, B. 2012. "Am I Pretty or Ugly? Why Teen Girls Are Asking YouTube
for Validation." *Time*, March 3. http://healthland.time.com/2012/03/07/am
-i-pretty-or-ugly-whats-behind-the-trend-of-girls-asking-YouTube-for
-validation/#ixzz2RJTk1zCV.

Roiphe, K. 1993. *The Morning After: Sex, Fear, and Feminism*. Boston: Little,
Brown.

Ronson, J. 2015. "Jon Ronson: How the Online Hate Mob Set Its Sights on Me."
Guardian, December 20. https://www.theguardian.com/media/2015/dec/20
/social-media-twitter-online-shame.

Ronson, J. 2016. *So You've Been Publicly Shamed*. New York: Riverhead Books.

Roscoe, M. 2016. "6 Ways Liberal Democracy Destroys the Goodness of Humanity." Return of Kings, April 4. http://www.returnofkings.com/84753/6-ways
-liberal-democracy-destroys-the-goodness-of-humanity.

Rose, N. 1999. *Powers of Freedom: Reframing Political Thought*. Cambridge: Cambridge University Press.

Rosin, H. 2012. *The End of Men: And the Rise of Women*. London: Penguin.

Rottenberg, C. 2014. "The Rise of Neoliberal Feminism." *Cultural Studies* 28 (3):
418–37.

RSDTyler. n.d. "How to Pick Up 18+ Girls As an Old Man (with No Money!)."
YouTube. https://www.youtube.com/user/RSDTyler.

Sandberg, S. 2013. *Lean In: Women, Work, and the Will to Lead*. New York:
Random House.

Savage, C. 2016. "Why Feminism Is a Terrorist Movement." Return of Kings,
April 4. http://www.returnofkings.com/77971/why-feminism-is-a-terrorist
-movement.

Savage, C. 2017. "Can Men Be Masculine without Being Warriors?" Return of
Kings, July 31. http://www.returnofkings.com/126230/can-men-be-masculine
-without-being-warriors.

Savali, K. W. 2017. "Black Feminists Don't Owe Hillary Clinton Their Support."
In *Wolf Whistle Politics: The New Misogyny in America Today*, edited by D.
Wachtell. New York: New Press.

Schaefer, K. 2017. "What Comes after Scandal and Scathing Reviews? Sophia Amoruso Is Finding Out." *Vanity Fair*, April 26. https://www.vanityfair.com /style/2017/04/sophia-amoruso-girlboss-netflix-nasty-gal.

Schrobsdorff, S. 2015. "Ellen Pao Was One More 'Difficult' Female Executive." *Time*, July 11. http://time.com/3954460/ellen-pao-reddit/.

Scott, J. W. 1991. "The Evidence of Experience." *Critical Inquiry* 17 (4): 773–97.

Sender, K. 2012. *The Makeover: Reality Television and Reflexive Audiences*. New York: New York University Press.

Sharpe, D. 2016. "Six Slut Tells Every Man Needs to Be Aware Of." Return of Kings, April 5. http://www.returnofkings.com/84445/6-slut-tells-every-man -needs-to-be-aware-of.

Shaw, A. 2014. *Gaming at the Edge: Sexuality and Gender at the Margins of Gamer Culture*. Minneapolis: University of Minnesota Press.

"Sign the Pledge." n.d. Confidence Coalition. Accessed April 2014. http:// confidencecoalition.org/commit.

Smith, C. 2012. "Teens Post 'Am I Pretty or Ugly?' Videos on YouTube." *ABC News*, February 23. http://abcnews.go.com/US/teens-post-insecurities -YouTube-pretty-ugly-videos/story?id=15777830#.UXbWK4LufuE.

Smith, S., K. Pieper, and M. Choueiti. 2017. "Inclusion in the Director's Chair? Gender, Race, and Age of Film Directors across 1,000 Films from 2007–2016." Media, Diversity, and Social Change Initiative, USC Annenberg. Accessed September 2017. http://annenberg.usc.edu/pages/~/media/MDSCI/Inclusion%20 in%20the%20Directors%20Chair%202117%20Final.ashx.

SPLC: Southern Poverty Law Center. 2012. "Misogyny: The Sites." *Intelligence Report* (spring). https://www.splcenter.org/fighting-hate/intelligence-report /2012/misogyny-sites.

Springsteen, B. 2012. "Bruce Springsteen Discusses 'Wrecking Ball'" [promotional video]. YouTube, February 17. https://www.youtube.com/watch?v =cEdX2IT41eE.

Srnicek, N. 2016. *Platform Capitalism*. Oxford: Polity.

Stern, S. 2004. "Expressions of Identity Online: Prominent Features and Gender Differences in Adolescents' World Wide Web Home Pages." *Journal of Broadcasting and Electronic Media* 48 (2): 218–43.

Stockman, F. 2017. "Women's March on Washington Opens Contentious Dialogues about Race." *New York Times*, January 9. https://www.nytimes.com /2017/01/09/us/womens-march-on-washington-opens-contentious-dialogues -about-race.html.

Straughan, K. 2013a. "Don't Be That Anti-rape Campaign." *A Voice for Men*, July 21. https://www.avoiceformen.com/mens-rights/false-rape-culture/dont -be-that-anti-rape-campaign/.

Straughan, K. 2013b. "Don't Be That Lying Feminist." YouTube. Accessed February 2016. https://www.youtube.com/watch?v=GHLMfGz3VAI.

Sturken, M., and L. Cartwright. 2003. *Practices of Looking*. Oxford: Oxford University Press.

Sun-Higginson, S., prod. and dir. 2015. GTFO: *A Film about Women in Gaming*. United States: Kickstarter.

Switzer, H. 2013. "(Post)Feminist Development Fables: The Girl Effect and the Production of Sexual Subjects." *Feminist Theory* 14 (3): 345–60.

This American Life. 2015. "If You Don't Have Anything Nice to Say, SAY IT IN ALL CAPS. Act One. Ask Not For Whom The Bell Trolls; It Trolls for Thee." January 23. https://www.thisamericanlife.org/545/if-you-dont-have-anything -nice-to-say-say-it-in-all-caps/act-one.

Thomas, D. 2015. "Why Is #MasculinitySoFragile?" *Los Angeles Times*, September 23. http://www.latimes.com/fashion/alltherage/la-ar-masculinity-fragile -20150923-htmlstory.html.

Thompson, L. 2018. "'I Can Be Your Tinder Nightmare': Harassment and Misogyny in the Online Sexual Marketplace." *Feminism and Psychology* 28 (1): 69–89.

Tiku, N. 2014. "How to Get Girls into Coding." *New York Times*, May 31. https://www .nytimes.com/2014/06/01/opinion/sunday/how-to-get-girls-into-coding.html.

Tilstra, L. 2016. "It's a Great Time to Be a Woman at Verizon." Verizon, March 14. http://www.verizon.com/about/news/its-great-time-be-woman-verizon.

Tolman, D. 2012. "SPARKing Change: Not Just One Girl at a Time." *Huffington Post*, July 5. http://www.huffingtonpost.com/deborah-l-tolman/sparking -change-not-just-_b_1506433.html.

"Transcript: Donald Trump's Taped Comments about Women." 2016. *New York Times*, October 8. https://www.nytimes.com/2016/10/08/us/donald-trump -tape-transcript.html.

Turner, F. 2006. *From Counterculture to Cyberculture: Stewart Brand, the Whole Earth Network, and the Rise of Digital Utopianism*. Chicago: University of Chicago Press.

Turner, F. 2009. "Burning Man at Google: A Cultural Infrastructure for New Media Production." *New Media & Society* 11 (1–2): 73–94.

Twomey, K. [ke2mey]. 2015. "Had *such* trouble doing good science today. What with the crying, and battling my way through hordes of suitors. So distracting. #timhunt." Tweet, June 10. https://twitter.com/ke2mey/status /608651538073051136.

Valenti, J. 2010. *The Purity Myth: How America's Obsession with Virginity Is Hurting Young Women*. Berkeley, CA: Seal Press.

Valenti, J. 2014. "If Everyone Is a Feminist, Is Anyone?" *Guardian*, November 24. https://www.theguardian.com/commentisfree/2014/nov/24/when-everyone-is -a-feminist.

Valentine, C. 2017. "Activist ShiShi Rose on the Women's March and Making Sure All Women's Voices Are Heard." *Paper Magazine*, January 20. http://www

.papermag.com/activist-shishi-rose-on-the-womens-march-and-making-sure
-all-womens-vo-2203417399.html.

Valizadeh, D. n.d. "About." Return of Kings. Accessed March 2018. http://www
.returnofkings.com/about.

Valizadeh, D. 2014. "No One Would Have Died If PUAHate Killer Elliot Rodger
Had Learned Game." Return of Kings, May 25. http://www.returnofkings.com
/36135/no-one-would-have-died-if-pua-hate-killer-elliot-rodger-learned-game.

Valizadeh, D. 2015a. "How to Stop Rape." *Roosh V*, February 16. http://www
.rooshv.com/how-to-stop-rape.

Valizadeh, D. 2015b. "What Is Neomasculinity?" *RooshV*, May 6. http://www
.rooshv.com/what-is-neomasculinity.

Valizadeh, D. 2016. "Announcement: The Meetup on February 6 Is Cancelled."
Roosh V, February 3. http://www.rooshv.com/announcement-the-meetup-on
-february-6-is-cancelled.

vanden Heuvel, K. 2012. "Katrina vanden Heuvel: Unleashing the Power of Real
Girls." *Washington Post*, July 17.

van Dijck, J. 2013. "Social Media and the Culture of Connectivity." *OUPblog*, February 25. https://blog.oup.com/2013/02/social-media-culture-connectivity/.

Walkerdine, V., H. Lucey, and J. Melody. 2001. *Growing Up Girl: Psycho-social
Explorations of Gender and Class.* Basingstoke, UK: Palgrave Macmillan.

Wang, A. B. 2017. "'Nevertheless, She Persisted' Becomes New Battle Cry
after McConnell Silences Elizabeth Warren." *Washington Post*, February 8.
https://www.washingtonpost.com/news/the-fix/wp/2017/02/08/nevertheless
-she-persisted-becomes-new-battle-cry-after-mcconnell-silences-elizabeth
-warren/?utm_term=.602e3c06b39a.

Weber, B. 2009. *Makeover TV: Selfhood, Citizenship, and Celebrity.* Durham, NC:
Duke University Press.

Weeks, K. 2011. *The Problem with Work: Feminism, Marxism, Antiwork Politics,
and Postwork Imaginaries.* Durham, NC: Duke University Press.

"Welcome to Africaid." n.d. Accessed February 18, 2018. Africaid.org.

West, L. 2015. "What Happened When I Confronted My Cruelest Troll." *Guardian*, February 2. https://www.theguardian.com/society/2015/feb/02/what
-happened-confronted-cruellest-troll-lindy-west.

Whitford, D. 2015. "Brianna Wu vs. the Gamergate Troll Army." *Inc.*, April.
https://www.inc.com/magazine/201504/david-whitford/gamergate-why-would
-anyone-want-to-kill-brianna-wu.html.

"Why Can't Girls Code?" 2016. *Girls Who Code.* Accessed February 2016. https://
girlswhocode.com/girlsdocode/.

Wiegman, R. 1995. *American Anatomies: Theorizing Race and Gender.* Durham,
NC: Duke University Press.

"Women Want to Be Led." 2016. *Reddit*, October 16. https://www.reddit.com/r
/TheRedPill/comments/57qyor/women_want_to_be_led.

Young, C. Forthcoming. "Becked Up: Glenn Beck, the New White Supremacy and the Hijacking of the Civil Rights Legacy." In *Post-Race Racial Projects*, edited by R. Muhkerjee, S. Banet-Weiser, and H. Gray. Durham, NC: Duke University Press.

Zacharek, S., E. Dockterman, and H. Sweetland Edwards. 2017. "The Silence Breakers." *Time*, December 18. http://time.com/time-person-of-the-year-2017 -silence-breakers/.

Zeisler, A. 2016. *We Were Feminists Once: From Riot Grrrl to CoverGirl, the Buying and Selling of a Political Movement*. New York: PublicAffairs.

Zevallos, Z. 2011. "Erotic Capital and the Sociology of Beauty." *Other Sociologist*, October 29. https://othersociologist.com/2011/10/29/erotic-capital/.

Ziering, A., prod., and K. Dick, dir. 2015. *The Hunting Ground*. The Weinstein Company.

Zurbriggen, E. L., R. L. Collins, S. Lamb, T. Roberts, D. L. Tolman, M. Ward, and J. Blake. 2007. "Report of the Task Force on the Sexualization of Girls: Executive Summary." American Psychological Association. Accessed August 2016. http://www.apa.org/pi/women/programs/girls/report-summary.pdf.

INDEX

Art of Manliness, 114–15
Atlantic, 104, 175
At-Risk girls, 28, 82, 109, 188n7
Audi, 7, 43
audience, 6, 10, 19, 43, 48, 53, 68–69, 84,
    101, 108, 144, 189n3
Australia, 120–21
authenticity, 151, 176

Bachelor, The, 123
backlash, 2, 16, 35–36, 40, 83–84, 129, 133,
    149, 164
Barbie, 71–72, 137–38
Battered Women's Support Services
    (BWSS), 57–58
BBC, 163–64
Beinart, Peter, 174–75
Bell, Kristina, 152–53
Berlant, Lauren, 89
Beyoncé, 7–8
Big Brother, 123
Black Girl Dangerous, 8, 16, 83
Black Girls Code, 132–33
Black Lives Matter, 14, 62, 104, 141
Blanc, Julien, 121–22
blogs, 1, 6, 8, 92, 122, 153, 163, 190n3;
    feminist, 16, 84; men's rights, 184
blood sport, 67, 87
Bluhm, Julia, 102
body image, 46–48, 72, 76, 80, 84, 89,
    98, 107
body positivity, 2, 9, 48, 66–68, 104, 181
body shaming, 2, 80–81
Bourdieu, Pierre, 112
boyd, danah, 69
Boys and Girls Club, 133
Brand, Stewart, 155
branding, 31, 44, 48, 77; self-, 29, 78
Bratich, Jack, 38
breast cancer, 50
Brock, André, 16
"bro" culture, 132–34, 155–56
Brown, Lyn Mikel, 102, 190n3
Brownmiller, Susan, 188n3

bullying, 47, 79, 81, 98, 162
Burke, Tarana, 16. *See also* hashtags:
    #MeToo
Burning Man, 191n7
Butler, Judith, 172–73
BuzzFeed, 120

Canada, 56–58, 120
Can-Do girls, 28–29, 31, 53, 82, 83, 108,
    188n6
capacity, 4, 28–30, 35, 45–46, 49–50,
    53–58, 67–68, 72, 77, 80–81, 85, 89–90,
    93, 97–98, 100, 105–9, 112–13, 131–34,
    151, 173, 177
capital: erotic 112; human, 98
capitalism, 11, 16, 92, 135, 148, 155; global,
    109; neoliberal, 23–24, 29–30, 44, 48,
    75, 95–96
Carlson, Tucker, 104
Castells, Manuel, 155
Chasing Amy, 153
Chatman, Dayna, 16
Chevrolet, 7
Chu, Arthur, 162
Citron, Danielle Keats, 67, 83–84
civil rights, 3, 21–22, 38, 162, 179, 182
class: middle, 80–83, 180; privilege, 91;
    working, 14, 28, 82, 110–11
Clerks, 153
Clinton, Bill, 65–66, 174
Clinton, Hillary, 33, 173–75, 179
Coalition for Men, 33, 117
coding, 29, 130–49, 168, 172
Collection of Confidence, The, 113
commodifiable body, 25, 102
commodification, 18, 21, 100
commodity, 95, 97, 99, 187n3; activism,
    12; brandable, 82; confidence as, 97,
    100–102, 109, 128; feminism, 7, 13,
    16, 38, 47, 169; fetishism, 16, 27, 47,
    158; objects, 37; self-esteem as, 81–82;
    shame as, 66–68; spectacle, 31, 68
Communications Decency Act, 86
Community, 153

competence, 3–4, 13, 19, 27, 40, 45, 95, 168–72

competition, 11, 123, 134; global, 147, 169

compliance, 128

concealed-carry law, 160

Condé Nast, 192n9

Confessore, Nicholas, 39

confidence, 3–4, 40, 45, 48, 54, 72, 92–124, 165, 172; culture, 125–28; economic, 93; industry, 115; sexual, 93, 121

Confidence Coalition, 98

Confidence Code, The, 94

con game, 97, 127

consent, 15, 16, 56–58, 65, 85–88, 164, 188n3

consumption, 12, 27, 44, 48, 75, 77–78, 118, 155

Cosmopolitan, 8

CoverGirl, 7, 50–54

creativity, 19, 138–39, 153, 155, 169

creepshots, 164

crisis, 158; of confidence, 93, 127–28; in girls, 42, 46–49; in masculinity, 38, 45, 96–97, 109–11, 156–58

Cruikshank, Barbara, 30

Crunk Feminist Collecive, 8, 16

Cruz, Ted, 175

Cullors, Patrisse, 62

cultural infrastructure, 191n7

culture: digital, 35, 39, 68–69, 89, 115, 127, 155, 166; popular, 15, 31–33, 81–82, 137, 158; rape, 54–56, 84, 153

custody rights, 33, 55, 58, 116–17. *See also* men's rights

Cyber Civil Rights Initiative, 86–87

Daily Beast, 120

Damore, James, 130

date rape, 54–58, 188n3. *See also* rape culture

Davis, Viola, 180

Dean, Jodi, 143

death threats, 32–33, 64, 71, 83, 117, 131, 133, 160, 163. *See also* harassment: online

defeat, 111, 177

DeGeneres, Ellen, 51, 54

Deleuze, Gilles, 23

democracy, 12, 30

Democratic Party, 176

Department of Justice, 182

Depression Quest, 145, 160

digital culture, 35, 39, 68–69, 89, 115, 127, 155, 166

digital media, 18–19, 26–27, 68–69, 116–17

Dior, Christian, 9

discrimination, 61, 140, 167; gender, 55, 88, 103, 142–44, 148, 179, 181–83. *See also* gender asymmetry; racism; sexism

disenfranchisement, 27, 39, 62, 82

DiSesa, Nina, 95

Disney, 71

divergence, 38

Dockterman, Eliana, 71

documentary, 41, 54, 143–48, 150–51, 191n5

domestic abuse, 50, 61, 184

domestic labor, 135

domestic terrorism, 188n8

domestic violence, 116–17

domination, 63, 165

"Don't Be That Girl" campaign, 57

"Don't Mancriminate," 36, 59–61

Dove, 7, 9, 48, 73, 75–76

doxing, 83, 133, 160, 165

Dragon Age, 144–45

Drudge Report, 65

Duca, Lauren, 103–5

Duffy, Brooke Erin, 19, 95

Dunbar-Hester, Christina, 132, 152

eating disorders, 46, 81. *See also* body image

economic subjects, 96

economization, 24–27

Edell, Dana, 102, 190n3

education, 41, 47–50, 98, 105–7, 135–37, 168, 172, 190n2; abstinence-only, 83

Egan, R. Danielle, 83

Elam, Paul, 117

mental illness, 34, 188n8
microaggressions, 36
middle class, 80–83, 180
Mills, Nicolaus, 66
mirroring, 38–40, 45–64, 113
misogyny, 2, 11, 19, 26, 147; defensive, 32,
    64, 118, 161–62, 178; networked, 34, 122,
    125–26, 132, 163; online, 156; popular,
    2–6, 31–40, 44–46, 54–64, 66–70,
    83–97, 109–20, 125–35, 151–56, 163–78,
    184; systemic, 151
Miss Universe, 176
Moore, Hunter, 85–86
Moynihan, Daniel, 110
Ms. Foundation, 8
Muslim, 188n8
My So-Called Life, 153

Nakamura, Lisa, 38, 126–27, 162
NASA, 191n2
Nasty Gal, 96, 190n1
"nasty woman," 175
National Basketball Association Champi-
    onships, 152
National Coalition for Men (NCFM), 117
"negging," 119, 123. *See also* pickup artist
    community; seduction communities
neoliberalism, 11, 40, 74–76, 114, 135, 184;
    antisocial, 184
neomasculinity, 119, 125
Neo-Nazis, 178
networked public, 70
networked spaces, 26–27. *See also* media:
    networked
networks, 35, 40, 118–19, 168
New York Times, 39, 65–66, 86, 100
NGOs, 98–99, 106
Nike, 48–50, 188n1
Nobel Peace Prize, 143, 188n5
nonprofit, 28, 73, 82, 103–7, 129–31, 139, 146
normalization, 24, 40, 78, 91, 103, 117–18,
    161–62, 178
NPR, 103
Nussbaum, Martha, 156

Obama, Barack, 137, 183; administration,
    175
objectification, 32, 63, 113, 120, 162
Occupy movement, 22
O'Neill, Rachel, 115, 121–23
Onion, The, 174

patriarchy, 32–34, 96, 135, 142, 147, 159,
    167, 173, 183
Penny, Laurie, 16, 130, 159
Peoples, Angela, 180
Phillips, Whitney, 151, 167
Pickup Artist, The, 121–22, 191n9
pickup artist communities, 115–16,
    121–27, 153, 172
Planned Parenthood, 182
pledge, 98–100
political correctness, 149–50
political economy, 135
politics, 22, 140, 175, 177, 184
popular culture, 15, 31–33, 81–82, 137, 158.
    See also media: popular
popular feminism. *See* feminism: popular
popularity, 13, 40, 88, 171, 183
popularization, 170; of bullies, 38
popular media. *See* media: popular
popular misogyny. *See* misogyny: popular
postfeminism, 18–21, 23, 54–58, 63, 113,
    172
potential, 101, 108
poverty, 108
power, 5, 16, 64, 156, 168–70, 188n1; rela-
    tions, 16, 22. *See also* empowerment;
    girl power
presence: digital, 87, 138, 190n2; norma-
    tive, 55, 139; web, 190n2
presidential election, 173–78
privilege, 13, 156–59; class, 94; economic,
    16, 27, 47, 158; male, 36–38, 61–62;
    race, 94; white, 20, 23, 134, 180
Procter & Gamble, 43, 52
Promise of Happiness, The, 15
Public Religion Research Institute, 175
public shaming, 85–89, 134, 142

Violence Against Women Act, 182
Violent Crime Control and Law Enforcement Act, 174
visibility, 10–17, 66, 91, 171, 176, 178, 183; critique of, 37; economy of, 2–3, 10, 13, 15, 18, 21–33, 38–40, 50–54, 62–78, 82–83, 87–98, 100–105, 107–13, 115–23, 127–28, 131–33, 140–43, 148, 150, 154, 157, 166–67, 173–79; politics of, 62, 140; practices of, 22; spectacular, 31, 157, 181
Voice for Men, A, 117
voters, 175–77
vulnerability, 48, 69, 172–73

Warren, Elizabeth, 182
Washington Post, 65, 100, 149
Watson, Emma, 8, 15
Weinstein, Harvey, 16
West, Lindy, 84
white fragility, 156–57
White House Council on Women and Girls, 137
whiteness, 12, 16, 32, 38–39, 81–82, 145, 156
white supremacy, 177–78

"Why Girls Can't Code," 139
Wiegman, Robyn, 21
Williams, Anthony, 118
Will to Empower, The, 30
"woman problem," 129–30, 136
women of color, 9, 14, 16, 35, 84, 168, 174, 180, 183–84, 191n7
Women's March, 14, 179–83
Wong, Yishan, 164
Wood, Elijah, 59
work, 95, 109–11. *See also* labor
working class, 28, 82, 110–11
World Association for NGOs (WANGO), 190n2
World Bank, 50, 190n2
Wu, Brianna, 33, 144, 159, 161

Young, Cynthia, 38
Young, Susan, 149
Yousafzai, Malala, 188n5
YouTube, 69, 78–90, 95, 139, 143, 159, 168

Zeisler, Andi, 169
Zuckerberg, Mark, 137, 153

Made in the USA
Las Vegas, NV
31 July 2024

93212177R00142